Welcome

THE
EVERYTHING
PROFILES SERIES ®

D0370728

Welcome to the EVERYTHING® Profiles line of books—an extension of the bestselling EVERYTHING® series!

These authoritative books help you learn everything you ever wanted to know about the lives, social context, and surrounding historical events of fascinating people who made or influenced history and religious thought. While reading this EVERYTHING® book you will discover four useful boxes:

Factum: Definitions and additional information
Discussion Question: Questions and answers for deeper insights
Symbolism: Explains a concept or symbol
Fallacy: Refutes a commonly held misconception

Whether you are learning about a figure for the first time or are just brushing up on your knowledge, EVERYTHING® Profiles help you on your journey toward a greater understanding of the individuals who have shaped and enriched our lives, culture, and history.

Visit the entire Everything® series at *www.everything.com*

The
EVERYTHING®
Mary Book

Dear Reader,

When we joined the Eastern Orthodox Church ten years ago, we struggled to understand the traditional Christian devotion to Mary. Over time, we've come to a deeper appreciation of the Virgin Mary and her place in the lives of billions of Christians around the world and throughout the ages. During the writing of this book we had the opportunity to gain a fresh glimpse of a woman who remains an enigma to so many.

Perhaps you're a little bit like us. If you ride the bus to work, maybe you've noticed a woman who boards at the same stop every morning, who sits across from you but keeps to herself. Encountering Mary is a little bit like striking up that first conversation with that stranger. It takes courage, but yields rewards.

We invite you to join us in a whirlwind tour of history, theology, imagery, and popular lore as we draw close to this familiar stranger. The Mary shared by Roman Catholics, Eastern Orthodox, Protestants, and Muslims is available to all. Her own simple "yes" continues to inspire millions as we struggle with our own spirituality, as we embrace the hope, pain, and possibility that defined her life and permeates our own earthly journeys.

Father John and
Jenny Schroedel

THE

EVERYTHING®

MARY

BOOK

The life and legacy of the Blessed Mother

Jenny Schroedel and
Reverend John Schroedel

Adams Media
Avon, Massachusetts

Publishing Director: Gary M. Krebs
Associate Managing Editor: Laura M. Daly
Associate Copy Chief: Brett Palana-Shanahan
Acquisitions Editor: Lisa Laing
Development Editor: Rachel Engelson
Associate Production Editor: Casey Ebert
Technical Reader: Dr. James B. Wiggins

Director of Manufacturing: Susan Beale
Associate Director of Production:
Michelle Roy Kelly
Cover Design: Paul Beatrice, Matt LeBlanc,
Erick DaCosta
Design and Layout: Colleen Cunningham,
Jennifer Oliveira, Brewster Brownville

• • •

An Everything® Series Book.
Everything® and everything.com® are registered trademarks of F+W Publications, Inc.

Published by Adams Media, an F+W Publications Company
57 Littlefield Street, Avon, MA 02322 U.S.A.
www.adamsmedia.com

ISBN 10: 1-59337-713-4
ISBN 13: 978-1-59337-713-7

Printed in the United States of America.

J I H G F E D C B A

**Library of Congress Cataloging-in-Publication Data
is available from the publisher**

Unless otherwise indicated, Scripture quotations are from *The Holy Bible, English Standard Version (ESV)* © 2001 by Crossway Bibles, a division of Good News Publishers.

This publication is designed to provide accurate and authoritative information with regard to the subject matter covered. It is sold with the understanding that the publisher is not engaged in rendering legal, accounting, or other professional advice. If legal advice or other expert assistance is required, the services of a competent professional person should be sought.
—From a *Declaration of Principles* jointly adopted by a Committee of the American Bar Association and a Committee of Publishers and Associations

Many of the designations used by manufacturers and sellers to distinguish their products are claimed as trademarks. Where those designations appear in this book and Adams Media was aware of a trademark claim, the designations have been printed with initial capital letters.

*This book is available at quantity discounts for bulk purchases.
For information, please call 1-800-872-5627.*

Contents

4 Spotting Mary in the Old Testament 41

5 Mary and the Councils 53

6 Images of Mary 65

7 Seasons of Salvation 79

11 Messages from Mary 135

12 Ancient Appearances 149

13 Modern Sightings 165

14 Mary in Catholic Thought 179

Top Ten Facts about Mary

1. Dante said that Mary's face is the one that most closely resembles the face of Christ.

2. Apparitions of Mary have been reported in every era in history and every country in the world.

3. The early church fathers compared Eve to Mary. As Eve was the mother of humanity who fell into sin, Mary was the mother of a new humanity.

4. The Christian representation of Mary helped early converts from paganism connect with the Church.

5. Mary is regarded as a helper for those who grieve and to those who are in need of comfort. Grieving parents have taken comfort in her because she lost her own child in a tragic way.

6. Despite the widely secular nature of the twenty-first century, pilgrimages to Marian sites seem to be increasing in frequency.

7. Many of the earliest churches devoted to Mary were built on old pagan holy sites.

8. Despite Mary's significant place in the lives of the Christian faithful for centuries, she is mentioned less in the Bible than in the Koran.

9. Many scholars think that Mary may have only been thirteen or fourteen years old when she gave birth to Christ.

10. Mary has garnered the praise of writers such as Dante, Jack Kerouac, Flannery O'Conner, and Sue Monk Kidd.

Acknowledgments

We are deeply indebted to our friends who assisted us in this effort by providing child care, moral support, and prayers: Joan Law, Ser Jackson, Bethany Torode, Rachel Schroeder, and Stephanie Baker. We also wish to thank our parents for their unwavering support. We are also grateful for the guidance and patience of our editor, Lisa Laing.

Introduction

You've probably seen evidence of devotion to Mary in our society—you may have seen the shrines that adorn backyards across America, an image of Our Lady of Guadalupe dangling from the rear-view mirror in a taxicab, or statues or icons of the Virgin Mary in people's homes. Perhaps you've wondered what is at the heart of this love for the Virgin Mary.

The phenomenon of devotion to the Virgin Mary is wider and deeper than you may imagine. Apparitions of her are reported to have occurred in every country in the world, spanning the centuries, and crossing cultural barriers. She has inspired more artistic renderings than any other woman in the history of the world and has nudged the pens of poets, the hearts of kings, and the history of nations.

Her influence even extends to our gardens. Did you know that in a very simplistic way the flowers and plants in your backyard witness to the history of Marian devotion, with its many peaks and valleys? Originally, flowers and plants were named for ancient pagan gods and goddesses. In the medieval era, hundreds of them were renamed with Marian names, which helped the faithful to draw close to her even in the fields. Think about the names of marigolds, lady's slippers, and Madonna lilies. After the Reformation, when devotion to the Virgin Mary was curtailed, these flowers were again renamed—or in some cases, their connection to Mary just became more subtle, so that only a serious devotee would be able recognize the connection. For example, the Milk Thistle was known before the Reformation as "Our Lady's Milk Drops," and forget-me-not was known as "Our Lady's Eyes."

Think of this book as a quilt of the Virgin Mary with many squares stitched together to tell the story of the history, legends, art, culture, and controversies that have been connected to Mary. Most of us know only our own square; by stepping back from that one square and glimpsing the whole quilt, we have an opportunity to glimpse the whole—to see patterns, shapes, and possibilities that may not have been apparent before.

It is an exciting process of discovery to learn how people have related to the Virgin Mary throughout the ages, how her presence has inspired and transformed lives, how her very being has helped Christianity to connect with the patterns and seasons of Earth, and how we can be strengthened as we face the great mysteries of life—birth and death.

As we remember the way that Mary walked through these thresholds, we find courage as we face our own thresholds. We see that there is more to life than meets the eye, that only by stepping back to see the whole can we begin to see patterns in the ways in which devotion to Mary crosses cultures, spans seasons, and transforms lives around the globe, both historically and in the present day.

If we come to Mary with humility, with an open and seeking heart, we are sure to learn something, no matter who we are and where we come from. This book discusses so many cultures and peoples. For some of us, it may help us to better understand our spouses, our in-laws, our neighbor's devotion and it may help us make sense of the bewildering variety and intensity of devotion to this lady whose life, in so many ways, still remains a mystery.

Foreword

There is simply no doubt about it. The woman who has had the most impact on the history, art, culture, and literature of the human race from the dawn of time till now is clearly Mary, the mother of Jesus. The ironic thing about this, however, is that good information about Mary is not always easy to come by. Usually what you can find is either incomplete, dry, or sectarian.

This book is none of the above. It represents something that has been desperately needed for a long time—a fascinating, comprehensive, provocative, and eminently readable introduction to every aspect of Mary and her 2,000-year relationship with the sons of Adam and the daughters of Eve.

The Everything® Mary Book does not stop with the various and sundry Christian perspectives on Mary. It also reviews the very important role she plays in the Islamic faith confessed by over a billion of the earth's inhabitants. In fact, the book makes a rather startling claim—that the Virgin Mary, far from being a bone of contention, is actually a bridge-builder of monumental proportions. This book explores Mary's ability to cross boundaries and build connection between Jewish and Christian Scriptures, Christians and Muslims, poor and rich, and men and women.

In fact, in a feminist age fascinated by the "divine feminine," Mary holds greater importance than ever. What she represents is the key to unlocking the secret of true feminine dignity and power, and how best to understand and access the feminine dimension of the Divine.

But make no mistake about it—this is no academic tome of mere theoretical interest. Its focus throughout is how Mary has impacted the faith and lives of *real* people. Here we learn about devotions as well as doctrines, art as well as literature, and folk customs along with their surprisingly profound meanings. Weeping icons, statues crowned with May flowers, apparitions, healing Marian springs, rosaries, and scapulars are covered along with what church councils, Protestant reformers, New Testament Scriptures and even the

Koran have had to say about the most modest, yet most pivotal, woman in human history.

This book will not only provide you with information *about* Mary, it will also introduce you *to* her. As you read about the ways she has influenced the lives of millions across the centuries from every religious tradition imaginable, you may just find her story striking a chord in you. Your knowledge of culture and religion will certainly be enriched, as will the quality of your own life and spirituality.

This book demonstrates that Mary is more than a plaster statue on a pedestal or an icon on a wall. She is a very real person who is strangely approachable, given her lofty role, because she is not very much different than we are. She experienced many of the same doubts, fears, and limitations that beset us every day. Perhaps that's why she's been such a sought-after prayer partner and an inspiring model. For Mary achieved what many of us, at least secretly, desire to achieve—loyalty to the truth, courage in the face of fear, and surrender to the One whose love and power surpasses everything we can possibly imagine.

Marcellino D'Ambrosio, Ph.D.
Adjunct Professor of Theology
Ave Maria University
Naples Florida

Chapter 1

Our Lady of Paradox

Many people are surprised to discover how little the New Testament says about Mary, especially in light of her profound influence throughout the ages. Although few, if any, would claim to know exactly what Mary looked like, artistic renderings of her appear in almost every culture in the world. Likewise, millions continue to be inspired or baffled by news of her "appearances." To express the inexpressible, the ancient church often used paradoxes to speak about Mary. This chapter will use paradoxes to introduce a teenage virgin from Galilee who changed the world.

Who Is Mary?

In C. S. Lewis's *Prince Caspian*, Lucy notices that Aslan seems to have grown since the last time she saw him. When she asks him about this he tells her that he only seems bigger because *she* has grown. It is like that with Mary. She seems simple at first glance and becomes more complex and significant the more you learn about her.

Throughout the centuries, Christians have debated about what to call Mary, how to view her life, and how to integrate her witness into their own spiritual journeys. The Roman Catholic and Eastern Orthodox Churches have retained a deep love for her. Although the two churches have not always expressed their devotion in the same ways, they have generally shared the guiding premise that every statement and image of Mary is ultimately intended to bring people closer to her son.

Icons depicting Mary holding her infant son express the reason that Mary is most revered. Her witness is not only one of profound courage and obedience, but is ultimately one of maternal love. Her love for her own son has often been seen as a role model for mothers as they seek to care for their own children.

symbolism

In some icons of the Virgin Mary, she holds the infant Christ with her left arm. Her right hand gestures toward the face of her son, guiding our eyes back to him. He leans into her, with the eager devotion of a child, expressing his quiet, steady love for her, and ultimately, for all of us.

Friends in High Places

Anne Rice's novel *Christ the Lord* offers a unique glimpse into the clannish culture in which Jesus was born. According to Rice's depiction, the nuclear family as we know it now was rarely seen in ancient times. Instead, a family would have multiple generations and relations (including first and second cousins) living under the same roof. When a family would travel, they would often journey as a tribe.

This image fits well with the lengthy genealogies offered at the beginnings of the Gospels of Luke and Matthew. These meandering lists of barely pronounceable names are read in many churches in the days and weeks leading up to Christmas. Some might wish to skip them and get on to the gist of the story—the no-room-at-the-inn scene starring the very pregnant Mary and Joseph. But these lists are important because they help place the newborn Jesus in the context of generations of faith, a community stretching through time and space.

Even today, every Christian life is rooted in a heritage of faith and has a sense of continuity with all of those who have come before, who have carried the Gospel with their lives through the centuries. In many churches, this "Great Cloud of Witnesses" (Hebrews 12:1) is understood to be full of holy people who, though deceased, nevertheless continue to pray and support those struggling to live for God. Throughout Christian tradition, this intangible, invisible community of saints has been made tangible and visible through icons and statues and other religious objects.

Those within the churches that believe in the living example of the "Great Cloud of Witnesses" have also continued the ancient practice of asking for the prayers of those who have gone before them, believing that those who now live with God know far better than the earthbound how to pray. Within this community, there is no prayer partner more beloved than the Virgin Mary.

So Few Words—So Much Influence

Despite Mary's significance for many Christians around the world, the Gospel accounts only provide the barebones of Mary's life. Many details from the Gospels about Mary's life have leaked into Christmas hymns and Nativity scenes and have been repeated year after year. Sometimes, the story seems so familiar that it can be hard to grasp the full impact of the event. Mary lived with her parents in Nazareth. During her engagement to a man named Joseph, an angel came to her and told her that she would conceive a child through the Holy Spirit. The angel told Mary that the child's name would be Jesus, because he would save people from their sins (Luke 1:31–32).

discussion question

What is the significance of the name Jesus?
The Hebrew name for Jesus, Y'shua, is a shortened form of the name Joshua (Y'hoshua). The name Joshua literally means "the Lord saves."

When Mary shared her frightening, awe-inspiring news with her fiancé, he did not rejoice. In fact, according to the Gospel of Matthew, he did not actually believe her, and secretly resolved to quietly end the relationship to prevent a scandal (Matthew 1:19). But Joseph's sense of betrayal and disbelief changed as a result of a dream in which an angel came to him, assuring him about the more-difficult-to-explain parts of the pregnancy (specifically, how Mary came to be pregnant when she and Joseph had not yet been married). The angel also told Joseph not to be afraid to take Mary as his wife.

Joseph's initial apprehension about Mary's news is reflected in early Christian icons of Jesus' birth. In these icons, Joseph is often portrayed with his back to Mary and the newborn Jesus, looking away from the infant Jesus toward a small demon. Because icons often include images of events that may have occurred at different times, the image of Joseph here jumps back in time to show his earlier temptation to disbelieve Mary. He seems lost in his own private world of doubts and fears. This image expresses the ancient belief that temptations tend to be most fierce when we are alone, and that sin increases isolation.

In one of the great giddy moments of the Gospels, Mary hears the news that her relative Elizabeth (who had been barren) is also pregnant. She journeys to Elizabeth's home, and as she steps through the front door, Elizabeth makes the first public proclamation about the miracle inside of Mary. Elizabeth calls Mary "the mother of my Lord" and the babe in Elizabeth's womb leaps with joy (Luke 1:39–45).

During her pregnancy, Mary traveled with Joseph to Bethlehem for the census (Luke 2:1–7). When they realized that the birth of the baby was near, Mary and Joseph attempted to find a room at an inn, but there were no openings, so Mary gave birth in a stable where animals were kept, and Jesus was laid in a manger (which is something like a cattle trough).

The accounts from Matthew and Luke differ in many elements, including the structure in which Jesus was born. Many Christmas hymns make it seem as if Jesus was born in a wooden barn, but according to ancient church tradition Jesus was actually born in a cave. This tradition is based on Luke's account (Luke 2:7), because shepherds would have likely kept animals in a cave. Matthew, however, refers to a house (Matthew 2:11).

factum

The oldest continually operating church in the Holy Land, the Church of the Nativity in Bethlehem, is located on the spot where many believe Jesus was born. Each year, thousands of pilgrims journey to Bethlehem to light a candle and pray beside the gold star that marks this holy spot.

After Mary gave birth, Jesus was circumcised and the family visited the temple in Jerusalem. Shortly after this, the family fled to Egypt to avoid Herod's wrath, and then returned after Herod's death (Matthew 2:13–23). They lived in Nazareth for thirty years until the beginning of Jesus' public ministry (Luke 2:39–40). Scholars believe that Mary was eventually widowed, because Joseph was never mentioned again.

From the cross, Jesus asked his beloved disciple John to care for Mary until her dying day (John 19:26–27). In Ephesus, there is a small stone house that Christian and Muslim pilgrims visit to this day, where many believe John and Mary lived for several years. You'll learn more about the house of Mary in Chapter 18. According to Scripture, Mary was also present with the apostles at Pentecost (Acts 1:14, 2:1).

These bare-bones accounts demonstrate how very little we know about Mary from the Gospels. They don't seem to explain the widespread influence of Mary. Because the Biblical accounts are so sparse, many Protestants are reluctant to say too much about Mary. Unlike the Reformers (discussed in more detail in Chapter 10) who generally expressed devotion toward Mary, modern Protestants often avoid saying anything about her that doesn't directly come from Scripture. Within the Roman Catholic and Eastern Orthodox Churches, however, devotion to Mary is so strong that hyperbole is often used in speaking about her—not unlike the way that some people rave about their own mothers.

The next sections will explore some of the ways in which the ancient church used to speak about this woman of so few words and so much influence.

Unwedded Bride

One of the paradoxes that has been used to describe Mary, especially in Byzantine hymnography, is the phrase "unwedded bride." This expresses something profound about Mary's relationship with God. Throughout the centuries, many have believed that by choosing Mary to be the mother of Christ, God entered into a unique, almost spousal relationship with Mary. Mary has been considered the Bride of the Holy Spirit in a relationship that echoes the Scriptural reference to the marriage between Christ and the Church (Ephesians 5:23–32). For Saint Paul, there was no imagery more potent than that of a wedding to express this joyful union between Christ and the Church.

symbolism

In the Gospels, the kingdom of heaven is compared to a wedding banquet, and the relationship between Christ and the Church is compared to a marriage between a husband and a wife. The use of nuptial imagery remains a common way for Christians to express the mystical depths of the relationship between God and his beloved creatures.

Mary was, of course, married to Joseph in the official sense of the word, but church tradition has held that, in a more transcendent sense, Mary was actually the spouse of the Holy Spirit. Because of the particular nature of Mary's role as the mother of Christ and her unique place in salvation history, both the Roman Catholic and the Eastern Orthodox Churches believe that Mary and Joseph's marriage was never consummated.

Currently there is much debate between Protestants, Catholics, and Eastern Orthodox over whether the Virgin Mary remained a virgin all of her life. Although most of the Reformers did believe that Mary remained a virgin (including Protestant reformers John Calvin, Ulrich Zwingli, Martin Luther, and John Wesley), Protestantism has generally moved away from this earlier belief, while Orthodoxy and Catholicism continue to teach that Mary was "ever-virgin."

Virgin Mother

The idea of a Virgin Mother is extremely difficult to grasp, because children are the fruit of a sexual union. But Christ's unusual entry into the world set him apart as the unconventional sort who would no doubt turn the world upside down.

Most Christians have been able to agree that Mary was a virgin when Christ was born, but the idea of her being ever-virgin has been hotly contested by many. Those who do not believe that Mary was ever-virgin have pointed out that the Gospel accounts mention that Jesus had siblings. Some also express concern about the passage in the Gospels that says that Joseph did not *know* Mary until after Christ was born (Matthew 1:25). Part of the problem here may be the particular connotations of the word *until* in English—in Greek, it simply means "up to the time of" and does not imply anything about what came afterward. The word *until* simply emphasizes the idea that Mary was a virgin when Christ was born.

factum

In the Bible, the term "to know" is often used to imply sexual relations. When Mary asks, "How shall this be, since I know not a man?" (Luke 1:34 KJV) she is saying, quite simply, that she is still a virgin. This term "know" implies that a rich intimacy is found in sexuality—an intimacy that creates physical, emotional, and spiritual union.

Although the Roman Catholic and Eastern Orthodox Churches share the conviction that the Virgin Mary was ever-virgin, each church has found ways to explain the fact that the Gospels speak of the "siblings of Christ." Their different explanations are based on the different sources they have generally relied on for the traditions surrounding Jesus' family.

The East follows the story in the Protoevangelium of James (an apocryphal book), which says that Joseph was a widower, and that they were Joseph's children from a previous marriage. It would not have been unusual for a young virgin to be betrothed to an older man. Christians in the West, following St. Jerome (A.D. 331–420), have usually regarded the siblings of Jesus as merely cousins.

Over time, more and more discussion has been generated about these basic questions. Some scholars have said that if Jesus did have siblings in the modern sense of the word, then it would be rather odd for Jesus to ask his relative John to care for his mother after his death (John 9:27).

Whichever account is accepted, it is clear that the Greek and Aramaic terms for brother are more expansive than the English term, which could account for some of the confusion surrounding these passages. In Aramaic and Greek, this term is more generic, sometimes meaning "relative" or someone who is part of one's extended family as opposed to a blood sibling. There are other scriptural examples of Biblical brothers such as Lot and Abraham, who were not brothers in the English sense of the word.

The cultural context of the Scriptures certainly offers a picture of family relations that is much more expansive than the American version of the nuclear family. Because of this, modern readers might be skeptical of the theory that the word *siblings* could actually refer to cousins.

Frail, but Powerful

In his 1898 painting of the Virgin Mary, Henry Ossawa Tanner depicts Mary as a young girl, seated on the rumpled sheets of her bed, looking vulnerable and afraid. She is looking toward a light-filled being in the corner of the room. The radiance of the angel seems to pull her face upward, toward some hope and purpose, as she is being told that she will bear the Christ child in her womb, risking alienation from her fiancé and community.

Mary must have understood the real risks of what was about to happen to her. As a betrothed woman, she could have been stoned to death for adultery. This is part of why Joseph, evidently a gentle man, planned to quietly end the relationship, to protect Mary (Matthew 1:19).

This painting also says something about the progression of the way Mary has been viewed throughout time. This image expresses an important truth about Mary. She is not a simple, one-dimensional character, aloof and separate from our struggles and experiences. She experienced the full complexity of human emotions and struggled for courage. Fear and wonder must have mingled on her face as the angel spoke, which is why she was told, "Be not afraid."

symbolism

In the early centuries, Christians often emphasized the ways in which Mary was set apart and holy. In more recent times, however, Mary has been better known for commiserating with the poor and oppressed and the ways she lived with empathy, compassion, and vulnerability.

But there is another side to Mary that is rarely emphasized in modern times. As much as she can be seen as vulnerable and frail, she can also be viewed as a woman of incredible strength and power because of her closeness with God. Her strength was seen as so great that entire armies—from Byzantium, through the Crusades, and up through the time of Imperial Russia—would ask for her protection before heading into battle. Mary was also seen as a protector for those heading out to sea, because she was viewed as able to quell the waves and storms as her son had.

When Christopher Columbus set sail for the Americas he named his ship the *Santa Maria,* for Mary. By naming ships after Mary, mariners often felt that they were evoking her special blessing upon them as they journeyed. It was widely believed that her prayers could hold back storms and protect those at sea in the midst of them, as her son did in the Scriptures.

The image of Mary as "Star of the Sea" or *Stella Maris* may be based on an error a scribe made when he was copying the works of Jerome. Although Jerome is often viewed as the first author to use this title, the title he actually used was *Stilla Maris,* which can be translated as "Drop of the Sea."

Revered and Shunned

Despite the widespread devotion to her through the ages, Mary has remained something of an enigma. Check your local bookstore and you may be surprised by how few titles there are related to the Virgin Mary. While most bookstores have large selections of books on Christianity, books on Mary are often difficult to find.

But perhaps this lack of literature speaks to the historical dilemma. People just don't know how to feel about the Virgin Mary. While Eastern Orthodox and Roman Catholics revere her, Protestants often feel uneasy about Marian Devotion, sensing that it could distract people from Christ. And while no woman has been a model to more women, some strains of feminism have expressed disdain for Mary, saying that her submissive attitude only fosters a culture of male oppression. Yet the paradox only grows, because to so many of the people who love her most, Mary is the ultimate female representation of strength and power—transcending time and transforming lives.

The final way in which our culture seems to have a paradoxical relationship with Mary is demonstrated through some of its popular images. While many images of Mary are created with great love and reverence, others seem to mock her. The "artistic" depiction of the Virgin Mary covered in dung and pornography, which went on display at the Brooklyn Museum of Art is one example of this. (You can read more about this in Chapter 15.)

factum

During the Reformation, bandits knocked off the heads and limbs from statues as a way of expressing their rage at some of the practices of the Roman Catholic Church. In our day, random vandals topple and shatter statues of Mary as a way of defacing all that she represents.

Another way that Mary is both loved and shunned is through statues. After Hurricanes Katrina and Wilma devastated Louisiana and Florida, many people cared gingerly for pieces of the statues of Mary that had been shattered by the storm. They felt that their loving care for these broken images translated into loving care for Mary and her son. But as much as people have respected these images, over the course of history people have also defaced and intentionally destroyed them.

As much as Mary is shunned, mocked, and feared, she is also adored and cherished. The wide variety of reactions to Mary is suggestive of the wide scope of realities that she represents. So much of who and what she was seems simple at first glance, and then becomes increasingly complex as she is explored. For this reason, paradoxes have offered an invaluable tool for glimpsing this woman who continually stretches beyond the grasp of our language and comprehension.

Chapter 2

Gospel Glimpses

The Gospels do not give much attention to Mary, because they are far more focused on detailing the works of Christ and the establishment of his ministry. References to her may be sparse, but each one has grown richer and deeper through time, as generations of Christian theologians have engaged and reflected upon the texts. This chapter will explore the different Gospel representations of Mary, as well as the unique approach taken by each of the Gospel writers.

Prophecies

The New Testament builds upon and expands the Old Testament. The writers of the New Testament were steeped in the Scriptural world of Judaism. One way many of the New Testament writers emphasize this connection to the writings of Judaism is by pointing to prophecies or other verses from the Old Testament that, according to the writers of the New Testament, were fulfilled in events the New Testament writers were recording.

Isaiah's Prophecy

One of the prophecies woven into Matthew's Gospel was taken from the Old Testament book of Isaiah (7:14). Matthew embedded this prophecy into his account of the birth of Christ (Matthew 1:18–24), which differs significantly from the account offered by Luke (Luke 1–2). Matthew's account offers the bare-bones of the birth, skipping the central story of the angel's visitation to Mary and emphasizing the way that the angel appeared to Joseph in a dream just as he was considering leaving Mary.

According to Matthew's account, the angel's words echoed the Old Testament prophecy from Isaiah when the angel said, "Now all this took place to fulfill the words of the prophet when he said, 'The Virgin will conceive and give birth to a son, and they will call his name Emmanuel, which means "God is with us,"' (Matthew 1:18–24).

This connection with the Old Testament prophecy helped to demonstrate that both Christ and the Virgin Mary were part of a divinely orchestrated plan, which was intimately connected to the Old Testament.

Jesus in the Temple

Another prophetic event in the Gospels is related to something that happened shortly after Jesus' birth. In this case, it is not an Old Testament prophecy but a prophecy that was first mentioned in Luke's Gospel that had implications for Mary's life and for later generations to come.

This prophetic event occurred when Joseph and Mary took Jesus to the temple as an infant. Simeon was there and he said to

Mary, "You see this child. He is destined for the fall and for the rising of many in Israel, destined to be a sign that is rejected—and a sword will pierce your own soul, too—so the secret thoughts of many will be laid bare" (Luke 2:33–35).

symbolism

In later Roman Catholic piety, images of Mary with her heart exposed became popular. These images offered a way of understanding the love she experienced for Christ and the suffering she endured for his sake. Many of these images show her heart pierced by a sword, based on the image from Luke's Gospel.

This passage from Luke's Gospel has many theological implications, which will be felt personally by Mary. Mary will suffer because of her love for her son. Just as Jesus experienced rejection and death, Mary will feel this pain acutely, as only a mother could.

Mary's Family Tree

One of the first ironic things that one might notice about the lengthy lists of names that trace Joseph's lineage back to King David is that these genealogies are specifically related to Joseph, who was not, according to Christian teaching, biologically related to Christ. At first glance, it seems strange that these writers would go to such great lengths to establish a royal line if this royal line were only connected to Joseph. However, in Jesus' time, the father's lineage would be of utmost importance for establishing legal parentage. Matthew emphasizes Jesus' adoption into this line. There is a church tradition that Mary was also a descendant of King David, but the Bible is ambiguous about this. In any case, all four of the Gospels—Matthew, Mark, Luke, and John—speak of Jesus as the son of David.

There is an interesting divergence between the way the Koran and the Gospels present these genealogies. In the Gospels, the genealogies seem to be chiefly intended to show that Jesus came from the royal house of David. In the Koran, however, Christ's genealogy offers a different set of Old Testament figures than any of the Gospels. These figures are not from the kingly line but from the line of prophets. This variation between the two texts parallels the different teachings about Christ. Within Christianity, Christ is the Son of God and a descendant from the royal line of David. In the Koran, however, Christ is a great prophet, but is not considered divine.

factum

Some theologians have pointed out parallels between the Virgin Mary and the Old Testament prophet Abraham. Both struggled with the question of how they would bear children, and both heard, "Fear not!" in response. Just as Abraham pleaded with God to save the people of Sodom and Gomorrah, Mary was seen as one who interceded for people seeking God's mercy.

Matthew's genealogy mentions four women: Tamar, Ruth, Rahab, and "the Wife of Uriah," or Bathsheba. Although all of these women's lives were significant, each of their names was at least slightly tainted by scandal.

Tamar, who was a widow without children, dressed up as a prostitute so that she could trick her father-in-law into sleeping with her in order to claim her legal right to continue the family line of her deceased husband. Ruth was not Jewish by birth, but her Jewish mother-in-law Naomi helped her into a marriage with Naomi's wealthy relative, Boaz, so that Ruth could also perpetuate her family line. Rahab was herself a prostitute, but she put her efforts toward helping the Jews to enter the promised land.

Finally, there is Bathsheba. King David spied her bathing naked one day as he was walking on his roof. David lusted after her to such an extent that he gave orders that she be brought to his palace, and he committed adultery with her. When she became pregnant, he commanded that her husband, Uriah, be put on the front lines of battle so that he would be killed and David could marry Bathsheba. (2 Samuel 11) The child born of her was Solomon, who later became king and was renown for his wisdom. It was Solomon who built the temple for God that David dreamed of, and through whom the royal line continued. All of these women used unconventional methods to accomplish extraordinary things that profoundly affected the history of the Jewish lineage.

In these women, many theologians have seen a suggestion of what was to come—another woman who would enter into an equally unconventional marriage for the greater good of her people.

The Brave Yes

Because stories of the Annunciation (the revelation to Mary by Gabriel that she will conceive and give birth to the Son of God) have become so familiar, many of us miss the unusual aspect of the conversation between the angel and Mary that is recorded in Luke. Mary's agreement with God's plan was not automatic. She had to struggle through the implications first (Luke 1:26–38).

The account in Luke begins with the story of Zachariah serving in the temple and having an angel appear to him to tell him that his prayers will finally be answered and that his barren wife (Mary's cousin, Elizabeth) will give birth. Zachariah is struck silent by the vision and is unable to report to anyone in the temple what he saw or heard. Only when he names the child, John, by writing the name on a tablet, does he regain his speech.

This story of miraculous conception sets the stage for Jesus' birth. According to Luke's account, when Elizabeth was six months pregnant, the angel Gabriel appeared to Elizabeth's relative Mary, telling her to not be afraid because she will bear a son, and her son will be great and will rule over the house of Jacob forever.

After Mary questions the angel, asking how this can be possible because she has not known man, the angel explains that the Holy Spirit will come upon her and the holy one in her womb will be called the Son of God.

After the angel explains how Mary's conception will occur, the angel goes on to report another miracle to Mary that may likely help her to see that she was at the center of concentric circles of miracles—that the child she had conceived came at a time of other extraordinary events.

symbolism

Many Christian interpreters see parallels between the Holy Spirit overshadowing Mary in the Gospel account (Luke 1:35), the Spirit descending like a dove at Jesus' baptism (Matthew 3:16, Mark 1:10), and the passage in Genesis about the Spirit of God hovering over the waters at the creation of the world (Genesis 1:2). Jesus' birth heralds the beginning of new creation.

The angel explained to Mary that her relative Elizabeth, who had been barren, had also conceived and was six months pregnant. The angel then said, "For with God, nothing will be impossible" (Luke 1:37).

Mary is amazed by this news and travels to the hill country of Judea to be with her relative. As soon as she greets Elizabeth, the babe leaps in Elizabeth's womb, and Elizabeth immediately recognizes the holiness of the moment, as she loudly proclaims the words that would later become the foundation of the Hail Mary prayer: "Blessed are you among women, and blessed is the fruit of your womb." Then she goes on to say, "But why is this granted to me that the mother of my Lord should come to visit me?" (Luke 1:43).

factum

> The Annunciation has been the source of much creative interpretation. The beauty of this encounter between Mary and Elizabeth caused the great contemporary poet Rainer Maria Rilke to write, "She had to lay her hand upon the other woman's body, still more ripe than hers . . . each one a sanctuary, sought refuge with her closest woman kin."

Both of these statements must have confirmed for Mary and Elizabeth that they were part of a Divine plan. After Elizabeth's greeting, Mary replies with the words that are now known as the Magnificat. In Eastern Christian usage, the Magnificat is the ninth chapter of the *Biblical Odes*, a book that was used liturgically and included in many Bibles right after the Psalms.

Here is this famous "Song of Mary":

My soul proclaims the greatness of the Lord; my spirit rejoices in God my savior.

For he has looked with mercy on the lowliness of His handmaiden; for behold, from now on all generations will call me blessed.

For the Mighty One has done great things for me, and holy is His name.

His mercy is on those who fear him from generation to generation.

He has shown strength with his arm;

He has scattered the proud in the imagination of their hearts.

He has thrown down the mighty from their thrones, but lifted up the lowly.

He has filled the hungry with good things, but the rich he has sent away empty.

He has helped Israel his servant, in remembrance of His mercy;
As He spoke to our fathers, to Abraham and to his seed forever.
(Luke 1:46–55)

With these words, Mary expresses her sense of wonder and joy at the news of her role in God's plan for the salvation of the world. Because of the way it proclaims God's salvation, these verses have sometimes been called "The Gospel of Mary."

Christ's Birth

Luke's and Matthew's accounts of Jesus' birth do not offer all the same details. For centuries, Christians have been piecing together different elements from each Gospel in an effort to create one cohesive account, but in reality, the Gospel accounts sometimes contradict each other. Likewise, only Matthew and Luke offer details from Christ's birth and only Luke mentions Jesus' childhood.

discussion question

Has there been an attempt to blend the Gospel stories together?
In the latter half of the second century, a man named Tatian attempted to create a synthesis of all the four Gospels called the *Diatessaron*. This was used by many Christians but was ultimately dismissed by the fifth-century Bishop of Cyrrhus, Theodoret. He believed that the Church needed to preserve the original Gospels in their full integrity.

Luke's Gospel is the only one in which a census forced the holy family to journey to Bethlehem, where Mary gave birth to her firstborn son, wrapped him in swaddling clothes, and laid him in a manger (Luke 2:7).

The next striking aspect of Luke's account occurred when the shepherds were minding their flocks at night and an angel appeared to them, announcing that a child named Christ had been born in Bethlehem. The shepherds, like Mary before them, were extremely frightened by the glory of the Lord that shone upon them as the angel spoke. But also like Mary's Annunciation, the angel offered reassuring words—he was again bearing good news that would bring joy to all the people.

The shepherds were then told to go to Bethlehem to find the babe wrapped in swaddling clothes and lying in a manger. Then, a whole host of angels surrounded the shepherds and began to sing, "Glory to God in the highest and on earth peace, good will toward men" (Luke 2:14).

When the shepherds arrived at Bethlehem, they found the babe just as the angel had prophesied. They were amazed at all the things they had experienced and shared their story with Mary and Joseph. Everyone marveled, and Mary "kept all of these things and pondered them in her heart" (Luke 2:19).

In the Gospel of Luke especially, Mary often seems to be storing up bits of information in her heart as she ponders the changes that are happening to her son as he grows toward his vocation. After Mary and Joseph lose Jesus in Jerusalem and then search for their twelve-year-old son for three days, they finally find Jesus in the temple. Mary says, "Son, why have you done this to us? Your father and I have been looking for you with great anxiety" (Luke 2:48).

Jesus responds with a statement that some contemporary scholars believe was one of rebuke when he says, "Did you not know that I must be in my father's house?" (Luke 2:49). According to Sally Cunneen in the book *In Search of Mary*, the response Mary gives to Jesus is interesting, because Mary does not scold Jesus for a remark that might have sounded arrogant coming from the lips of a twelve-year-old. Instead, she keeps silent, and according to Luke's Gospel she kept all these things in her heart (Luke 2:51).

In the Gospel stories, Mary, like her son Jesus, seems to be growing toward understanding. She holds experiences in her heart because she needs time to understand them. Mary seems amazingly flexible in this way—she is able to adjust to her son's evolving ministry even when it causes him to say or do things that might have appeared rude coming from any other child. She recognizes that there is a larger purpose at work in her son, even if she does not claim to fully understand the implications of it or the shape that it will take over the next several years.

The Wedding at Cana

In this story, found only in the Gospel of John, Jesus and Mary are at a wedding. It seems that Mary is one of the wedding coordinators, and when the wine begins to run out, she becomes alarmed. She tells Jesus that they are out of wine. Jesus responds to his mother's prompting with some very blunt words. He says, "Woman, what have I to do with you? My hour has not yet come" (John 2:4).

Mary, however, does not seem to be offended. Her son eventually responds to her concern, though. The wine that he creates from the water is so good that one of the guests comments that usually one puts out the best wine first, and when it has been consumed puts out the lower-quality wine, but at this wedding, the best was saved for last. This miracle is significant, because it is one of Jesus' first acts at the very beginning of his public ministry. Because this was a significant turning point for Jesus, his reluctance may have been warranted—when he said "My hour has not yet come," he might have had in mind everything that was to happen to him in the future.

This story has also been quoted as an antecedent to the later mystery of the Eucharist in both the Roman Catholic and Eastern Orthodox Churches, in which bread and wine become body and blood. Another echo of this story is seen when Jesus is stretched out upon the cross and a soldier pierces his side with a sword and both blood and water stream from the wound.

Perhaps the most popular bit of folk piety, however, that rose from this passage is the idea that Mary is a great intercessor because in this story at least, she was able to get Jesus to do the thing she most wanted him to do, even though it went against his initial wishes. People reading this story in the Bible see a different side of Mary, who is a strong and determined woman who has the power to get things accomplished.

Mary at the Cross

According to the book of John, Jesus' mother was said to be at the cross during Jesus' Crucifixion, along with Mary Magdalene, and another Mary. According to John's account, Jesus speaks from the cross and commits his mother to the care of his beloved disciple. He says to John, "Behold your mother," gesturing at Mary, and then he says to Mary, "Behold your son" (John 2:4).

According to John's account, from that time forward John took Mary to live with him in his own home. According to Church tradition, John moved to Ephesus after the Crucifixion.

At the wedding at Cana, in which Mary asked Jesus to turn water into wine, he states, "Woman, what have I to do with you? My hour has not yet come" (John 2:4). Jesus addresses his mother as "woman." While many people have viewed this statement as profoundly disrespectful, some recent scholars have suggested that when Jesus called Mary "woman," he was addressing her as one of his disciples, as opposed to his mother. It would have been an honor to be considered one of Christ's disciples.

This statement seems to connect well with the verses in Acts which mentions that after the Crucifixion, Mary went to the upper room with the disciples to pray. She was present as if she was a disciple—she bore a responsibility to Christ that went beyond her biological connection to him and related directly to the spiritual responsibility she felt to continue to bring his message into the world.

discussion question

If the Virgin Mary had children other than Jesus, why were none of them present at the cross with her?
Although this issue is sometimes debated among Protestants, Roman Catholics, and Eastern Orthodox, Christians have pointed to the Crucifixion passage as evidence that Jesus had no blood siblings, because siblings would have been a more logical choice as guardians of Mary than his disciples.

Mary and the Apocalypse

The book of Revelation, also known as the Apocalypse of John, describes a "woman clothed with the sun" who labors with child (Revelation 12:1–6). She stands upon the sun and has twelve stars upon her head. She cries out in anguish as she gives birth to the child.

The child she brings into the world is a male child who will rule all the nations with an iron scepter. This woman is never explicitly identified as Mary in the Biblical text, but many Christians have drawn out the parallels. Many of the Marian apparitions seem to confirm this interpretation, especially because of the solar miracles associated with her visitations at Fatima and Medjugorje. This image also parallels the prophecies given to Mary at the Annunciation when she was told that Jesus will rule over Judea forever and his kingdom will have no end.

Although the passages in the New Testament related to Mary are sometimes sparse and occasionally contradictory, these passages became the basis for much of the piety that would surround Mary for generations to come. Each passage offers fresh insights into her heart, her person, and her unique role in her son's ministry.

Chapter 3

Mary in the Apocrypha

Besides the books that eventually became collated into the New Testament, many other books were written around and after the time of the apostles. While these books never achieved the full status as canonical (or universally accepted) books of the Bible, some of them came to have a wide influence and were much loved by Christians, while others were considered dangerous and shunned. This chapter will explore the stories of Mary found primarily in one apocryphal book, the Protoevangelium of James.

What Is the Apocrypha?

The term *Apocrypha* can refer to two very distinct bodies of texts. First, the Old Testament Apocrypha connotes a group of texts that are part of many Greek versions of the Old Testament around the time of Christ, but are not considered authoritative in Judaism or the Protestant churches today. These texts, however, remain part of the officially accepted Roman Catholic and Eastern Orthodox versions of the Old Testament. Because the Reformers used the Hebrew text instead of the Greek as the basis for their translations, these apocryphal books are not generally accepted by the Protestants, although the Anglicans tend to use the books to some extent.

The Old Testament Apocrypha

The Old Testament, as we know it now in most English-language Protestant texts, reflects the decision of a council of non-Christian Jewish rabbis around A.D. 90. Because these were non-Christian rabbis who met after the Church had already begun to be established, their decisions did not have weight for the early Christians. To make matters more complex, there has been some debate between the Roman Catholic and Eastern Orthodox theologians about which of these texts are authoritative. The Roman Catholic scholar Jerome did not believe that some of these books should be used at all.

The New Testament Apocrypha

The focus of this chapter, however, is on those texts that are sometimes called the New Testament Apocrypha. These have a much different origin and status than the Old Testament Apocrypha, and vary greatly in character and content. Some of them, particularly the Protoevangelium of James, were accepted as useful even if not fully canonical, while other texts, such as the Gospel of Thomas, which showed many Gnostic tendencies, are full of ideas that were contrary to the Christian gospel and were shunned as heretical.

The Gnostics were an offshoot of early Christianity—early enough that some parts of the New Testament are crafted as an argument against them, particularly 1 John. Gnosticism is a diverse phenomenon, but it can be broadly characterized by a few traits held in common by these disparate (and quarreling) groups. Gnostics:

- Understood themselves to possess a secret knowledge ("gnosis") that others did not have
- Believed that the God spoken of in the New Testament was different from, and superior to, the God of the Old Testament
- Viewed the body, and the material world in general, as insignificant or evil, fundamentally opposed to that which is spiritual

Because of the belief that the body and the material world are evil, many Gnostics sought liberation from the flesh through extreme ascetic practices. Although these sometimes resembled orthodox practices—trying to become liberated from the tyranny of the flesh through fasting and abstinence from sexual intercourse—Gnostics practiced asceticism for different reasons. While Christians believed the world was fundamentally good, but fallen, Gnostics viewed the world as something to be escaped entirely.

factum

Some Gnostics took their beliefs and practices in an opposite direction from the majority of Gnostics, believing that if what happened with the flesh was meaningless, there was no reason to avoid indulging the lusts of the flesh.

As noted above, Gnostics also generally taught that there was a deep division between the Old and New Testaments—that the God of the Old Testament was inferior to the God of the New, and that this inferior God had created the material world, and that childbirth merely prolonged people's enslavement to this lesser world. These teachings were considered heretical by the early church because Gnosticism viewed the body as evil, and viewed death as the ultimate separation of the body and soul, while more mainstream Christians taught that although the body and soul were separated at death, they would be reunited at the Resurrection. Although the lusts of the flesh were to be overcome, the body itself was to be sanctified, not despised. Marriage and procreation were defended as good things—as gifts from God.

The Making of Scripture

The first canon of Scripture, or list of official books, was drawn up by a Gnostic teacher named Marcion in the second century A.D. His list of books included only parts of the Gospel of Luke and some of Paul's letters, and specifically excluded the Old Testament. It was only in the fourth century that a final and authoritative list of the books of the New Testament was agreed upon. This wasn't arbitrary, though.

The books that were finally accepted had to meet certain criteria. They had to:

- Be written by one of the apostles or their close associates
- Conform to the understanding of the Gospel message passed down by the apostles or to those they appointed as successors in the churches and those who came after them (thus giving birth to the doctrine of Apostolic Succession)
- Be more or less universally known and accepted in all of the churches

Thus it could be said that the current New Testament was not invented in the fourth century, but rather was formally recognized and sealed by the church leaders at that time. One amazing thing about this process was how much agreement there actually was with regard to which books were to be included.

Mary's Conception

The story of Mary's conception is not recorded in the any of the New Testament canonical books. Authors of noncanonical books such as the Protoevangelium of James attempted to provide the details that were lacking in the Gospels by writing their own narratives, which would have likely included elements from the oral tradition. This is especially likely with the Protoevangelium of James, because this book was written around A.D. 150, only eighty years after the destruction of the Temple of Jerusalem.

The memories of the events that occurred in the Gospel, as well as the stories that were not recorded in the Gospels but reflect the lives of those most intimately connected with Christ, would have still been fresh in the memory of the society as well as in the mind of the author of the Protoevangelium.

The Question of Authorship

Most scholars believe that the Protoevangelium was compiled by a single author, who attached the name of the apostle James to it to give it an air of authority. The Protoevangelium offers more details about the life of Mary and birth of Christ than any other text, although the bulk of these details are not viewed as straight historical facts.

discussion question

How widespread is knowledge of the Protoevangelium of James? The Protoevangelium of James is perhaps the most widely accepted and frequently copied of the apocryphal books and has been translated into more than twenty languages. It has also inspired many artistic renderings as well as church feasts in the East.

Some scholars have suggested that the genre of the Protoevangelium of James is closest to a Midrash, which is literature from the Jewish rabbinical tradition based on the original sacred texts. According to scholar Addison Wright, the authors of Midrash sought to make the Biblical stories "understandable, useful and relevant" to later generations by means of creative, extended reflections upon the Biblical texts.

The Protoevangelium is valuable because it offers useful insights into the life and theological significance of the Virgin Mary. It is also very moving and even humorous and tragic in turns, as the characters are shown in their full human complexities.

The Holy of Holies

In the Protoevangelium, Mary is brought to the temple when she is only three years old, and she remains in the temple until adolescence. Upon her arrival, she is brought by Zachariah, the high priest, into the Holy of Holies, the innermost part of the temple where the Ark of the Covenant was once housed. This place was considered so holy that even the high priest would only enter once a year, on Yom Kippur, the Day of Atonement. According to tradition, the Holy of Holies was not illuminated by the sun or by artificial light, but shone with the Glory of God. This text helped form an association in the minds of early Christians between Mary and the temple. Like the physical temple, God dwelt within Mary. Unlike the temple building, God took on her own flesh and was, in a sense, even physically present within her womb.

factum

The depiction of Mary's parents, Joachim and Anna, in the Protoevangelium seems to echo that of another Old Testament apocryphal couple named Joachim and Susanna. This couple is described in a book called *Susanna*. They were also wealthy and unable to bear children.

Joachim and Anna

According to the Protoevangelium, Mary's parents, Joachim and Anna, were a wealthy and generous couple who had struggled with

infertility for many years. The Protoevangelium is also very intentional about stating that Joachim was from the Royal line of David,
which would mean that Mary, and ultimately her son, Jesus, would
also be descendants of David.

When Mary's father Joachim goes to the temple to make an offering, his offering is rejected by the priest Rubin because Joachim
and his wife had not yet been able to produce a child. Joachim
was aggrieved by this, but when he studied the Old Testament
Scriptures he discovered that it was true that all of the great people
in the Scriptures had, in fact, produced offspring. Instead of returning home to his wife, Joachim decided to go out into the wilderness
and fast and pray for forty days.

It is significant that Joachim was away for forty days because of
the significance of the number forty in the Bible. The number forty
in the Old and New Testaments is intended to signify many years,
but it is not necessarily related to the literal numerical value. Noah
was in the ark for forty days and nights (Genesis 7), the Israelites
wandered for forty years in the wilderness (Exodus 16:35), Moses
was on the mount for forty days and nights (Exodus 24:18), and
Jesus fasted for forty days (Matthew 4:2).

When Joachim disappeared for forty days, Anna did not immediately guess that her husband had gone to the wilderness to pray.
Instead, she feared the worst, imagining that she was both infertile
and a widow.

Anna prayed and moped at home, while one of her servants
made matters worse by pointing out to her that her infertility was a
curse. Anna went into her garden and looked up at a tree and saw
that there were newly hatched baby birds in the nest. She felt that
everyone in the world was able to have babies except her.

She made this plea to God, "O God of our fathers, bless me
and hear my prayer as thou did bless the womb of Sarah . . ." This
prayer connects her own plight to the ancient story of Abraham and
Sarah's struggle with infertility. Like Abraham and Sarah, Joachim
and Anna were ultimately blessed with a miracle, but they had to
struggle for it first.

An Angel Appears

While Joachim was in the desert and Anna was praying at home, angels appeared to both of them to tell them that they would have a child. According to the angels, this child would be "a gift of the Lord." Anna responded to this message with great joy, and made a promise that she would dedicate her child to the Lord's service for the rest of her life. Joachim immediately made an offering of lambs, kids, and calves. He then rushed to the gates of Jerusalem to embrace his wife. Anna does conceive and bear a child, who is born exactly nine months, minus one day, after her parent's embrace.

symbolism

The embrace shared by Anna and Joachim has become the subject of many icons. In these icons, one can often see the wedding bed just behind the embracing couple, as if to report that Mary was indeed conceived in the traditional way.

According to a medieval text that is partially based on the Protoevangelium of James and called *The Golden Legend* (see Chapter 9), just after Anna gave birth she asked her midwife about the sex of her child. When the midwife replied that Anna had given birth to a little girl, Anna said, "On this day is my spirit exalted."

This passage is especially interesting because a similar tale is also told in the Koran, although in the account in the Koran, Anna is initially distressed and disappointed to discover that she has given birth to a girl, because she had hoped for a boy.

Child Mary in the Temple

According to the Protoevangelium, Anna watched her daughter closely. Just after the infant Mary took her first seven steps, Anna scooped her up and said, "As the Lord my God lives, you shall walk no more upon this ground until I take you to the temple of the Lord."

From that day forward, Anna kept Mary in her room, which she set apart as a sanctuary and allowed only "undefiled" people to enter. When Mary was a year old, her father had a great feast in celebration of her birthday, and the priests and high priests came and blessed Mary.

When Mary was two years old, Joachim and Anna debated over whether or not they should send her to the temple in fulfillment of Anna's promise to God. They decided to wait because they felt it would make the two-year-old Mary sad if they left her at the temple.

At age three, Mary was taken to the temple to live as a virgin. Joachim and Anna wanted to offer her to the temple as a dedicated virgin, but they were afraid that she might not be able to stay there. To their amazed wonder, however, the priest received Mary, kissed her and said, "The Lord has made your name great among all generations. At the end of days, the Lord will reveal in you his redemption for the sons of Israel."

The priest then placed Mary on the third step leading to the altar, and the spirit of God filled her and she danced with Joy. According to the Protoevangelium, "The whole of Israel loved her." Mary then lived in the temple for many more years, and according to tradition, was fed by an angel.

The account of Mary being miraculously fed is quite similar to the account offered by the Sufi Muslim mystic, Jalal-ud-Din Rumi. According to this account, the priest Zachariah continually brings food to Mary, but each time he does so, he finds an exact replica of the food he is bringing to her. Finally the priest asks where the other food is coming from and Mary responds, "Whenever I feel hungry, I ask God, and whatever I ask for, God sends. His generosity and compassion are infinite; whoever relies wholly on God finds that his help never fails."

Rumi's account of Mary being miraculously fed is very similar to the account offered by the Koran, which you will learn more about in Chapter 18. There are many parallels between the Christian extra-Biblical texts and the Koran.

According to the Protoevangelium, Mary lived in the temple for many years, but had to leave when she was twelve years old, because as soon as she began to menstruate, her blood could defile the temple. This concern was based on ancient views of purity which held that blood (and other bodily fluids) must be kept out of the temple because of the risk of pollution.

Mary's Engagement

After Mary had to leave the temple, priest Zachariah then went into the Holy of Holies and prayed to God about what to do. The response to his prayer came through an angel, who told him that he should assemble all the widowers from Judea. They would all bring their rods and drop them and then Zachariah would take all the rods into the temple and pray over them. Whoever received that last rod back would take Mary as his wife.

This process of selection was a little bit like the "casting of lots" which occurred in both the Old and New Testaments (see, for example, 1 Samuel 14:36–42 and Acts 1:24–26). Occasionally, lots (coins, polished sticks, dice, or cards) were tossed in an effort to make difficult, significant decisions. When lots were cast, nobody could complain of favoritism. According to Proverbs 16:33, "The lot is cast into the lap, but its every decision is from the Lord."

factum

The dove has symbolic value in Scripture. After the flood, Noah sent a dove to check for land. When Christ was baptized, a dove hovered over him. In Christian tradition, the dove represents the Holy Spirit. The dove was also present in the apparitions of Mary in Zeitun, Egypt, in which doves flew from a form resembling the Virgin Mary.

When the selection process commenced, a trumpet sounded and all the widowers came running. Joseph's rod was the last to be returned, so he was selected to be Mary's husband and guardian. As he received the rod, a dove flew from it and landed on his head.

Joseph, however, initially refuses to take Mary as his wife, because he feels that if he takes such a young bride, he will be seen as a laughing stock among his people. The priest, however, offers Joseph reassurance, and Joseph finally agrees to take Mary. The priest then performs the betrothal service, which is something like an engagement, only more binding.

Mary's Work

According to the Protoevangelium, Mary was part of a group of twelve virgins who were asked to return to the temple to help weave the holy veil for the tabernacle. Mary was pleased with this work and considered it a great honor to be entrusted with the very valuable scarlet and purple threads for her weaving.

During this time, Mary went out to a well to draw water and was startled by the appearance of an angel who said to her, "Hail, thou art highly favored, the Lord is with thee, blessed art thou among women." When Mary returned home, the angel appeared to her again, and spoke words that echo the account of the Annunciation in Luke.

One of the differences between the Gospel account of the Annunciation and the accounts of the Annunciation in the Protoevangelium of James is that in the Protoevangelium, Joseph responds more harshly to the news that Mary is pregnant, accusing her of being deceitful like Eve.

Joseph mentions that Mary, of all people, should never have done what she did, because she was raised in the Holy of Holies. This statement is important because it forms the basis for one of the central teachings about the Virgin Mary as a temple of the Holy Spirit, and yet, ironically, it seems to be thrown in as an afterthought—it is only in the course of Joseph's rant that Mary being raised in the Holy of Holies is ever stated explicitly.

Mary and Joseph then went before the priest Zachariah, who also accused them of immorality. They were required to do the ancient "bitter water test," which is described in the Old Testament book of Numbers (5:11–31). This test was meant to show whether a wife had been unfaithful or not (since Mary was betrothed, any infidelity would have been considered adultery). According to the results of this test, Mary was found innocent.

Mary's Vision

Mary and Joseph then had to travel to Bethlehem, where Mary would give birth to Jesus. While they were traveling, Mary had a vision in which she saw two infants, one weeping and one rejoicing. This vision seemed to echo the vision Rachel experienced soon before she gave birth to Esau and Jacob. In Rachel's vision, she sensed that there would be great struggle between her twins.

discussion question

How can Mary's vision be interpreted?
The struggle between the two infants from Mary's vision has been viewed as a metaphor for the tensions between Judaism and Christianity. It is also viewed as a representation of the fact that although Christians rejoiced at the birth of Christ, Jews soberly continued to await the Messiah.

Soon after the couple finally arrived in Bethlehem, Mary gave birth to Jesus while Joseph was away. Shortly afterward, Joseph saw a cloud surrounding the manger and realized that Mary had given birth. The Protoevangelium ends with the Slaughter of the Innocents, which was also recorded in the Gospels (Matthew 2:16). In the Slaughter of the Innocents, Herod hears that the Messiah had been born and becomes furious, so he decrees that every firstborn child shall be killed. According to the Protoevangelium, Mary hides Jesus in the manger until Herod's soldiers pass by.

Mary's relative Elizabeth fled to the mountains with her baby John, and he was also spared, although her husband, the high priest, Zachariah, who served in the temple, was often questioned about his son's whereabouts. When Zachariah refused to give any clues about his son, he was killed, causing great grief in the Jewish community. Eventually, Simeon was appointed as Zachariah's replacement, and Simeon believed in the promise that he would not die until he had seen the Savior with his own eyes.

Jesus' Siblings

There are two traditional ways of understanding who the Scriptural "brothers" of Jesus were. According to one tradition, rooted in the Protoevangelium of James, these "siblings" are from Joseph's prior marriage (because Joseph was a widower). This perspective is the standard explanation found in Eastern Orthodox Churches.

Roman Catholic theologians, on the other hand, have been more inclined to say that that these siblings were cousins. This statement is based in the teaching of Saint Jerome, a Biblical scholar who didn't like the way the Protoevangelium of James described the siblings of Jesus as stepbrothers.

factum

Saint Jerome preferred the argument that the siblings of Jesus were cousins because he felt that it was most appropriate for both Mary and Joseph to have been virgins. Saint Jerome felt that it would have been improper for Joseph to have fathered other children even if he did remain chaste with Mary.

Ever since Jerome's statement, Roman Catholic theologians have been more inclined to emphasize the Pseudo-Gospel of Matthew, a later text that shares many elements with the Protoevangelium. According to the Pseudo-Gospel of Matthew, the siblings of Jesus were actually his cousins. The pseudo-Gospel of Matthew is also distinct in that it offers more information about Mary's education in the temple. Stories from the Protoevangelium became popular in the West many years later, when they were incorporated into *The Golden Legend* (see Chapter 9 for more information).

Mary's Death

Likewise, there are two main traditions related to Mary's death. One of the great unsettled debates within Christianity surrounds the question of where Mary lived out her final years. According to many people, most notably the second-century writer Saint Irenaeus of Lyon, Mary died in Ephesus. Irenaeus based his belief on the immediate disciples of the apostle John. Because this traditional teaching is based on the passage from John in which Jesus commits Mary to John's care from the cross, and because it is widely believed that John moved to Ephesus to preach after the Crucifixion, a strong case can be made for this position.

Another tradition holds that Mary died in Jerusalem. This tradition is reported in the medieval text the *Legenda Aurea* (or *the Golden Legend*). This text was compiled in the thirteenth century, by the Dominican Archbishop of Genoa, Jacobus de Voragine. According to this account, Mary lived in a house on Mount Zion for many years after the death of her son.

According to this account, one day, as the Virgin Mary was again pondering her son's death, an angel appeared to her and announced her death. But Mary protested, because she wanted to see the apostles one more time. In response to Mary's request, Saint John was brought on a white cloud from Ephesus, and all of the other apostles came as well. Just as Mary was believed to have given birth to Jesus without suffering, according to the *Golden Legend*, Mary also died without suffering, as her soul flew directly into the arms of her son.

An account called the Transistus, or Passing, offers an additional detail about Mary's death. In this account, Saint Thomas also arrived just after Mary's death on a cloud from India. Because the apostles knew that Thomas was a doubter and needed to be reassured with evidence, they took him to Mary's empty tomb. But Thomas explained that he didn't need to see the empty tomb, because he had already spotted Mary ascending when he was passing by on his cloud.

These accounts of Mary's death are all attempts to fill the gaps about an event that we know very little about. Some of the traditions are more reliable than others, and much of the mystery remains. No relics of Mary's body have ever been found. While some have suggested that they could have been lost, this is unlikely, considering how much care and attention have been given to relics throughout Christian history.

The search for Mary's relics began more than 1,500 years ago when Constantine's mother Helen began her excavations in Palestine in the fourth century to try to find relics from the life of Christ. Drawing from the collective memory of local Christians, Helen was able to successfully locate the cross on which Christ died, but she never found the Virgin Mary's body.

symbolism

Several icons show a large Jesus holding his mother wrapped in her burial shroud as if she is a tiny baby. This image is an exact reversal of the Nativity icon, which shows a tiny Jesus wrapped in swaddling clothes. Most icons of the Virgin Mary and child show a small Jesus held in his mother's arms.

In 1950, the Roman Catholic Church officially proclaimed that the Virgin Mary was taken up into heaven after she completed the course of her earthly life. Although the Eastern Orthodox believe that Mary was assumed into heaven, they teach that she "fell asleep" first (and thus celebrate the feast of the Dormition instead of the

Assumption). Roman Catholics are divided on whether Mary died or not before being assumed. The Eastern Orthodox celebrate Mary's Dormition, or falling asleep, on August 15.

Although it was widely believed among the early Christians that Mary was taken directly up to heaven without suffering the separation of body and soul that is customary at death, there is little certainty surrounding Mary's death. The earliest written mention of her ascension is found in a text that dates from the fourth or fifth century. It is difficult to know for sure how strongly this teaching was affirmed in the oral traditions before that time.

According to the fourth-century writer Ephiphanius, no one knows exactly what happened to Mary at the end of her life. As we can see, this debate continued well into the Middle Ages and continues even now, particularly between Protestants and Catholics. In 1950, Pope Pius XII declared the Assumption to be a formal dogma of the Catholic Church. The lingering questions that surround the Virgin Mary's death remain part of the larger body of mysteries that continue to surround her life.

Chapter 4

Spotting Mary in the Old Testament

I n novels, many writers employ a literary device called foreshadowing in which they offer a hint of what is to come later in the book. The early Church Fathers viewed the Old Testament in a similar way. According to their thinking, there were both Christ types and Mary types in the Old Testament that foreshadowed the appearance of Christ and Mary in the New Testament. This chapter will explore ways in which the early Church Fathers saw Mary in the Old Testament.

Multiple Meanings

In contemporary times, people often debate about literal interpretations of different Biblical stories. For example, whether the world was created in a literal seven days or whether the term "day" in Genesis 1 might not correspond perfectly to the twenty-four-hour-days experienced on Earth.

The earliest Christians, however, did not hold to a strictly literal interpretation of the Scriptures. Because they believed that the Scriptures were wholly true and inspired by God, they believed that many stories of the Old Testament implicitly spoke about the truths that were revealed more fully in the events surrounding Jesus' life.

discussion question

What is typology?
In a Christian context, typology is way of reading the Bible in which Old Testament figures, events, or prophecies are interpreted through the lens of Jesus Christ. Practically speaking, typology allowed Christian interpreters to fully integrate some of the more difficult parts of the Old Testament in a Christian context.

The Church Fathers saw multiple meanings in every passage, especially in the lives of the great ancestors of the faith, such as Abraham, Isaac, Jacob, and Moses. They interpreted everything through the lens of Christ, and saw references to Jesus and Mary throughout the text.

In allegorical interpretations of the Scriptures, passages contain additional meanings apart from the plain sense of the text. These meanings would have been readily understood within the whole context of faith. One of the most famous and universally accepted uses of allegorical interpretation was used in the Song of Songs, the great love poem of the Old Testament. This book was seen as not just a love poem between two individuals, but more profoundly, a love poem between God and Israel, God and humanity, or in later understanding, humanity and Jesus Christ or the Virgin Mary.

Typological interpretations allowed later thinkers to look back on earlier texts and to understand them as precursors of things that were yet to come. Typology was also used more broadly by many Christian thinkers to refer not only to the Old Testament, but also to elements of other religions, showing how they were all fulfilled in Christ.

One example of this kind of typological interpretation is Jonah, who was often viewed as a type of Christ because he spent three days in a dark, deathlike place (the belly of the fish) and then was brought back into the light of day. Similarly, the sacrifice of Isaac (Genesis 12) is understood to foreshadow Jesus' on the cross. Just as Abraham was called to offer his only son as a sacrifice, so too, according to Christian belief, God gave up his only son for the life of the world.

These typological and allegorical interpretations extended beyond Christ to his mother Mary, who came to be seen by the Church Fathers in many of the most significant events of the Old Testament. Typological interpretation allowed for a clear sense of Mary's significance as well as the way in which her actions helped to bring many of the Old Testament stories together into a more complete picture of creation, fall, and redemption.

The Burning Bush

In his work *On the Birth of Christ*, the fourth-century Church Father Saint Gregory of Nyssa wrote eloquently about the Virgin Mary and her connection to the burning bush from the Old Testament. He said, "What was prefigured at that time in the flame of the bush was openly manifested in the mystery of the Virgin . . . As on the mountain the bush burned but was not consumed, so the Virgin gave birth to the light and was not corrupted."

These images captured the imaginations of many of the early and medieval Christians, who felt that the Virgin Mary's body was something like the bush, which burned with the flames of the presence of God, yet miraculously survived. According to the Old Testament account, through that flaming bush, the angel spoke to Moses, who discovered that he was standing on holy ground.

Saint Gregory of Nyssa believed that not only did Moses experience this miracle as an encounter with God, but that he may have even been able to see into the future in that moment in which the presence of God burned within the bush. For Saint Gregory, even Moses was looking toward what was to come. The image of Mary as the burning bush has been depicted both in Eastern Orthodox iconography and in Western medieval art.

symbolism

In Nicholas Froment's 1476 painting, *Moses and the Burning Bush*, Mary holds the infant Christ and is seated on a flaming rose bush. Moses is also in this image, tending his flock of sheep as an angel appears to him. Froment depicts the connection between Mary and the burning bush that had been made by many early Christians.

This image of Mary in the burning bush is part of a larger collection of images that connects Mary to the natural world. In the Middle Ages, hundreds of plants and flowers were named for Mary's different attributes. The natural world was seen as a school through which the Church could educate people about the life of Mary and of Christ. You'll learn more about the connections between the Virgin Mary and the natural world in Chapters 16 and 19.

Jacob's Ladder

The story of Jacob's Ladder from the book of Genesis is read in the Eastern Orthodox Church on the Feast of the Nativity. In the minds of the early Church Fathers, this image pointed to the Virgin Mary. Just as in Jacob's dream, where a ladder ascends to heaven and angels climb down the ladder, so, in Christian tradition, God climbs down the ladder toward Earth through Mary, who becomes the ladder—the bridge between heaven and Earth.

When Jacob awoke from sleeping on his stone pillow, he declared, "How awesome is this place! This is the gate of heaven!" (Genesis 28:17). This proclamation is read by Christian interpreters to connect Jacob's vision to Mary because in other writings, Mary's womb is "the gate of heaven." She is also viewed by many early Christian writers as the house or the temple of God, because God dwelt in her and made her holy. The images used by the fathers and in the Scriptures are all related, complementing each other and each offering a fuller picture of the Virgin Mary.

The Ark of the Covenant

The Virgin Mary is also viewed as the Ark of the Covenant because God dwelt within her. She also carried within her womb the creator of all things, and she herself became "the holy of holies." This image is closely connected to the apocryphal story from the Protoevangelium of James, in which Joseph accuses Mary of adultery. Her close association with the temple was directly linked to the fact that in the Christian tradition Mary is viewed as the temple. While all Christians are in some sense the temple of the Holy Spirit when they bear the Word of God, Mary's role as a temple of the Holy Spirit was unique, because only she nourished Christ in her womb.

The fourth-century bishop of Alexandria, Athanasius, also wrote eloquently about the Virgin Mary, making strong connections between her and the Ark of the Covenant. He was an extremely influential writer, expressing many of the mysteries of the Incarnation in powerful, lucid terms. He wrote, "O [Ark of the New] Covenant, clothed with purity instead of gold! You are the Ark in which is found the golden vessel containing the true manna, that is, the flesh in which divinity resides. You surpass them, for it is written: 'The earth is my footstool' (Is 66:1). But you carry within you the feet, the head, and the entire body of the perfect God."

The East Gate of the Temple

Another image often used for the Virgin Mary was the East Gate of the temple. Like the other Old Testament types, this image highlights the way in which Mary's role in salvation history is intrinsically linked to Christ. Mary is the portal through which the Lord entered his creation. Because of this, exploring the Old Testament typology becomes a means of contemplating the Incarnation.

According to Jewish tradition, the Messiah would enter through the East Gate (see, for example, Ezekiel 43:1–5). Christians also celebrate Jesus' entry through the East Gate into Jerusalem on Palm Sunday (Luke 19:35–38).

The Golden Gate

In the Book of Acts, the East Gate is called the Beautiful Gate (Acts 3:2–10). Because of the way Jerome translated the book into Latin, it is also known as the Golden Gate. This is appropriate, not only because of the way this gate was once decorated, but also because, according to the Bible, it was the place where the glory of God (the Shekinah) entered the temple.

This gate is also said to be the place where the Last Judgment will take place. This is based on passages from both the Old and New Testaments, as well as other traditions. Jews, Christians, and Muslims have traditionally buried their dead outside of this gate so that they could be close to the Lord when he returns to judge the living and the dead (see Zechariah 14:4–5 and Matthew 24:27). This is why there are many cemeteries to this day on the Mount of Olives, just east of the Temple Mount. The Mount of Olives is located on the east side of Jerusalem and is a popular holy site for Jews, Muslims, and Christians. Among Jews, the Mount of Olives has been a popular burial site since the time of the first Temple. According to Jewish tradition the Messiah is to enter Jerusalem through the nearby

Golden Gate and those who are buried on the Mount of Olives will be the first to be resurrected. Today many important churches are located on this mountain, and according to Christian tradition, this was the last place where Jesus prayed before he was taken captive by the Romans.

The imagery of the East Gate was also connected to the teaching of Mary's ever-virginity. Ezekiel writes, "And the Lord said to me, 'This gate shall be shut; it shall not be opened; and no man shall enter by it because the Lord God of Israel has entered by it; therefore, it shall be shut'" (Ezekiel 44:2).

There is a further significance connected to this temple door facing east. Christians have traditionally prayed facing east, and it is from the east that the sun rises—an image that the Church has often connected to rising of the "son."

A Garden Enclosed

The image of a gate that remains closed is closely connected to the images of Mary as a "garden enclosed" (Song of Solomon 4:12). This image would also have been connected to her ever-virginity. She became, in the minds of Christians, a sealed-in garden that no man could enter after God did. This image was also featured in medieval tapestries and paintings, in which Mary is shown surrounded by animals and flowers that had a particular connection to her (such as roses and lilies) and surrounded by a walled-in gate. She would be shown near her infant child Christ, if not holding him.

The image connecting Mary to the East Gate of the temple is similar to the image of the door, which is featured in the writings of Saint Romanos. In his hymn for the Nativity of Christ, he writes that Mary "opens the door and receives the company of the magi. She opens the door—she the unopened and yet in no way robbed of the treasure of her purity. She opened the door, she from whom was born the door." This passage symbolically connects Mary, who was herself a door, since it was through her that God came into the world, with Christ, who is himself "the way," or the door, to eternal life (John 14:6).

The Root of Jesse

The rod (or root) of Jesse was interpreted by early Christians as a Christlike figure. This imagery was connected to David's royal line, from which both Joseph and, according to Church tradition, Mary were descendants. The lineage grew through the ages and blossomed in the persons of Mary and Christ. Isaiah 11:1–10 says, "There Shall come forth a Rod from the stem of Jesse, and a Branch shall grow out of his roots . . . and in that day there shall be a Root of Jesse, who shall stand as a banner to the people; for the Gentiles shall seek him and his resting place shall be glorious."

According to the Church Fathers, the Virgin Mary (not just her husband Joseph as is shown clearly from the Gospel lineages) was a descendant from the house of David. This lineage was important to the Church Fathers because it connected Mary's son, Jesus, with the royal line. In Romans 15:12, Saint Paul explicitly makes the connection between Christ and the root of Jesse.

The root-of-Jesse imagery is similar to the vine imagery from the Gospel. The Gospel that states, "I am the true vine, and my father is the vine grower. He removes every branch in me that bears no fruit. Every branch that bears fruit he prunes to make it bear more fruit . . . Just as the branch cannot bear fruit by itself unless it abides in the vine, neither can you unless you abide in me" (John 15:1–4). In this passage, Jesus is the vine and his followers are the branches. Mary, as the mother of Jesus, would have been the first to receive this seed from God and to nurture the vine as it grew. According to the book of Isaiah, "a staff shall spring forth from the root of Jesse, and a flower shall come up from his root; and the Spirit of God will rest upon him" (Isaiah 11:1).

The image of Mary as springing from the root of Jesse was also another reference to the miracle of her ability to bring life into the world although she was a virgin. Many times, in both the writings of the fathers and the Koran, much is written about Mary's ability to bring forth life without any seed from man. This gift is a sign of divine favor as well as miraculous intervention. Saint Jerome brought out the paradox of this event by marveling at the miracle that she, who never had the seed of man, was able to bear fruit—she herself was the fruit of the earth but she bore the Lord in her womb.

factum

> Within Islamic thought, there is also a connection between Mary and fruitfulness. In the Koran's account of the birth of Jesus, Mary went to an isolated place to give birth. When the pain of childbirth became intense, she reached up and grabbed a fig tree, which immediately bore sweet figs to nourish and refresh Mary.

The Buttery Mountain

The Church Fathers also made a connection between Mary and a mountain. She is like a mountain in the sense that she stretched toward the heavens with her life. Her life is viewed as higher than any of the other saints, because she was chosen for the ultimate calling of bearing God in her womb.

These interpretations are sometimes connected to Psalm 67, in which God dwelt inside of a mountain in the same way that Jesus dwelt inside of the Virgin Mary's womb. Psalm 67:17 describes this mountain as "God's mountain, a rich mountain, the mountain in which God has been pleased to dwell."

Some translations of this verse have used the word *fertile* instead of *rich*— a translation that strengthens the Marian association. This image of the "buttery mountain" has also been translated in a way that may sound strange (and not very appetizing) to modern ears. The other image was "a Curdled Mountain." In the Eastern Orthodox Church these mountain images are used in a Vespers hymn for September 6, "O immaculate one, Daniel describes you as a great mountain, while Habbakuk calls you a mountain shaded by virtues, and David regards you as a curdled mountain, from which God has become incarnate and redeemed the world."

This was another reference to the Virgin Mary's fertility, which was connected to the ancient understanding of how babies were made. In the ancient world, it was believed that babies were made when the seed of the man mingled with the blood of the woman, causing that blood to "curdle" into a kind of cheese. This image was also stated in Job 10:10, "Did you not pour me out like milk and curdle me like cheese?"

Saint Romanos, who wrote beautiful chanted sermons in the sixth century, picked up on this image and puts the words in Christ's mouth as he speaks to his mother on his way to the cross saying, "Do not make the day of my passion bitter, because for it I, the sweet one, came down from heaven, like the manna, not onto Mount Sinai, but into your womb. For within it, as David prophesied, I was curdled like cheese." Christ goes on to make the reference even more direct in Saint Romanos's hymn, saying, "Understand, honored Lady, the curdled mountain, I now exist because being word I became flesh in you."

The Rose of Sharon

The Rose of Sharon image was used by Saint Jerome and is taken from the Song of Solomon (also known as the Song of Songs), "I am the Rose of Sharon and the Lily of the Valleys" (2:1). These images suggested the Virgin Mary's purity and beauty. The image of a rose with petals not fully opened was connected to her virginity and youth. Just as young flower does not open completely until it has reached maturity, the Virgin Mary was chosen to become the Mother of God when she was still a pure, young girl.

There is some ambiguity surrounding this particular passage in the Song of Songs. The Song of Songs is a passionate love poem from the Old Testament. Traditional rabbinic Jewish interpretation understood it to symbolize the special relationship between God and Israel, while Christians have generally taken it to refer to the love between Jesus and the Church (as spoken of in Ephesians 5), or more recently, between Christ and the individual Christian soul. Many have also seen it as speaking of Mary's relationship to God.

Some of the confusion that has come about related to this poem is the fact that it can be difficult to parse out *who* is speaking. In some cases it seems that the bride is speaking, while in other cases it seems as if the bridegroom is speaking. The confusion surrounding this passage has extended into later commentaries on the passage, because while some people took the reference to the Rose of Sharon and the Lily of Valley to be a reference to Mary, still others thought it was a reference to Christ.

symbolism

The Rose of Sharon imagery is also a symbol for the bride. In this case, these references would have called Mary to mind as the spouse of the Holy Spirit, chosen by God for a very unique and significant purpose, set apart from the rest of creation, united to God through her perfect obedience.

Several centuries later, Saint Thérèse of Lisieux picked up on this imagery when she wrote, "Thou art the flower with petals still unclosed; I gaze upon Thy beauty undefiled. Thou art the Rose of Sharon long foretold, Still in Thy glorious bud, Thou heavenly Child!" This reference can be confusing, because it sounds as if it is referring to Mary. But clearly, in this passage, it is only the final verses that refer to Mary. "Thy dearest Mother's arms, so pure and white, form for Thee now a royal cradle-throne; The morning sun is Mary's bosom bright, thy sunlit dew her virginal milk, my own!"

In the minds of the Church Fathers, Mary pulled together the disparate aspects of creation and wove them into a single seamless garment, bringing harmony to a world broken by sin. These images come together beautifully in the seventeenth century when

Johannes Scheffler, under the penname Angelus Silesius, wrote, "Ark, fortress, tower, house, garden, mirror, fountain; The sea, a star, the moon, the rose of dawn, a mountain; She is another world so can be all things freely."

These images provide just a sampling of the many visual images that were used both by early Christians and during the medieval period to point to the multiple connections between the Old and New Testaments, and the ways in which these images come together in representations of Mary. All of these images serve to create a rich tapestry of belief that provides a helpful backdrop for understanding the multiple facets of devotion to Mary.

Chapter 5

Mary and the Councils

During the first few centuries after the death of Christ, there were sometimes fierce debates over what constituted legitimate Christian teaching. In order to bring unity and clarity to the churches, the famed Roman emperor, Constantine the Great, called the first church council, which met in Nicea in 325. This chapter will offer a basic framework of some the earliest church councils and the ways these councils helped to form an early understanding of Mary's place within Christianity.

No Easy Answers

People often assume that more unity existed in the early Church than actually did. In truth, the earliest Christians had to struggle to define their faith. Throughout history, Christians have struggled to distinguish between true and false teaching. Even some books in what is now known as the New Testament were the subject of heated debate among early Christians. Together, these believers had to struggle and prayerfully discern which books would be included in the final canon, and which would be kept within the tradition of the Church, but not given authoritative status.

Likewise, many of the central teachings of Christianity became more defined through time. For example, although the doctrine of the Trinity—the belief that there are three divine persons, Father, Son, and Holy Spirit, who exist and work together in unity—is rooted in Scripture, it would not necessarily be plainly apparent from a reading of the Bible.

In this context of division, church councils were often called by the Roman (Byzantine) emperor as a way to unify the churches. This was in the interest of the civil authorities since, as Christianity became more widespread, doctrinal disputes had a marked effect on civic peace. These councils provided a forum for Christians to meet and struggle through the different issues, seeking a prayerful consensus on matters that were critical to the life of faith.

discussion question

Why were councils called ecumenical?
These councils were called ecumenical because they brought together representatives from all over the Christian world. The word *ecumenical* comes from the Greek word *oikos,* or house, so what is ecumenical pertains to the whole ecumene, meaning the household of the Empire, or the inhabited world.

Sometimes the battles about theology were quite fierce. People believed things with all their hearts and fought for them, only to have their views rejected by the Church as a whole. There is an old saying attributed to Tertullian that "the blood of the martyrs is the seed of the Church," meaning that the teachings of the Church come from the blood, sweat, and tears of the earliest Christians. Long before official councils were called, bishops had been assembling to dispute and define theology for their flocks. One of best-known and earliest examples of this is the Council of Jerusalem, which is spoken about in Chapter 15 of the book of Acts.

Constantine

The earliest Christians struggled under the continual threat of persecution. This situation changed dramatically, however, when Constantine issued the Edict of Milan, also known as The Edict of Toleration, in A.D. 313. Under this edict, freedom of religion was proclaimed, and Christianity was even specially favored. Some years later, under Theodosius the Great (379–395), Christianity would become the official religion of the Empire.

factum

Like many secular rulers before and after him, politics and religion were intermixed for Constantine. He was concerned with unifying both Church and Empire. Constantine was baptized on his deathbed in A.D. 337, having legalized Christianity while still a catechumen (a student preparing for Baptism).

About six years after the Edict of Milan was issued, a *presbyter* (a Greek term meaning "elder," usually translated as "priest") named Arius of Alexandria began to teach concerning the Word of God (John 1:1) that "God begat him, and before he was begotten, he did not exist." Athanasius was at that time a newly ordained deacon, secretary to Bishop Alexander of Alexandria, and a member of his household. His reply to Arius was that the Father begat the Son from all eternity—this was not an event in time. Arius was condemned by the bishops of Egypt (with the exceptions of Secundus of Ptolemais and Theonas of Marmorica), and went to Nicomedia, from which he wrote letters to bishops throughout the world, stating his position.

Calling a Council

Constantine sought to resolve the dispute by calling a council of bishops from all over the Christian world. This council met in Nicea, just across the straits from what is now Istanbul, in A.D. 325, and consisted of 317 bishops. Athanasius accompanied his bishop to the council, and became recognized as a chief representative for the view that the Son was fully God, co-equal and co-eternal with the Father.

The party of Athanasius was overwhelmingly in the majority. (The western, Latin-speaking, half of the Empire was very sparsely represented, but it was solidly Athanasian, so that if its bishops had attended in force, the vote would have been still more lopsided.)

Those at the council first attempted to find a formula from Holy Scripture that would express the full deity of the Son, as well as his equality with the Father. However, the Arians cheerfully agreed to all such formulations, having interpreted them already to fit their own views. Finally, the Greek word *homoousios* (meaning "of the same substance, or nature, or essence") was introduced, chiefly because it was one word that could not be understood to mean what the Arians meant, which was that the Son was somehow less divine than the Father. On the contrary, it made absolutely clear that the Son's divinity was exactly the same as the Father's (the only difference being that the Son was begotten of the Father, that his divinity derived from the Father, the "source" of the Godhead).

Ultimately, this council sought to formulate a creedal statement that would express the consensus belief, which was that Jesus Christ was eternal with the Father, and not "made" or "begotten." This creed was called the Nicene Creed.

symbolism

The term *catholic* comes from a Greek word that can mean both "whole" and "universal." The Church of the councils used this word both to refer to "those things which were held by Christians everywhere" and to the idea of the fullness or holistic character of the faith.

Here is one version of the Nicene Creed as it is often said in churches today:

We believe in one God, the Father Almighty, Maker of heaven and earth, and of all things visible and invisible;

And in one Lord, Jesus Christ, the Son of God, the Only-begotten, Begotten of the Father before all ages, Light of Light, True God of True God, Begotten, not made, of one essence with the Father, by Whom all things were made:

Who for us men and for our salvation came down from heaven, and was incarnate of the Holy Spirit and the Virgin Mary, and was made man;

And was crucified also for us under Pontius Pilate, and suffered and was buried;

And the third day He rose again, according to the Scriptures;

And ascended into heaven, and sits at the right hand of the Father;

And He shall come again with glory to judge the living and the dead, Whose kingdom shall have no end.

And we believe in the Holy Spirit, the Lord, and Giver of Life, Who proceeds from the Father, Who with the Father and the Son together is worshipped and glorified, Who spoke by the Prophets;

And we believe in One, Holy, Catholic and Apostolic Church.

We acknowledge one Baptism for the remission of sins.

We look for the Resurrection of the dead,

And the Life of the world to come. Amen.

You may recognize the basic wording, which has been translated in a variety of ways. This statement of faith is often said in conjunction with baptism, as it offers a helpful summary of Christian belief. Many Christians have memorized and said it every day of their lives in an effort to remain faithful to the teachings of the Gospel.

The Filioque Clause

A long-standing dispute between the Eastern Orthodox Church and the Protestant and Catholic Churches is related to an addition to the creed. This is called the Filioque clause. The word *filioque* means "and the Son" in Latin and refers to the part of the creed that says, "the Holy Spirit, the Lord, the Giver of Life, Who proceeds from the Father and the Son" (in the West). The phrase, "and the Son" was first added at the Synod of Toledo in Spain in A.D. 447. It was adopted by Charlemagne in the ninth century, and finally by Rome in 1014 (at the request of the German emperor Henry II). The East never accepted this addition, both questioning its theology, and citing concerns about the way it was adopted (without the approval of an Ecumenical Council).

Ephesus, A.D. 431

Even as the Councils sought to define the creeds, the nature of the Trinity, and the person of Christ—both divine and human—discussions arose about titles for his mother, the Virgin Mary. The most important council in relation to the Virgin Mary was the council at which her name, Theotokos, was officially declared. The word Theotokos is rooted in the two Greek roots *theos* (God) and *tokos* (bearer). This term can be translated as "The one who gave birth to God," although a more simple (and widely used) translation is "Mother of God." ("Mother of God," however, is a more direct translation of the phrase *meter theou* which is also used in Greek, so some prefer to keep this distinct in their translations.)

Within the Eastern Orthodox context, the single most important title associated with the Virgin Mary was the title Theotokos. By the fourth century, this title was so widely used among Christians that the famed anti-Christian emperor Julian (whose short reign lasted from A.D. 361 to 363), referred to by Christians with the unflattering title of "the Apostate," complained about it.

Although the term *Theotokos* was used as early as A.D. 230 by Origen of Alexandria, and was widely used in the fourth century (there are references from Athanasius, Gregory the Theologian, Cyril of Jerusalem, John Chrysostom, Augustine, Gregory of Nyssa, and many others), it had never been universally sanctioned, and some Christians vehemently opposed it. This title for the Virgin Mary also appears in the most ancient prayer to Mary that exists, dating back to at least A.D. 300. This prayer was originally written in Greek and is preserved on a scrap of parchment. This short prayer, commonly known in the West by its Latin name, *Sub Tuum Praesidium*, reads, "We flee to your protection, O Holy Mother of God; Do not despise our petitions in our necessities, but deliver us always from all dangers, O glorious and blessed Virgin."

As significant as the title Theotokos was for many of the early Christians, those who opposed this title felt that they must object to it because it seemed crazy to them. They asked a question many might ask today, which was "How could God have a mother?"

Some feared that this title made it seem as if the Virgin Mary existed from the beginning of time, whereas those who used this title and were devoted to it always understood that it was to be used in a very specific way—Mary gave birth to God only in the sense that she gave birth to Christ. She did not conceive and give birth to God the Father.

Some who believed in the divinity of Christ didn't particularly like this title because they felt that it might be confusing to some, making it sound as if Mary came before God the Father, while others felt that it was very important as a way of expressing the teaching that Jesus united the human and divine natures in this one person. So much controversy surrounded this title that a council was held in which some of the questions surrounding it were formally addressed. The two central figures on opposite sides of the debate were Cyril and Nestorius.

Nestorius and Cyril

Nestorius, who had been appointed patriarch of Constantinople in A.D. 428, was deeply concerned that the title Theotokos could lead to exaggerated beliefs about the Virgin Mary. When he was in Constantinople, a famous speaker named Proclus preached an exuberant sermon about the Virgin Mary. When Proclus exclaimed that the Virgin Mary was the Theotokos he struck a sour note with Nestorius, who stormed up to the pulpit and accused him of mingling Christianity and pagan mythology.

Nestorius always felt squeamish about this term. He felt that it was more theologically acceptable to call Mary *Christokos*, Christ-bearer, or simply *anthropotokos*, "human-bearer." Nestorius felt that it was essential to view the Incarnation in terms of two natures that remained separate. He did not like the idea of two natures mingling, and he was put off by the idea that God was born in a manger. He also struggled to believe in a God who died and rose again.

factum

The sparring between Nestorius and Cyril was not just rooted in theology. There was also long-standing competition between the two places they represented, Alexandria and Constantinople. These geographical tensions very likely contributed to the bitter fight between the two men.

The most powerful opponent of Nestorius was Cyril, bishop of Alexandria. After Nestorius publicly criticized Proclus, Cyril not only came to the defense of Proclus, but he also sent several letters to important people, accusing Nestorius of separating the Christ into two separate people. Nestorius refused to take back his words. Both in writing and verbally he would not call the Virgin Mary Theotokos. He felt bitter, even, that others would press him this way.

Cyril taught that it was absolutely essential to retain the unity of the human and divine persons in Christ. The symbol of this perfect unity was the Virgin Mary as the "Theotokos," or God-bearer. Nestorius countered that he did not like the idea of the divine nature of Christ seeming to overwhelm his humanity, while Cyril hoped to hold the two natures in perfect balance, seeing them as two natures functioning, unified, in one person. The battle between Nestorius and Cyril was so fierce that it could only be settled by calling together the leaders of the Church to talk through the issues at hand.

The Third Ecumenical Council was held at Ephesus in June of A.D. 431. Nestorius had hoped that through this council he could convince others that he was right, but from his perspective, the council did not go well at all. Although the council had been called by Pope Celestine at Cyril's urging, Pope Celestine actually died before the council began. Cyril had been given permission to open the council, and Nestorius's views were condemned.

Nestorius was both excommunicated and deposed, meaning that he was kicked out of the Church and he lost his job as patriarch of Constantinople. To further his shame, the very man he had so sharply criticized for his flowery sermon, Proclus, was appointed to replace Nestorius as patriarch of Constantinple.

Results of the Council

The Third Ecumenical Council had a variety of results. Following the decree from the council that it was acceptable to call the Virgin Mary, Theotokos, people from the town marched through the streets, cheering. That night, after the council, those who led Cyril to his lodgings shouted, "Praised be the Theotokos, Long live Cyril!"

The official pronouncement of Mary as Theotokos at Ephesus was worded quite strongly. Cyril said, "If anyone does not confess that Emmanuel is God in truth, and therefore that the Holy Virgin is the Mother of God (Theotokos), let him be anathema."

discussion question

In what sort of place was the Third Ecumenical Council held?
This council was held in a large church that was dedicated to the Virgin Mary. About 200 bishops attended. The ruins of this church can still be seen in Ephesus.

Ever-virgin

The term *ever-virgin* was used officially at the Fifth Ecumenical Council in Constantinople in A.D. 553. This term is connected to the belief that the Virgin Mary was a virgin both before she gave birth to Christ and afterward. References to Mary's ever-virginity can be found, for example, in the writings of Peter of Alexandria, Epiphanius, Athanasius, Didymus the Blind, Jerome, Cyril of Alexandria, Leo, Sophronius of Jerusalem, John of Damascus, John Cassian, Ephrem of Syria, and the Second Council of Constantinople in A.D. 553, which said, "If anyone shall not confess that the Word of God has two nativities, the one from the Father, from all eternity, without time and without body; the other in these last days, coming down from heaven and being made flesh of the holy and glorious Mary, Mother of God and ever-virgin, and born of her: let him be anathema."

The word *anathema* means "cut off from the community." It is used by Saint Paul in 1 Corinthians 16:22, "If anyone does not love the Lord Jesus Christ, let him be anathema." It becomes a kind of technical term used as a way to denounce a person's immoral behavior or false teachings.

These terms—*theotokos, panagia,* and *aeiparthenos* (ever-virgin)—were continually used in traditional Christian liturgies, especially after these disputes, as a way to seal the declarations in people's hearts and to bring clarity to their prayers. There is an ancient saying that "the rule of prayer is the rule of belief" (*lex orandi, lex credendi*)—in other words, theology and prayer reinforce each other, so they shouldn't be separated.

Mary as All-holy

Another term used for the Virgin Mary is "all-holy" (*panagia* in Greek). This title was not officially decreed at a council, but was invoked at the Seventh Ecumenical Council, which occurred at Nicaea in A.D. 787. At this Council, the Virgin Mary was called a title that is very close to Panagia in meaning, which was "most pure."

The use of the word Panagia also has very ancient roots. It may be have been used to describe Mary by Origen in the middle of the third century. By the early fourth century, this name was clearly linked to the Virgin Mary by Eusebius.

The term *panagia* provides a helpful perspective on the unity of teaching between East and West. Even though the Orthodox Church does not hold to the doctrine of the Immaculate Conception (see Chapter 14), this term articulates views that the Virgin Mary did not sin during her earthly life, but rather, she lived a pure and holy life. It does not, however, imply that something unique occurred at her conception that released her entirely from the consequences of sin that occurred in the Garden of Eden. Just as all Christians must struggle to live lives of purity and grace, Eastern Orthodox theologians emphasize that the Virgin Mary was Panagia not so much because of the miracle of her birth, but because of her consistent desire to choose a holy and pure life.

factum

The idea of Mary as the Mother of the Church is related to her role as the first to accept Christ. Mary's motherhood is also related to the idea that spiritual ties could be as strong (or stronger) than biological ones. This is illustrated at the cross, when Christ said to Mary, "Behold your son" while gesturing to Saint John.

In A.D. 787, the Seventh Ecumenical Council, held at Nicea, once again restated that the Virgin Mary is *Theotokos* and *panagia*.

All of these councils sought to bring clarity to the confusions surrounding Jesus Christ, to define essential theological positions, and to help bring unity to the Church. The Virgin did play a prominent role in these councils, as the titles ascribed to her had tremendous implications for how Christians understood Jesus and the way in which he brought about the salvation of the world.

Chapter 6

Images of Mary

No woman in history has inspired more artists than the Virgin Mary. Within Eastern Orthodoxy, she has been captured by a very particular form of stylized art called iconography. Icons are two-dimensional images of holy people or events, which nevertheless are meant to capture or present some kind of spiritual reality to the faithful. They find their context in the midst of church life—in the cycles of feasts and fasts and days of remembrance, as well as in relation to the whole scope of Christian theology. This chapter will explore the meaning of icons within Eastern Orthodoxy, especially when they are used to depict the Virgin Mary and the infant Christ.

Heaven on Earth

The use of icons within the Eastern Orthodox Church cannot be understood apart from the whole context of worship. Eastern Orthodox services strive to reflect heavenly realities in their services with candles, incense, icons, and *a cappella* singing. In this way, Eastern Orthodox worship engages not just the mind or heart, but all of the senses. Images of saints and Biblical events cover the church walls. These icons are an integral part of the services because they help make present the holy people and saving events from the history of Christianity.

The Eastern Orthodox Church is the second largest Christian group in the world (after the Roman Catholic Church). It is made up of more than twenty national churches that are in communion with each other. The Eastern Orthodox Church has many ethnic manifestations around the world but shares a common theology.

factum

One can visit any branch of the Orthodox Church—Greek, Romanian, Georgian, and so on—for a Sunday service, and while the worship may have some ethnic and cultural variations from one church to the next, it will be essentially the same service, a liturgy that is more than 1,500 years old.

Other than Christ, there is no single figure within Eastern Orthodox iconography who is depicted more than the Virgin Mary. Her face is beloved because it was her face that most resembled Christ's face—she was his closest biological kin, and it was she who experienced the quickening of Christ in her womb.

Orthodox Christians also find theological support for creating and honoring icons through the event of the Incarnation. According to Orthodox theology, if Christ could take on human form, then he could be depicted in earthly ways. Within the East, however, statues have never been embraced. Eastern Christians have been historically wary toward statues because of their lifelike qualities.

According to official Eastern Orthodox teaching, it is unacceptable as well to create images of God the Father because no living human has seen God the Father. An exception is made for depicting, for example, the "Ancient of Days" figure of the prophet Daniel's vision in Daniel 7:9 because this refers to what he *saw* rather than being a depiction of God himself. Similarly, the Holy Spirit may be depicted as a dove in the icon of Theophany (the Baptism of Christ, from Matthew 3:16 and Mark 1:10), or as tongues of fire in the icon of Pentecost (Acts 2:3) but otherwise is not to be depicted.

Encountering Icons

When Eastern Orthodox Christians enter their churches, they will often greet the many icons around the church, kissing them, bowing before them, and taking a moment of silent prayer before them as they light candles. While some might view the practice of kissing icons or bowing before them as idolatrous, the Eastern Orthodox do not view it this way. The Eastern Orthodox believe that the icon makes present the holy person or event in the same way a photograph might. They believe that the honor that is paid to the image passes through the image to the holy person the image represents. In this way, they can continue to show honor and love for those who have departed this world but continue to live with Christ.

Images Not to Be Worshipped

Icons are not worshipped, because worship is reserved for God alone. This position was emphasized at the Seventh Ecumenical Council, which took place in Nicea, Asia Minor, in A.D. 787, and was held in response to this controversy about the use of icons. According to the iconoclasts (those who opposed the use of icons, literally the "destroyers of icons"), icons were idolatrous and should be destroyed. Many others, especially the monks, believed strongly that the icons were valuable for the faithful because they helped teach and make present the lived theology of the Church. The Council made a sharp distinction between *proskynesis* (a relative respect or veneration that could be shown to images, saints, and other human beings, literally, a bowing before), and *latreia*, which is the worship due to God alone.

One of the great ironies of history is that new battles are not always being fought but often the same battles are waged from age to age. In our age, the Eastern Orthodox, Roman Catholic, and Anglican Churches generally hold to an anti-iconoclastic perspective, believing that images can help glorify God. Certain other churches, however, still hold to a strict iconoclastic perspective, teaching that images are idolatrous. Some contemporary Protestant churches have an iconoclastic perspective that loosely resembles the thinking of the historical iconoclasts.

Because Eastern Orthodox Christians believe that icons are an invaluable link to these heavenly realities, they refuse to destroy or abandon their images. To this day in Eastern Orthodox Churches, icons are treated with great respect and love because they help connect the Eastern Orthodox faithful to "The Great Cloud of Witnesses" from Hebrews 12:1.

Icons also serve as a tangible reminder of intangible realities. Icons accompany the Eastern Orthodox believer through every phase of life. They are often presented to an infant at baptism, hung on the wall of one's home, and kissed and used for daily prayer. At the end of life, when the person dies and is placed in the casket, the much-loved icon is tucked into their hands as a sign of God's continual presence.

Icons are powerful images in the life of the Eastern Orthodox Church because they make the communion of saints—the fellowship of all the Christian faithful who have departed this life, and even now participate in the Resurrection—present to the faithful, expressing heavenly realities in a language that is rich, visual, and transcendent. Because icons are so precious, the faithful generally treat them with great care, and do not set them on the ground or use them in ways that might be viewed as careless. If an icon accidentally falls to the ground, the person who caused it to fall will usually quickly snatch it up and kiss it before placing it back on the stand or wall.

symbolism

Within Orthodoxy, symbols are intimately connected to the realities they represent, in the same way that in American culture, coins and bills are directly linked to an actual amount of gold, which is why it is illegal to deface or destroy American dollars or coins.

Because icons are intended to show eternal realities, the figures on the icons usually have sober expressions that go beyond the realm of human passion. Their faces are often full of love, but they do not laugh or smile. The gaze of holy people through icons is steady and unchanging, much like the changeless realities they intend to represent.

Icons are also called "windows to heaven" because they offer a glimpse into heavenly realities. For this reason, the Eastern Orthodox Christians create prayer corners in their homes with icons of Christ, the Virgin Mary, and the particular saints that are significant for each family member.

Creating an Icon Corner

Icon corners offer a way to make heavenly realities present. They also serve as a reminder that all Christians are called to keep watch for the return of Christ. Many families also keep a "lampada" or small, oil-filled lamp, burning at all times before the icons.

Icons also express profound realities related to each person's unique vocation. Just as in Genesis Adam and Eve were created in the image of God, all human beings reflect this image. According to Eastern Orthodox theology, the ultimate call is to make this image shine forth more and more clearly in our own lives (and to see it more clearly in others) as one grows closer to God. The saints depicted in icons are shown in their glorified or resurrected state—fully complete in the divine life. In this way, the images of the saints reveal our own calling to be saints.

factum

In Orthodox Churches, the priest censes the icons. The smoke that rises at Vespers, an evening prayer service, echoes the words of the Psalm 140: "Let my prayer arise in thy sight as incense." Because the Orthodox Church teaches that humans are "living icons" the priest also censes the people, who bow in response, acknowledging the image of God in the priest.

Icons often depict saints—people who fully embraced the reality of Christ in their own lives and now live with God in heaven. In the Eastern Churches, icons of the Virgin Mary and infant Christ are of primary importance because they reflect the Incarnation, the way in which God took human form and dwelt on this earth, placing himself in a profoundly vulnerable position.

The Craft of Iconography

Icons are quite unlike most art, because they are not only subject to artistic discipline but the creator of icons (or iconographer) must follow guidelines while working. Iconographers usually learn their craft under the guidance of an experienced iconographer. These apprenticeships help guarantee that new generations of iconographers follow the ancient form. Iconographers are expected to fast and pray when working, so that their icons become the fruit of prayer as much as the end result of their artistic endeavors.

Creating Icons

The process of creating icons is laborious. Most iconographers prepare their own boards for painting, and also mix their own egg-tempura paint. Icons also depart from Western art in the perspective they employ. In most Western art since the time of the Renaissance, a "vanishing point" perspective is used. This makes objects at a distance seem smaller than those that are closer. Vanishing-point perspective is something like the illusion created when one stares at train tracks and the tracks at the farthest distance seem to come together.

Inverse Perspective

In iconography, the opposite perspective, inverse perspective, is used, so that the vanishing point is in the viewer. The person who gazes at the icon becomes the central focus of the icon. This perspective engages the viewer and helps him to see that he is not on the outside of theological realities but at the very heart of the Biblical stories. The inverse perspective suggests that each Christian stands at the center of narrative—that our lives are directly connected to the history of Christianity.

symbolism

The iconographer's work is sometimes referred to as "writing icons." Some people prefer this terminology because it captures the idea that icons constitute a specific symbolic language, and contain a lot of theology. Similarly, the act of deciphering the symbolic language of icons can be called "reading," just like a person might search a holy book for spiritual insights.

Another interesting distinction between Western art and iconography is an iconographer begins his work with a layer of dark earth tones (called "the chaos"), slowly adding lighter colors as the icon develops, so that when the icon is complete the holy person seems to radiate light. (In Western art, it is more typical to begin with light colors, and slowly add the darker ones.) This process is symbolic of the dynamic movement of the Christian life—always toward the light and away from the darkness.

The craft of iconography follows strict guidelines of form and style so that from generation to generation, holy people and events remain recognizable. Saint Paul, for example, is almost always shown with an elongated and hairless forehead because, according to tradition, he was mostly bald. Likewise, children are often portrayed as little balding adults to demonstrate their wisdom. The Virgin Mary is most often shown with a red robe and a blue mantle, which is the inverse of what Christ wears. The blue is associated with Christ's divinity, and the red with his humanity.

Icons of the Virgin Mary

It is rare to see an icon of the Virgin in which she is shown by herself, without Christ present. This also illustrates an important theological point about human nature: we fully become ourselves through relationships. Our relationships are integral to our identity, which is why traditional Christianity has recognized only two "stable" states for the human person—marriage or monasticism. In both situations, the challenges of interacting with others are a catalyst for spiritual growth and increased maturity.

There are a variety of types of icons of the Virgin Mary. There are three types that are the most famous, known in Greek as:

- The *Hodegetria*, translated as "the One who points the way"
- The *Orans*, or "the Virgin of the Sign"
- The *Eleousa*, or "the Virgin of Loving Kindness"

All of these images show Christ as an infant with Mary, but each one has particular theological significance. Rowan Williams, Archbishop of Canterbury, authored a book called *Ponder These*

Things which offers some beautiful, thought-provoking insights into these three main Marian icon types.

factum

Though Islam prohibits the use of images in worship, when the prophet Muhammad destroyed the images he found in the Kaaba in Mecca, he left one image untouched—the image of the Virgin Mary, which he could not bear to deface. Similarly, when the Turks invaded Greece, they defaced many icons in the churches, but often left the ones of Mary intact.

Eleousa Icons

In the *Eleousa*, the infant Christ appears as almost any child—eagerly, desperately, even, seeking the loving attention of his mother. The infant Christ pushes his cheek against his mother, and she leans into him with a look of tenderness on her face. Her eyes are often shown with bags beneath them, perhaps to express the weariness of loving this child who was born to die. Whatever the bags beneath her eyes express in terms of theology, the image certainly resonates with the parents of any young children. The task of parenting is awesome and, at times, overwhelming.

In this icon, the infant Christ clutches his mother's veil in his fist in the same way any infant might grab onto his mother's clothing or hair, his face pressed to her cheek with the eagerness of a child seeking his mother's love. One leg seems to be digging into her, as if he is trying to climb up her side as small children love to do. The Virgin Mary holds the child close, gathering him up in her embrace.

According to Rowan Williams, this icon is not only an image of the tender love between Mary and Christ, but is also an image of God's seeking, eager, love for humanity. One can also view this icon as a reminder of Christ's searching, intense, personal love for every person in the world.

Orans Icons

In the *Orans* or "Virgin of the Sign" icon, Mary stands in prayer with her arms raised up and Christ is shown in her womb. Often, there are one or more seraphim surrounding Mary, expressing the presence of the angels in prayer and the mystery of redemption. This image has been considered for centuries to be an image of the Church, in which each person is called to "give birth" to Christ in their own way by faithfully responding to his call.

As Mary prays in the ancient tradition of the church with arms raised, we are reminded that through prayer God becomes present in our lives and in our world.

Sometimes in this image, the Virgin Mary will hold a shawl over her hands, which is symbolic of her protective veil over the Church. You will learn more about the Virgin Mary's veil in Chapter 12, because it is associated with one of the ancient apparitions of the Virgin.

Hodegetria Icons

The *Hodegetria* or "She Who Points the Way" style of icon originated in Byzantine times. This icon offers an effective balance to the concern some hold that churches that honor the Virgin Mary occasionally fall into idolatry. In this icon, the Virgin Mary holds Christ with one arm, but with her other arm she gestures toward him, as if to say, "Look to him." In most icons of this type, Christ gazes at his mother and his hand is raised in blessing.

Icons for Parents

One of the moving things about this icon is how fully Christ and his mother engage each other. The icon seems to suggest that Mary is best known by the way that she points to or guides people to her son, while at the same time, one is better able to understand Christ in light of his love for his mother. In this icon, neither Christ nor his mother seem to call attention to themselves. Both draw the viewer in with their eyes, and each directs the eyes of the viewer to the other person, so that one's eyes move from child to mother and then back again to child.

symbolism

One of the beautiful themes in icons of Christ and Mary is universal among parents and children. When children are small, they depend upon their parents, but as they age and grow increasingly independent, their parents tend to depend on them.

One of the most striking depictions of this role reversal can be seen in the icons from Mary's death, in which she is a small form wrapped in linen, held in the arms of her much larger son Christ. The burial shroud she wears closely resembles the swaddling cloths worn by the infant Christ. In a sense, she has become the infant and he has become the parent.

Images from Christ's infancy show him as a small child, leaning into his mother's arms. As much as Mary was the first person to embrace Christ in her own life, she is ultimately the one who shows us what it is to be embraced by Christ. These images demonstrate the cycle of life, which moves from dependency to interdependency and then back again to dependency.

When Icons Weep

Accounts of the phenomenon of weeping icons are widespread, and several icons have been reported to have begun weeping in North America within the past decade. When an icon weeps, moisture tends to form on the surface of the icon, then begins to gather as tears in the eyes. The oil-like tears then drip down the face of the icon. This "holy oil" is then used to anoint the faithful. Often, so much oil streams down the icon that it soaks through the icon and leaves a stain on the back.

One such weeping icon is located in Chicago. Weeping icons have also been reported in New York and Texas. In most cases these icons are of the Virgin Mary, but sometimes icons of Christ or the saints have also been reported to weep. In 1996 in the Church of the Nativity in Bethlehem an icon of Christ began to weep red tears. The tears were first seen by a Muslim woman who was startled by them and could not imagine why she, a Muslim, would be the first to witness the weeping icon. She immediately brought the local monks to see the icon and they felt that they were witnessing a miracle. The weeping icon was viewed by thousands of pilgrims over the course of the next several days.

factum

In the early seventies in Akita, Japan, a statue of the Virgin Mary wept 101 times. This statue produced tears, sweat, and blood that were tested in a local laboratory. Scientists discovered that the blood, sweat, and tears were from a human source—the tears were type AB while the blood was type B.

Witnesses often describe the tears shed by icons as having an oily consistency and sometimes exuding a sweet smell that some describe as a heavenly aroma. This aroma is similar to the sweet aroma that is said to rise up from the bodies of saints, most notably Saint Demetrius in Thessalonica, Greece. The Eastern Orthodox Church has historically connected these oil-like tears with myrrh, which is the aromatic spice associated with the beginning and end of Christ's life—the three wise men brought gold, frankincense, and myrrh when Christ was a newborn, and after he died, three women went to his tomb to anoint his body with myrrh.

Chapter 13 describes the miracle that occurred at Damascus, Syria, in which a young woman experienced olive oil coming from her fingers as she prayed, as well as myrrh-like tears coming from her icon. It was also reported that over 100 copies of this icon also began to weep.

The Gift of Tears

Many people wonder why icons or statues seem to weep, especially those of the Virgin Mary. There have been no conclusive responses to this question from the Eastern or Western Churches, although many theories have been suggested.

Within the Eastern Orthodox tradition, the gift of tears has been viewed as a rich manifestation of the Holy Spirit. The gift of tears is an experience of weeping that arises out of prayer. This gift is not associated with emotional upheaval, but is said to be spiritual, and associated with the weeping of repentance and the compassion of God.

The prevalence of this gift within the Eastern Church is something like the widespread manifestation of the "gift of tongues" in some contemporary Pentecostal and Charismatic Churches.

symbolism

The gift of tears is associated with drawing near to God. In particular, in the ninth century Saint Symeon the New Theologian made a connection between weeping and the dwelling of God in our hearts. The weeping icons seem to mirror those who have experienced this gift.

Many in the East believe that the phenomenon of the weeping icons of Mary is associated with her role as an intercessor (someone who prays to God on behalf of other people). Because she prays so fervently for those in the Church and in the world, some believe that it makes sense that she would also weep through her icons.

Others have suggested that the tears are related to the state of the world today, which is full of brokenness and pain. Another theory about the weeping icons is that they are signs of God's continued love, which pours out through the icons and the prayers of the Virgin Mary to the faithful. The myrrh-scented tears are also sometimes viewed as a sign of the mingled sorrow and joy that is often associated with the Virgin Mary because at Christ's birth, one of the three Magi brought myrrh to present to him. Because of its bitter, balsamic smell, myrrh is also traditionally associated with mourning. Many interpreters see the myrrh as a foreshadowing of Christ's death. The myrrh-stained icons speak both of sorrow and joy— sorrow at the suffering of the world and its separation from God, but joy at the grace of God that brings salvation, and at the divine love that abides eternally.

Those who have witnessed weeping icons report that they are incredibly beautiful, and many also report having experienced healing from the myrrh-scented oil that drips from them. The icons of the Virgin Mary express profound realities about her person, her role in the church, her relationship with her son, and her protective role. These icons demonstrate the tremendous variety of theology that comes from the pivotal events in the Virgin Mary's life, and also all of the theology that she made possible through her willingness to say "yes" to God.

Chapter 7

Seasons of Salvation

Within the liturgical calendar, shared to some to degree by Anglicans, Roman Catholics, and Eastern Orthodox, there are several major cycles that span the year. One of the most significant is related to the Virgin Mary. This chapter will explore this cycle as well as her place within the liturgies of all three churches. The Church, just like Earth, marks time through the passing of seasons, returning year after year to the same patterns, which grow deeper and more meaningful with time.

Cycles of Faith

The books of the Bible are filled with references to the natural cycles of the earth. While the Christian faith offers a taste of the transcendent, it also takes its form in an earthly way. Early on, Christians saw a confirmation of their faith in the cycles of nature. The Bible is full of references to the natural world, such as "unless a grain of wheat falls into the earth and dies, it remains alone; but if it dies, it bears much fruit" (John 12:24, *ESV*). Christians saw a reflection of divine truth in the natural patterns of the earth. Furthermore, the church drew out these patterns in the arrangement of an ordering of feast days. Christmas Day, for example, was set on the winter solstice, just before the days would get longer and brighter after the bleak month of December. Easter has been traditionally celebrated at sunrise, in an effort to connect with the rising sun, which has been viewed as a powerful natural image of the Son of God who rose from the darkness of death.

Natural Associations

The piety surrounding the Virgin Mary was also rooted in the natural world. She has been associated with the sea, stars, soil, flowers, and snow. Her body, which went through nine months of pregnancy following the Annunciation, experienced one of the great seasons of the female life. She is intimately connected with the beginning and end of life, and the feasts that are devoted to her are largely connected with these critical thresholds. These thresholds are connected to the seasons of our bodies, the seasons of the earth, and the seasons of the Church.

Liturgical Calendars

In particular, liturgical churches such as the Roman Catholic, Eastern Orthodox, and Anglican are anchored by events that repeat themselves year after year. Life in these churches is cyclical, meaning that the same Scriptures are read on the same Sundays year after year, the same feasts are celebrated on the same days, and the same colors are used during particular seasons to visually mark the event that is being celebrated.

These churches move through time and through seasons. Historically, there have been special seasons in these churches connected to the Virgin Mary. These seasons encapsulate her conception, her birth, the Annunciation, Christ's birth, and her death. The seasons are intimately connected with the fundamental realities of life—conception, birth, and death. These feasts have been celebrated in a way that at least partially corresponds to the realities they represent. In particular, in the Eastern Orthodox Church the Virgin Mary's birth is celebrated exactly nine months minus one day after her conception. This placement of the feasts is intended to show that she was human, although quite extraordinary, coming a day early—fulfilling the dreams of her parents and ushering in a new era of faith. (In contrast to this, the time from Jesus' conception—Annunciation on March 25—and his birth on Christmas is exactly nine months.)

fallacy

Those who worship in liturgical churches do not feel that the repetitive nature of the church seasons are dull. Just as the first snow of winter inspires awe as do the first buds of spring, liturgical seasons repeat themselves but remain fresh for those who are open to them.

Mary in Anglicanism

Of all Protestant churches, the Anglican Church (known in America as the Episcopal Church) has historically had the deepest relationship with the Virgin Mary. This is because the Anglican Church was not founded primarily for theological reasons but because of practical concerns related to the English king of the sixteenth century, King Henry VIII, who reigned from 1509 to 1547. In his quest for a male heir to take over the throne after his death, Henry VIII sought the permission of the Roman Church to divorce his wife so that he could marry again.

When the Pope would not grant King Henry the divorce he requested, Thomas Cranmer, the king's ally, was appointed as Archbishop of Canterbury (the seat of highest authority in the Anglican Church), and immediately allowed the divorce. Because Pope Clement VII did not approve of the divorce or of King Henry's flagrant disobedience, he excommunicated him. King Henry's response to the Pope's act of excommunication was to remove England from the control of the Roman Catholic Church and to start the Church of England (called the Anglican Church).

Although the new Anglican Church embraced some aspects of the newly forming Protestant theology, the Church of England retained many of the forms and devotions of the Roman Catholic Church. King Henry never really intended to have a clean break from Rome; he had the short-term goal of attaining the freedom to do as he chose in regards to divorce.

In one of the most wrenching ironies of history, Henry VIII was never successful in producing a male heir who could be king. Despite his efforts with six wives, Henry only had one son, Edward VI, who was sickly and died when he was just fifteen years old. Still, the difficulties surrounding Henry's quest for a male heir had a profound impact on the history of England and the history of Christianity.

The Act of Supremacy

In 1534, King Henry VIII established The Act of Supremacy. Under this act, the Church in England was placed squarely under the authority of the king. Under King Henry VIII, who was quite conservative, the Church retained many of the liturgical practices and piety of the Roman Catholic Church, while mixing in some Protestant sentiment for good measure. During this time, Thomas Cranmer wrote *The Book of Common Prayer,* which contained specific articles of faith. During the early era of Anglicanism, the Church demonstrated varying degrees of warmth toward the Virgin Mary.

On August 15, the day on which the Roman Catholics celebrate the Assumption and the Eastern Orthodox Celebrate the Dormition (or falling asleep of Mary), the Anglicans also remember this event by praying, "O God, who hast taken to thyself the blessed Virgin Mary, mother of thy incarnate Son: Grant that we, who have been redeemed of his blood, may share with her the glory of thine eternal Kingdom; through the same thy Son Jesus Christ our Lord, who liveth and reigneth with thee, in the unity of the Holy Spirit, one God, now and forever. Amen."

discussion question

How many wives did King Henry VIII go through in his effort to produce a male heir?
King Henry had six wives: Catherine of Aragon, Anne Boleyn, Jane Seymour, Anne of Cleaves, Catherine Howard, and Catherine Parr. Henry divorced Catherine of Aragon and Anne of Cleaves, beheaded Anne Boleyn and Catherine Howard, and outlived Jane Seymour. Catherine Parr, Henry's last wife, lived to tell her tale.

One of the chief distinctions between the Anglican Church and the Roman Catholic and Eastern Orthodox Churches, however, is that although the Anglican Church heartily embraced the idea that the saints in heaven continue to pray for those on earth, from very early on, the Anglican Church expressed reservations about asking for the prayers of the saints. Although the Anglican Church retained much of the forms, calendar, and piety of the Roman Catholic Church, it had a strong desire to separate itself from some of the perceived "excesses" of the Roman Catholic Church.

Contemporary Anglicanism

In contemporary times, there are pockets of devotion to the Virgin Mary within the Anglican Church. Historically, the more robust Marian devotion that remained under Henry VIII gradually gave way to a more subtle Mariology, but Mary still has a position of esteem within the Anglican Church. Many Anglican chapels have been devoted to her, and she still occupies a place within their calendar.

In 1931, a Society of Mary was formed within the Anglican Church. This group describes itself as "Episcopalians dedicated to the Glory of God and the Holy Incarnation of Christ, under the invocation of Our Lady, Help of Christians." This group exists with the desire to promote devotion to the Virgin Mary within the Episcopalian context, although its membership is not limited to Episcopalians.

Within the Anglican Church, there are six major feasts of the Virgin Mary. Many of these feasts are not celebrated in all parishes, but they exist in the richness of the liturgical calendar. Depending on the spiritual emphasis of each individual parish, these services may or may not be celebrated.

The Major Feasts of the Virgin Mary in the Anglican Church

The Purification of Saint Mary	February 2
The Annunciation	March 25
The Visitation	May 31
The Day of Saint Mary (known in the West as Assumption and in the East as the Dormition)	August 15
The Nativity of Mary	September 8
Our Lady of Walsingham	October 15
Mary's Conception	December 8

The Seattle Statement

Historically, there has been enough common belief surrounding the Virgin Mary between the Roman Catholics and the Anglicans that in 2005, a statement called Mary, Grace and Hope in Christ (often referred to as the Seattle Statement) was formally presented. This statement was the fruit of many years of dialogue between a small group of Anglicans and Roman Catholics who sought to find common ground between the two churches in relation to the Virgin Mary.

The Seattle Statement offers an interesting glimpse into the fruits of ecumenical discussions surrounding the Virgin Mary, although this statement is not generally viewed as authoritative because it has not yet garnered universal approval within these churches. Instead, it is seen as a starting place for discussion on an issue that has at times been divisive.

This statement affirms the positions that the two churches hold in common in relation to Mary. In particular, it says that it is theologically acceptable for both Anglicans and Roman Catholics to pray to the Virgin Mary. It also states that the Roman Catholic dogmas of the Immaculate Conception and the Assumption can be viewed as consistent with Anglican methods of Biblical interpretation. On the Roman Catholic side, admissions are made that there have been some "past excesses" related to the Virgin Mary. Although they may not be explicitly opposed to the dogmas of the Immaculate Conception and the Assumption, Anglicans were primarily concerned with the way these dogmas came about—through Papal pronouncements instead of through a more organic kind of consensus. This issue was a major sticking point between the two churches. In another statement that was released in 1981, the Anglicans expressed deep concerns about a dogma that is binding to all believers and is proclaimed on the basis of papal authority.

In 2002 the current Archbishop of Canterbury, Rowan Williams, published a beautiful book about praying with icons of the Virgin Mary and infant Christ titled *Ponder These Things*. In this book, he expresses a classic Christian position on the relationship between Christ and Mary. "It is not only that we cannot understand Mary without seeing her as pointing to Christ: we cannot understand Christ without seeing his attention to Mary," he writes, continuing, "Jesus does not appear to us as a solitary monarch, enthroned afar off, but as someone whose being and loving is always engaged, already directed toward humanity."

The Roman Catholic Cycles

Roman Catholicism has historically had an extremely robust love for the Virgin Mary. Of all the churches, the Roman Catholic Church has the most days set apart for her commemoration. In fact, the entire month of May is set aside as Mary's month, and traditionally during this month, statues of Mary are crowned with flowers. October is also set apart as a month of the Rosary. The first Saturday of each month is also dedicated to Marian Devotions, a practice which began in the Middle Ages.

The Four Principle Marian Feasts of the Roman Catholic Church

The Immaculate Conception	December 8
The Assumption	August 15
The Divine Motherhood of Mary	March 25
The Annunciation	March 25

Almost fifty days are marked on the calendar with special Marian emphasis, although these Marian feasts are not equally important.

Apparitions and Calendars

Many days of remembrance are related to the phenomenon of Marian Apparitions—times in which Mary appeared to Christians offering healing, warnings, or messages. Apparitions that have received formal approval from the Church have sometimes found places of designation on the Roman Catholic Calendar. Days are set apart for remembering Mary by her many titles—such as Our Lady of Lourdes (February 11), Our Lady of Fatima (May 13), Our Lady of the Snow (August 5), and Our Lady of Knock (August 21). These dates create a formal way for the church to remember these apparitions.

Titles to Be Remembered

On the Roman Catholic calendar there have also been days set aside for the purpose of remembering specific titles of the Virgin

Mary that have had implications for those within the Church such as Our Lady Help of Christians (May 24), Our Lady, Mediatrix of All Graces (May 31), and Our Lady of the Most Blessed Sacrament (May 13). All of these feasts help refresh the memory of the faithful as they move through the Church year, offering fresh insights into Marian possibilities.

On top of these many Marian Feasts, the Roman Catholic Church also has several major Marian feasts on the same days which are set apart in the Eastern Orthodox and Anglican Churches. In particular, Mary's Assumption is celebrated on August 15, the Annunciation is celebrated on March 25, and the Immaculate Conception is celebrated on December 8 (the same day on which the Eastern Church celebrates her conception, without using the word "immaculate").

symbolism

It is interesting to note the unity of major Marian feasts between the Roman Catholic, Eastern Orthodox, and Anglican Churches that symbolize events in Mary's life. Although these feasts do not always share the same name (and each name may have meanings specific to the context of a particular tradition) the commonalities demonstrate a significant amount of unity.

After Vatican II (a major council of the Roman Catholic Church that took place from 1962 to 1965), there were several adjustments made to the Roman Catholic calendar. Important distinctions were made between the different feasts to help distinguish which feasts were most important, making some of the less significant feasts optional, although all of the feasts do help to complete the picture of the Virgin Mary's role in the Roman Catholic Church.

The Orthodox Cycle

The Eastern Orthodox Church may not have all the same feast days of Mary found in the Roman Catholic Church, but the Virgin Mary certainly plays a powerful role in the seasons of the Orthodox year. Her feasts are always linked to the Christian message, each one demonstrating something about what it is to be a Christian, what it is to be open to the Gospel message, what it is to become a temple of the Holy Spirit, and what it is to experience conversion and salvation.

Within the Eastern Orthodox context, there are four feasts that are most important in relation to the Virgin Mary, although there are other minor feasts connected with the Virgin Mary's life and some of the miraculous icons associated with her.

The Four Principle Marian Feasts of the Eastern Orthodox Church

The Nativity of the Virgin	September 8
The Presentation of the Theotokos in the Temple	November 21
The Annunciation	March 25
The Dormition	August 15

The feast of the Nativity of the Virgin commemorates the day that Mary's parents, Joachim and Anna, conceived her. This feast does not have a Scriptural basis, but the tradition surrounding this feast is deep and beautiful. It is the celebration of the beginning of the reversal of the curse that occurred in Eden. Joachim and Anna, who were barren, conceive the Virgin Mary after prayerfully pleading with God that they could become parents. Just as Mary's life will begin to reverse the curse of Eden because of her willingness to give birth to the Redeemer, the curse of Joachim and Anna's life, their infertility, was reversed at the moment of conception.

The feast of Presentation of the Theotokos in the Temple is the celebration of the day the Virgin Mary was brought into the temple by her parents, who had promised to devote her to God. According to Church tradition, the Virgin Mary was raised in "the Holy of Holies," she herself preparing to eventually become, in a very unique way, the temple of God by giving birth to Christ.

The feast of the Annunciation is the most universally celebrated feast. This one commemorates the day the angel came to the Virgin Mary and told her that she was to bear a child who would be God Incarnate.

The feast of the Dormition celebrates the memory of the Virgin Mary's death, or in the Eastern Orthodox Church, "her falling asleep." This belief is rooted in the idea that Christians do not die but only sleep in anticipation of ultimately waking with God. In the case of Mary, both the Eastern Orthodox and Roman Catholics believe that the Virgin Mary ascended into heaven.

Liturgical Traditions

Within the Eastern Orthodox tradition, prayers devoted to Mary are very common. She is remembered at the end of the various cycles of intercessions, hymns, and dismissal prayers. For example, most litanies end with the priest remembering the three great titles associated with the Virgin Mary as well as her place among the saints. He prays: "Calling to remembrance our all-holy, most-pure, most blessed and glorious Lady, the Mother of God and ever-virgin Mary, with all the saints, let us commend ourselves and one another and our whole lives unto Christ our God."

According to the late Eastern Orthodox theologian, Father Alexander Schmemann, a mention of the Virgin Mary offers the final note of Eastern Orthodox prayers. "This pattern applies to all liturgical units: the daily, weekly, and yearly cycles . . . Whatever the theme of any particular celebration, its last word, its seal, will always be the Theotokos."

factum

The belief that Mary ascended directly to heaven has been enforced by the fact that no relics have ever been found from the Virgin Mary's body. The relics associated with her are linked to her clothing and breast milk. Unlike other saints who have left behind their bones and bodies, there is no physical evidence of the Virgin Mary's body.

Akathists and Novenas

Akathists and Novenas are special prayer services in the Eastern Orthodox and Roman Catholic Churches. These services are often devoted to a particular saint, and in many cases this saint is Mary. One of the most beloved Akathists in the Eastern Orthodox Church is in honor of Mary, and is usually referred to simply as "The Akathist Hymn." This hymn dates back to about the middle of the sixth century, and is usually attributed to Saint Romanos the Melodist.

The word *Akathist* literally means "not sitting." Akathist hymns give honor to a particular holy person, and for this reason, people stand while praying them. The Akathists alternate between repetitive verses and unique stanzas. "The Akathist Hymn" uses poetic language to demonstrate the cohesiveness of the Scriptural message. Many Old Testament images that are often linked to Mary are mentioned in the Akathist. Mary is called the "Heavenly Ladder by which God came down," a reference to Jacob's Ladder, as well as the "Tabernacle of God the World." The Akathist also features language that demonstrates the way in which the Virgin Mary is symbolic of all of creation. She is seen as the earth, while Christ is the life-giving wheat that comes from it. Likewise, just as Christ will ultimately become "The Bread of Life" through his sacrifice on the cross, the Virgin Mary is seen in this hymn as the table upon which the feast is spread. These images express the multiple ways through which creator and creature were unified in the person of Christ, all of this made possible by the Virgin Mary's willingness to bear the seed of God in her womb.

The Akathist also describes Mary as the star causing the sun to shine. Star imagery surrounding the Virgin Mary comes up quite frequently. Just as a star led the shepherds to the manger where the Virgin had given birth, and the Virgin Mary is often adorned with stars in her icons, the term *Stella Maris* or "Star of the Sea" is frequently used as an image of Mary's guiding presence through the storms of life.

Stations of the Cross

The Stations of the Cross is a primarily Roman Catholic devotional practice that is sometimes performed by Anglican and other churches. This devotional practice, which goes all the way back to the Middle Ages, is also referred to as "The Way of the Cross" or "Via Dolorosa."

discussion question

How did the Stations of the Cross develop?
The devotional practice of Stations of the Cross developed during the Middle Ages when wars made it impossible for Christians to visit the Holy Land. Pilgrimages were a central part of the life of faith, so the Stations of the Cross was developed as a way of having a "mini-pilgrimage" right in one's local church.

You may have seen a Catholic Church decorated with fourteen images related to these central events in the life of Christ. The events are best commemorated on foot, as a person walks through the stations, pausing to pray and contemplate each step that Christ took. The Stations of the Cross can also be done in an outside space. A wooded area or garden is especially well-suited to this meditative and prayerful devotional practice.

For Roman Catholics, the Stations of the Cross are often associated with Lent and Good Friday, but they can be performed at any time of the year, both at church and at home. Nowadays, you can even walk with Christ in a virtual way through an online Stations of the Cross (*www.catholic.org/clife/prayers/station.php*).

The Stations offer an opportunity to literally follow in the footsteps of Christ during the most critical hours of his life. This devotional practice requires one to stop and prayerfully consider each step of Christ's journey to Calvary.

The liturgical and devotional practices surrounding the Virgin Mary offer a rich way to draw close to Christ as one considers the experience of the woman who was clearly closest to him—his mother.

A survey of these feasts and cycles offers a glimpse into the unity and diversity of liturgical traditions surrounding the Virgin Mary. These traditions have developed over time, as Christianity has spread around the globe. The feasts of Mary have served as a way to contemplate the Incarnation, the mystery of God becoming human. They bring an element of humanity to the Church, a glimpse of the feminine through Mary, and help keep worship rooted in the seasons and the earth.

Chapter 8

Mary among the Saints

Because the Virgin Mary had such a profound role in the history of Christianity, and because she was chosen to do the thing that no other person has ever been chosen to do before or since—to bear God Incarnate in her womb, you might think of Mary as a woman apart from the other saints. While Mary is special in her own right, she is better understood within the context of the Church. This chapter will explore Mary's unique role in this regard.

Mary, Mother of the Church

The title of Mary as Mother of the Church is an ancient description that has had many controversies surrounding it. This idea was based on the premise that had Mary not said "yes" to God, there would have been no Christian Church. Her very willingness to become the mother of God also made her, in effect, the very first Christian and the mother of the Church. This term also implied that Mary was the very first to do the work that all Christians are called to do, which is to birth Christ into the world by living in a way that faithfully expresses his love for humanity. Mary has also been called the Mother of the Faithful.

Motherly Icons

The theme of Mary as the Mother of the Church is also present in icons. In one icon, she is shown with Christ still in her womb giving a blessing. This icon has been interpreted by some as symbolic of her role as Mother of the Church because it offers a glimpse of how Mary gave birth to Christianity.

Many of the reported apparitions also testify to Mary's ongoing concern for the Church. Not only has one of the themes of the apparitions been that Mary often asks for churches to be built in specific locations, such as Lourdes, Guadalupe, and Rome, but she also shows an ongoing concern for people within the Church.

Sibling Rivalry

Another theme that has surfaced through the apparitions is that of the Virgin Mary's concerns about divisions in the Church. If Mary is the Mother of the Church, then it is only fitting that the painful separation between the Eastern and Western Churches would not go unnoticed by her.

Whether one ascribes authority to these apparitions or not, it is notable that at least one of the themes seems to be entirely consistent with the Virgin Mary's role as Mother of the Church. Just as a mother does not wish her children to fight with each other, the Virgin Mary (along with her son, Jesus) surely longs for the Church to one day become one again, to struggle toward this end in prayer and in dialogue.

symbolism

In the apparitions that occurred in Damascus, Syria, the Virgin Mary said that anyone who divides the Church is in sin. She also promised to bring special blessings to both the Eastern and Western Churches when Easter is finally celebrated on the same day in all churches.

Controversy about the title "Mother of the Church"

The title Mother of the Church has certainly not been without controversy, even during this century. At Vatican II, there was a good deal of discussion about whether this title should be used in the official documents or not. In his homily in December 2005, Pope Benedict recounted the moment when the final proclamation was made by Pope John XXIII. He said, "There is a moment fixed indelibly in my mind, when on hearing his words, 'Mariam Sactissimam declaramus Matrem Ecclesiae' ('Let us declare Mary the Most Holy Mother of the Church'), the [Council] Fathers leapt out of their chairs and stood applauding, paying homage to the Mother of God, our Mother, the Mother of the Church. In fact, it is with this title that the pope summed up the Marian doctrine of the Council and gave the key for its understanding."

Mary, Bride of Christ and Sign of the Faithful

The Virgin Mary has often been referred to as the Bride of Christ, especially in medieval Western devotion. This term may seem strange, in particular because the Virgin Mary is most obviously the mother of Christ. But when you consider the first title, that Mary is considered the mother of the Church, coupled with the scriptural idea that the Church is the Bride of Christ, you can see how the images of Mary and the Church are sometimes used interchangeably.

The other idea that is closely linked to this one is that the Virgin Mary acts in perfect harmony with her son. Clearly Mary is Christ's mother, but she is never above him, and she never dominates him. Instead, she cooperates with him. The two of them function in perfect unity in the way that a healthy married couple might. This may be part of the reason why when couples are married in the Eastern Orthodox Church the wedding icons given to them are often of Christ and the Virgin Mary. The perfect harmony of their relationship provides an image of how all of our relationships should be.

The Virgin Mary is also seen as a sign for the faithful because her life was a perfect witness. She pointed the way for all believers by living in dynamic obedience to the will of God. Her desire to open herself to God's will for her entire life is an image of the life that all Christians are called to—a life of surrender, brave faith, and obedience to the will of God. The Virgin Mary is also seen as a sign to the faithful because her example offers guidance to all those who seek it—especially those who are living in difficult circumstances.

Mary's life was a sign that things are never quite as they seem— an unmarried, pregnant teenager from Nazareth was able to show how the coming of Christ represented shifting realities in both the temporal and ultimate sense. The Virgin Mary was also seen as a sign because her story made the spiritual world a visible and real part of the mundane realities of secular life.

Champion Leader

The Virgin Mary is not seen only as the epitome of motherhood and femininity—she is also represented within the Church as a woman of great strength. So common is the image of Mary as powerful protector that her strength is often evoked by young men going into battle. People have felt that if they dedicated battles to her, she would help them to be victorious. One of the classic battle images associated with the Virgin Mary has to do with her battle with snakes or the dragon (which can symbolize the devil and temptation).

In Revelation 12, a woman groans in childbirth and a dragon waits for the child to be born, threatening to consume the child when he emerges from the womb. The woman seems to represent Mary, based on the description of the woman being clothed by the sun and with the moon at her feet. When the woman gives birth to a boy, the child is taken away to God and the woman flees into the wilderness, where she "has a place prepared by God"(Revelation 12:6). The child seems to represent Christ, because he is described as "a male child, who is to rule all the nations with a rod of iron" (Revelation 12:5). The image of this woman not being conquered by the dragon is similar to one that shows up frequently in Western art, in which the Virgin Mary conquers the serpent from Genesis 3, reversing the curse that resulted from Adam and Eve eating the forbidden fruit. In this art, instead of being seduced by the snake, Mary steps on it and conquers it. This image also serves as an example of the life of victory to which all Christians are called.

The Protection of the Mother of God

The other side of this emphasis on the Virgin Mary as the Champion Leader or Woman of Valor is that she has also, historically, been evoked as a protector for those who are struggling in times of political unrest. Many countries, such as Poland and Russia, believe that the Virgin Mary was responsible for protecting them during times of invasion, driving away foreign enemies and preserving peace.

In some cases, countries were invaded by large armies and were able to stand up to overwhelming forces and prevail over them. Often the successful defense was directly attributed to the Virgin Mary. There has been a long-standing belief connecting the Virgin Mary's love for people with her willingness (and ability) to protect them. Medjugorje, Bosnia, although torn apart by wars, seems to have been miraculously protected through some of the bloodiest battles during World War II. The village has remained intact and virtually unharmed. Medjugorje continues to be the location of some of the most famous apparitions.

Constantinople

The Great Eastern Christian city of Constantinople was also miraculously protected multiple times by the intercessions of the Virgin Mary. Throughout history, when rumors of war reached the emperor, processions around the city would be held. The emporer or Patriarch might carry an icon of Mary or her clothing-related relics. The crowds would pray and sing and wait to see what happened.

In 860, for example, Russians attempted to invade the city with a fleet of 200 ships. They were forced to withdraw after the Virgin's Robe was processed around the city and a great storm rose up and scattered their fleets.

An icon of Mary was again brought out in 1453 just as Constantinople was about to fall to the Ottoman Turks. Emperor Constantine XI commanded that this icon be carried through the city as a way of offering prayers and comfort to the Christians there. During this procession, however, the sky filled with ominous clouds and the icon slipped and fell. Immediately, the streets were deluged with hail and rain and the procession halted. The city fell to the invading armies and is now known as "Istanbul."

discussion question

Who is thought to have been assumed into heaven?
According to 2 Kings 2:9, Elijah was whisked to heaven by a whirlwind, accompanied by chariots and horses of fire. His disciple, Elisha, was also blessed enough to receive Elijah's gift of prophecy after Elijah departed.

The Blachernae Palace Church possessed this very valuable relic associated with the Virgin Mary, and in that church, an apparition directly linked to this particular relic was reported. On October 1, A.D. 911, this church was having an extremely long prayer service called an All-night Vigil.

It is said that during the service, Saint Andrew looked up and saw the Virgin Mary kneeling in prayer in the church, weeping and praying for all Christians. Saint Mary was not alone but was in the company of Saint John the Baptist and Saint John the Theologian. She was radiantly beautiful.

As the Virgin Mary prayed and wept, she eventually came close to the bishop's throne and continued to weep and pray. Saint Andrew could hardly believe his eyes as he watched the Virgin Mary complete her prayer and then spread her veil over all the people who were praying in the church. The veil was luminescent.

Saint Andrew watched in astonishment and then he nudged his companion, Epiphanius, to ask him if he also saw the Virgin. Epiphanius replied, "I do see, holy father, and I am in awe."

symbolism

Within the Eastern Orthodox Church, the Virgin Mary's veil is a much-loved symbol that represents the Virgin Mary's tender care and her ability to protect the faithful through her intercessions on their behalf.

The feast of the Pokrov (Protective Veil of the Mother of God) is celebrated on the day that the apparition is reported to have occurred, October 1. Although the event occurred in Constatinople, the feast is also zealously celebrated in Russia, where many churches are named for this feast, and an entire city, Pokrov, was named in memory of this event.

Mary and Weather

Historically, the Virgin Mary has also been connected with weather in the minds of the faithful. Many sailors, in particular, have believed that the Virgin Mary saved their lives when they prayed to her during stormy weather.

In Russia, where long, harsh winters are one of the undeniable realities of life, the connection between the need for the protective care of the Mother of Christ and the feast of Pokrov has been strong. A variety of folk traditions that have had particular significance for agricultural families surround this day.

In Russia it is widely believed that the first cold blast of winter wind blows on the day of this feast, which coincides with the time in which the weather begins to change from autumn to winter. The feast of Pokrov also marks a significant deadline—before this day, all harvesting and fieldwork must be completed, so people can settle in safely for the coming winter. One Russian folk saying captures the sentiment of Pokrov well. According to this saying, "On Pokrov, before dinner is autumn, after dinner is winter."

Traditionally, Russian families waited until this day to burn their first wood for warmth, believing that if they did not kindle their hearths until Pokrov they would be able to stay warm all winter long. The first fires of winter were often lit with a sort of prayerful devotion as the family committed itself to the tender loving care of the Virgin Mary in the face of the long, bleak winter that was to come.

Mary as Intercessor

Some of the most ancient images of the Virgin Mary come from the catacombs in Rome (catacombs are underground burial places found in many parts of the world) where Christians would hold their services during times of persecution. Most of the images from the catacombs do not directly show Christian themes because the Christians needed to keep their identities hidden.

One of the images of Mary recovered from the catacombs dates back to the fourth century. She is shown with her arms raised in the "orans" position. The image of raised arms symbolized prayer, and there were many depictions in the catacombs of figures in the orans position from the period during the persecution of Christians in the first few centuries after Christ. But in this fourth-century fresco image, a child is shown in the woman's belly. In contrast with the less defined images of earlier times, this would have been a more explicit reference to the Virgin Mary bearing Christ in her womb. This image demonstrates the classical relationship between the Virgin Mary and the Church.

Mary's arms are raised in prayer as a demonstration of her ministry of ongoing intercession, as she is praying for the good of the faithful. In this position, Mary demonstrates not only who she is, but what all Christians are called to become—intercessors for the sake of the world.

Another, more contemporary Western image of Mary that demonstrates her role as intercessor was first manifest through an apparition experienced by Catherine Laboure in France in 1830. This image was later engraved on the Miraculous Medal, which has been distributed all over the world (you'll learn more about the Miraculous Medal in Chapter 14). In this apparition, the Virgin Mary lifted up a golden globe topped by a cross, as if she was praying for mercy for the world. Then, the globe disappeared and she spread out her arms. Her fingers shone with luminous rings from which streaks of light poured down about the earth, illustrating the blessings that she pours upon those who seek them.

There are so many images of Mary as intercessor that it is impossible to detail them all here. But it is helpful to understand that all images of Mary are connected. Her role as intercessor is also connected to her role as Mother of the Church, demonstrating to all what it means to live a life of prayer, love, and action.

Star of the Sea

Another classic title for the Virgin Mary is *Stella Maris*, or Star of the Sea. This title is most often attributed to a manuscript written by

Saint Jerome, from the fifth century. Saint Jerome, however, actually used the term *Stilla Maris* instead of *Stella Maris*, which would have been translated as "a drop of the sea" instead of "star of the sea." Many historians believe that this linguistic confusion could have been caused by a copyist's error. The term *Stella Maris* was nonetheless used by many other later Christians, including Isidore of Seville.

There are also some ancient Christian hymns from the eighth to the eleventh centuries that used this title to describe Mary, such as "Ave Maria Stella" and "Alma Redemptoris Mater."

One of the Scriptural verses that is sometimes used to explain this term comes from a story in 1 Kings 18:41–45. In this passage, a small cloud appears above the sea. The cloud is interpreted as a hopeful sign to people suffering through a drought. Seeing the cloud, they know the rains will come and the drought will end. This Biblical image is almost a perfect reversal of other events connected to the title Stella Maris, specifically the image of Mary helping those who are trapped at sea during a storm—here, she gives hope of rain instead of stopping the storm. Mary is often viewed as a person who gives hope to the hopeless and help to those who are in despair.

factum

The connection between Mary and stars may also relate to the appearance of the star of Bethlehem, which guided the Magi to the baby Jesus.

The star imagery that is associated with the Virgin Mary has multiple dimensions. A six-pointed star is a reminder that Mary is from the line of David (as the Star of David has six points). Mary is also associated with the qualities assigned to stars—most specifically the use of stars for navigation. Stars lead you to your destination, and allow you to always know in what direction you are heading, guiding followers to the truth.

The association between Mary and stars gave birth to much imagery of the Virgin Mary as a protector of sailors. Many sailors have prayed to the Virgin Mary and felt that she miraculously protected them. In one legendary tale (which reflects some anti-Muslim bias, unfortunately), three men were on a boat, and a storm rose up. Two of the sailors cried out to Mary to protect them—these men were Christians. The other man, who was a Muslim, cried out to Allah for safety and then began to chastise the other sailors of crying out to Mary instead of Allah. As he scolded them, a great wave rose up and tossed him into the sea while the other two survived.

The image of Mary as "Star of the Sea" is also closely connected to some pagan-goddess imagery, particularly that of Isis, who came from the sea and was able to preserve seafarers. The parallels between the Virgin Mary and Isis have been especially significant because Isis had a sacrificial child (see Chapter 19 for more information about Mary and the goddess Isis).

The image of storm-tossed sailors calling out to the Virgin Mary for assistance can be understood metaphorically as well—the world itself is a stormy sea that is difficult to navigate and dangerous. As Saint Bernard said:

> *"Take not your eyes from the light of this star if you would not be overwhelmed by the waves; if the storms of temptations arise, if you are thrown upon the rocks of affliction, look to the star, invoke Mary . . . In dangers, in distress, in doubt, call on Mary. She will not be far from your mouth, or your heart; and that you may obtain her intercession, omit not to imitate her conduct. When you follow her, you will not go astray; when you invoke her, you will no longer be in doubt; when she supports you, you will not fall; when she leads you, you will surely come to eternal life, and will find by your own experience that she is justly called Maria—that is, Star of the Sea."*

The Heart of Mary

The significance of the Virgin Mary's heart is deeply connected to the heart of her son, which is called "The Sacred Heart." The Sacred Heart imagery is often connected to four apparitions from the 1670s, which were experienced by Saint Margaret Mary Alacoque.

The Sacred Heart

The name for Jesus' heart connects the heart of Christ to his ongoing love for humanity. It is often shown with thorns as an expression of Christ's suffering for the sake of the world, as well as the suffering he experiences when his love and message of salvation is rejected. The Sacred Heart of Christ has been widely connected to Roman Catholic devotional practices; to meditate on his heart is to contemplate his love and to draw closer to him in love.

Especially within Catholicism, there has been much discussion of the Virgin Mary's heart. In Paris, one of the most beautiful churches, set high on a hilltop overlooking the city, is named Sacre Coeur, which can be translated as "Sacred Heart." Many Western Christian monastic orders and parochial schools have been dedicated to the heart of the Virgin Mary. This piety may at least partially be connected to the idea that through the Virgin Mary's heart, one is able to glimpse her suffering, love, compassion, and unceasing prayer.

The Virgin Mary's heart is also a frequent theme of Western art and apparitions. This image came through strikingly in the vision that reportedly took place at Rue de Bac in Paris when a young postulant named Catherine had a vision of the Virgin Mary, which was ultimately made into the Miraculous Medal (you will learn more about the Miraculous Medal in Chapter 14). One of the significant elements of this apparition is that Catherine saw two hearts beside each other. One was encircled in thorns while the other was pieced by a sword. These two hearts were intended to represent the heart of Christ (as he suffered the pain of persecution), and the other heart was intended to symbolize the heart of Mary, which was prophesied in the New Testament. When Mary and Joseph took the infant Christ to the temple for his dedication, Saint Simeon greeted the Holy Family and prophesied to Mary that a "sword would pierce her soul" (Luke 2:33–35). This prophesy has been most often connected with the suffering the Virgin Mary would experience as she watched as her son was rejected and crucified. In popular piety, it is sometimes said that, besides Christ, no one suffered more than Mary at the Crucifixion.

Two Holy Hearts

These two hearts, shown so closely together, both pierced, also express the way in which the hearts of Jesus and his mother were linked. Within Catholicism, there has been much piety surrounding the Immaculate Heart of Mary. This piety finds inspiration from a number of passages in the Gospels, especially Luke 2:19, which says, "But Mary treasured up all these things [that had happened to her], pondering them in her heart," and Luke 2:35, where Simeon prophesies to Mary, "a sword will pierce through your own soul also." This second passage seems to be fulfilled in John 19, where Mary stands at the foot of the cross, and in which Jesus' side is pierced.

Within the Roman Catholic tradition, there is even a feast day on August 22 to celebrate the Sacred Heart of Mary. A special prayer is said on this day, which shows the significance of the Virgin Mary's heart within the Roman Catholic Church: "ALMIGHTY, everlasting God, Who didst prepare in the Heart of the Virgin Mary a worthy dwelling-place for the Holy Ghost; mercifully grant that we, devoutly contemplating the festivity of the same Immaculate Heart, may be enabled to live according to Thy Heart."

The Virgin Mary's heart has a significant place in the faith of many Roman Catholics because a glimpse of what she felt in her heart offers an understanding of who she is. The symbolic representations of Mary prevalent in the Church help to flesh out a picture of a woman who was fully human but fully transformed by her complete willingness to live for God.

Chapter 9

Medieval Mary

Many of the devotional practices surrounding Mary that grew up in the East eventually found their way to the West and blossomed in fresh ways during the medieval period. This chapter explores the artistic and poetic forms and devotional practices that developed during this era, which is known for its courtly romances, the Crusades, and flowering of mysticism.

The Cult of Courtly Love

Many of our modern ideas about romance are rooted in the medieval cult of courtly love, which developed from a mingling of many sources. These sources include older traditions of Arab love poetry, which first found their way to Spain and then became popular in Europe by the eleventh century. During the Middle Ages, these passionate expressions of love blossomed.

Courtly love was a school of thought in which courtiers could learn how to be charming and graceful. Famed poets, or troubadours, were attached to specific wealthy courts. They created poetry and songs to entertain and educate those in the court.

According to the model of courtly love, love was important as a catalyst for growth and transformation. When the notion of the transformative power of love migrated to Europe, it was easy for medieval Christians to apply this practice to Christianity. The Virgin Mary came to be seen as a lady worthy of devotion, and as people drew closer to her, they felt that their love for her made them bolder, braver, and more faithful.

Troubadour Poetry

Troubadour poetry became popular in Europe during the twelfth century. The Troubadours were a class of musicians and poets based in France, Italy, and Spain who wrote poems and music about chivalry and love. They were most prominent between 1100 and 1350. Many of their writings focused on sexual love.

By the thirteenth century, both the Arab love poetry and the troubadour poetry found a new subject—the Virgin Mary. The Virgin Mary served as an ideal subject of love poetry because she was viewed as paradoxically accessible and unattainable.

Courtly love was full of grace, longing, and devotion. According to the mores of the time, love made people better than they would otherwise be; and to love another person would be to raise that other person above oneself. Love was always restless, always seeking, and never fully satisfied. The desire to acquire the beloved only intensified with time. Mary could be sought, but never captured; passionately loved, but never possessed.

May Day Celebrations

One of the ancient romantic traditions rooted in the cult of courtly love is still celebrated today. May Day celebrations offered a way to integrate the pre-Christian practice of crowning a "lady" into the Christian tradition of devotion to the Virgin.

The ancient May Day celebrations included various courting rituals and were a celebration of the springtime and the pagan deities associated with fertility and the land. Increasingly, as the Church sought ways to translate these folk festivals into events that would be compatible with Christianity, they adapted to the rituals of the culture.

symbolism

Today, the ancient tradition of crowning a lady is still practiced during the month of May—but the lady crowned has become the Virgin Mary. Many American Catholics who attended parochial schools during this past century have fond memories of crowning the Virgin Mary with a wreath of flowers during the month of May (which is designated Mary's Month).

Many of the references to the Virgin Mary as "Our Lady" reflect the medieval obsession with courtly love. *Our Lady* serves as the counter-term to Our Lord. This title is suggestive of the pious notion that Mary was a royal lady who must be wooed and honored.

The Face That Resembled the Face of Christ

Mary was also the subject of more love poems during this time period than any other woman, and imagery surrounding her figured mightily into Dante's *Divine Comedy*. It was through the *Divine*

Comedy that Dante first coined a famous description for Mary's face, stating that it was "the face that most resembled Christ."

This idea that by peering into the face of Mary one might able to glimpse her son powerfully influenced both the art and theology of the day. Increasingly, artistic images (such as the Black Madonna images, which you will learn more about in Chapter 19) demonstrated the startling resemblance between the mother and her child. In these images, both mother and son were carved from a single block of wood and their resemblance was undeniable.

During the Middle Ages, Mary often seemed more accessible than Christ. For peasants, her femininity would have provided some continuity with the ancient goddesses they worshipped and prayed to as they tilled their fields. For the ranks of celibate monks, the presence of Mary as a "safe" woman in their lives might have fulfilled some need for female companionship—the famed Saint Francis of Assisi, for example, adored the Virgin Mary. Just as his monastic life called him to take vows of poverty and chastity, Saint Francis found a positive way to interpret these restrictions. Instead of viewing his life in terms of deprivation, he saw himself as united to these values in the way that a married person might be united to their spouse. Specifically, he felt a particular closeness with Mary, whom he thought of as his Lady, "Holy Poverty."

The Flowering of Western Art

For the teachers of theology, images of the Virgin Mary helped them convey her role in the history of salvation. Mary's role in art and piety was profound during this time, perhaps prone to excess, but certainly worth exploring if we are to understand the presence of Marian devotion in our world today.

During the Middle Ages, most people were not able to read or write the Latin that was used for theological documents, prayer books, and the Mass. Because they did not have access to the printed word, art and architecture served as the theological textbooks of the day.

According to Sally Cunneen in her book *In Search of Mary: The Woman and the Symbol,* the people of the Middle Ages would have readily understood the bulk of the images from the Old Testament that had been viewed by the Church Fathers as "types" of Mary. They would have been able to grasp Mary as the burning bush who had the presence of God within her but was not consumed; Mary as Jacob's Ladder, the link between heaven and earth; Mary as the Ark of the Covenant; and Mary as the flowering of the root of Jesse.

These images were powerfully woven together in churches, manuscripts, and sermons. The visual continuity of these images allowed medieval communities to grasp some of the earliest theology in a fresh way. The medieval period also brought about one of the most significant transformations related to the Virgin Mary. If piety helped create the art that made the Virgin Mary appear more elevated during the Middle Ages, the art also informed the increasing piety that helped Mary be more accessible and available.

The *Pieta*

One piece of art that powerfully influenced the devotion of the Middle Ages was Michelangelo Buonarroti's *Pieta*, the famed marble image created in 1499 in which Mary holds the body of her limp, crucified son. Unlike the stylized and richly symbolic icons of the East, this image was intentionally realistic. Although any mother would agonize during a moment like this, Mary's youthful face remains dignified and full of grace. Her incredible expression of calm speaks to the courage and serenity that is so often associated with her.

Like the images of Mary that link her role in the New Testament to some of the famed events from the Old Testament, the *Pieta* is a visual depiction of the early sentiments that come from the poetry of the East that would have expressed the sorrow of the mother at the death of her son. In his book *Mary Through the Ages,* Jaroslav Pelikan connects the image of the *Pieta* to the poetry of Romanos the Melodist, in which Mary and Jesus discuss his death. She begs him to let her be present at the cross because she wants to remain close to him through his darkest hour. Christ encourages her to lay aside her grief because she is "in the bridal chamber."

discussion question

Where is the *Pieta* now?
Housed in the Chapel of the Pieta in Saint Peter's Basilica in Rome, the *Pieta* is one of Michelangelo's most famous works (and the only one he signed). It is also one of the most recognizable pieces of religious sculpture. Michelangelo carved the *Pieta* when he was only twenty-four years old.

The Hope of a New World

The *Pieta* is not merely a grief-filled image. It is also a profoundly hopeful one. Christ's death must occur so he can fulfill prophecies of his resurrection, so that he can return like a bridegroom seeking his bride, the Church. He expresses his desire to return to his mother, Mary, who was often viewed as an image of the Church.

Mary grieved the death of her son, and shared in his sufferings as only a mother could. It was she who would have been most able to grasp that even in his death there were the fresh seeds of a promise. Even as she held her deceased son in her arms, she must have sensed that his death was the beginning of new life for the world.

The image of the *Pieta*, which showed Mary with Christ in her arms after his death, is also connected with Saint Teresa of Avila, who had a vision of Christ in her own arms after his death. Through this vision, Saint Teresa experienced what it would have been like to be Mary, holding her dead son in her arms.

Our Lady of Legends

During the Middle Ages, legends of Mary were widespread and influential, and were treasured for their spiritual significance and teaching value. These ancient legends also helped inform the piety of the day, shaping people's liturgical and private devotional practices.

The Legend of Theophilus

One of the most popular legends from the Middle Ages involved a sixth-century archbishop named Theophilus who lived in what is now Turkey. He was a humble man who served as archdeacon for the Archbishop of Celia. When he was unanimously elected to serve as bishop, he turned down the post because of his humility.

Later, however, when Theophilus was forced to step down as archdeacon for no clear reason, he was so filled with rage that he turned to the devil. The devil encouraged him to sign a pact in which he would renounce God and the Virgin Mary in exchange for the position as bishop. Theophilus signed the pact with his own blood.

He became bishop, but his conscience troubled him. After he fasted for forty days, the Virgin Mary appeared to him and chastised him for what he had done. After he repented, she agreed to intercede before God on his behalf. Later, she appeared to him in a dream and tore up the pact. He awoke surrounded by scraps of parchment. He made a confession to his bishop and died in peace.

This legend offers a glimpse into the medieval perspective of the Virgin Mary. During the Middle Ages, she was increasingly viewed as the woman who had the power to cancel the works of the devil, to make right even lives that had gone horribly awry.

factum

The medieval notion of Mary's ability to restore lives was expressed well by the eleventh-century writer Peter Damian, who offered this prayer to Mary: "Pay what we owe, avert what we fear, obtain what we wish, and accomplish what we hope."

Increasingly, Mary was viewed as this type of mediating (some might even say meddling) mother who makes things right for her children. Despite her exceptional example of piety and purity, she was not generally viewed as a figure of judgment but of mercy and reconciliation. Christ, on the other hand, was most often portrayed as a stern judge. According to Sally Cunneen, in her book *In Search of Mary,* many of the surviving medieval images of Christ show him as the stern Shepherd who separates the sheep from the goats. It was during the middle ages especially that Mary came to be associated with mercy while Christ came to be associated with judgment.

Images of Mary generally shifted during the Middle Ages as well. The early art from this period often emphasized Mary's greatness, while the art produced later emphasized her tenderness. As she came to be seen as increasingly tender and accessible, prayers to her for intercessions increased as well. Some people even prayed to Mary instead of Jesus.

The influential writer Bernard of Clairvaux expressed this progression away from the son and toward the mother this way, "If you fear the Father, go to the Son; if you fear the Son, go to the Mother."

The Golden Legend

Another influential text that developed during the Middle Ages was called *The Golden Legend.* This collection of stories of the lives of the saints was most likely compiled around 1290 by Jacobus de Voragine.

The Golden Legend was much loved for the way it both humanized and spiritualized the lives of holy people. For example, it drew from a variety of ancient and apocryphal texts to fill in many biographical details about Jesus and Mary which had not been supplied by Scripture.

The Golden Legend was something like a medieval encyclopedia of the saints, containing stories of varying pedigree. These stories were valued for the way they offered spiritual lessons to the faithful, but were not always accepted uncritically. Some of the details supplied in these accounts were more fanciful than historical, more symbolic than miraculous.

Mary and Medieval Mysticism

The monastic communities of the day did a great deal to encourage and increase Marian devotion, in part by establishing additional feast days for Mary. In particular, Saturday came to be set apart as a day for commemorating Mary. This decision was based on multiple traditions related to Mary. According to one, because the world was completed on the seventh day and Mary was an essential part of the ultimate plan of redemption, it was appropriate to commemorate Mary on that day.

One of the reasons that the seventh day seemed fitting as a day to commemorate Mary was related to the Genesis account. According to Genesis, after God created the world, he rested on the seventh day. Likewise, it was sometimes said that, when the infant Christ came into the world, he was able to find rest in the arms of his mother.

symbolism

Saint Alcuin was a Benedictine monk who was the Minister of Education. He was attached to the court of Charlemagne, and under his direction, each day of the week came to commemorate and symbolize a different event in Scripture. A Mass was to be celebrated on each day, and two were to be celebrated for Mary on Saturday.

The Venerable Bede, an eighth-century English monk who was a famed historian and theologian, wrote some of the earliest Western sermons devoted to Mary. A twelfth-century devotee of Mary, Saint Bernard of Clairvaux, who served as Abbot of Cistercian Monastery for thirty-eight years, also wrote beautiful and influential sermons about the Virgin Mary.

Saint Bernard

Saint Bernard was titled the "mellifluous doctor" because of his poetic writing, especially about the Virgin Mary. His first few writings about the Virgin Mary were composed when he was only twenty-five years old. He had loved her since he was a small child because, according to one legend, once while he was praying to the Virgin in a church, he received three drops of her milk as a sign of her love for him.

factum

> Sometimes Bernard used particularly romantic terms to describe the Virgin. In one sermon he wrote, "Our Queen has gone before us, and so glorious has been her entry into paradise that we, her slaves, confidently follow our mistress, crying: 'Draw us after you, and we shall run in the fragrance of your perfumes.'"

Bernard had a tender relationship with Mary for all of his life. He called her the "aqueduct" of God's grace. Through his sermons, Bernard made connections between the Virgin Mary and the bride in the Song of Songs.

Saint Bernard's devotion to Mary was so great that he often attributed things to her that some might only be comfortable attributing to Christ. He encouraged people in every kind of distress to call on Mary, and he firmly believed that she would assist people in their time of need. Some of his reasoning seemed to follow the medieval notion of Mary as interceding mother.

Saint Bernard is also credited with helping to perpetuate the image of Mary as the Star of the Sea. Many contemporary scholars see this particular title for Mary as one that is based upon a scribal error that occurred during one of Saint Jerome's translations. Yet, the image of Mary as the Star of the Sea was valuable because it provided some continuity for the local people between the ancient pagan deities who were associated with the sea and the figures of Christianity.

One of the ancient goddesses associated with the sea was Isis. Many throughout history have drawn parallels between the Virgin Mary and Isis (a connection you will learn more about in Chapter 19). Because of Saint Bernard's great and sometimes effusive devotion to the Virgin Mary, he was sometimes criticized as carelessly reviving the ancient goddesses for the local people. Some people felt that he was not careful enough to make a clear distinction between the Virgin Mary and the ancient goddesses.

Female Mysticism

The medieval period was also a time in which many women entered the monasteries. By the twelfth century, the monastic life was an increasingly popular choice for women. Monasticism not only offered an opportunity to devote one's life completely to the service of God, but it also offered women the opportunity to join tight-knit communities of women, to make valuable contributions to their society, and to escape the rigors and dangers of childbearing.

Some of the female nuns of this age authored some of the most beautiful writings about the Virgin Mary. One of the most famous medieval mystics was Hildegard of Bingen, who experienced multiple visions of the Virgin Mary during the twelfth century.

symbolism

Hildegard of Bingen emphasized the ways in which the Virgin Mary restored to women the dignity that had been compromised through Eve's sin. Just as Eve was viewed as the mother of all, Mary became the mother of the new creation.

Hildegard was sickly as a child, suffering from migraine headaches. She had her first taste of the monastic life at just eight years old when she was sent to live at a hermitage where she could receive her education. Eventually, she became an influential leader, or abbess, within her community. She composed songs for her monastic sisters, many of which she wrote, like the visions she experienced all of her life, were specifically centered on the Virgin Mary.

Hildegard's songs echoed some of the central themes of Marian devotion. Mary's virginity served as the link between heaven and earth, and the Virgin birth was as significant as the cross because of the way that it connected humanity to divinity.

In one of her writings on Mary, Hildegard addressed Mary this way: "You are the luminous matrix through which the Word breathed forth all virtues, as in the primal matrix it breathed into being all that is."

The Crusades

One of the most tragic chapters in the history of Christianity is related to the Crusades, which occurred during the Middle Ages. The Crusades were a series of eight military expeditions launched by Western Christians in an effort to reclaim the Holy Land from Muslims, whom the Christians deemed infidels. The Crusaders waged war against others too. During the Fourth Crusade in 1204, for example, the Crusaders sacked the city of Constantinople and zealously killed many of the Eastern Christians there. Just as the bitter memory of the Crusades continues to fuel hostility between the Islamic and Christian worlds, so too the memory of Western Christians attacking Eastern Christians remains a stumbling block in attempts to reunite the Eastern Orthodox and Roman Catholic Churches (which some believe is one of Mary's goals).

Writers such as Sally Cunneen have suggested that perhaps one of the most profound ironies of the Crusades is that Mary was sometimes invoked by English armies for her strength and cited by these armies and their leaders as a reason to engage in holy war. The First Crusade was initiated in 1095 by Pope Urban II. At a famed Marian shrine, in Claremont-Ferrand, France, Pope Urban encouraged his soldiers to pray to Mary for victory and promised that those who participated in Saturday Marian devotions would be forgiven for their sins. The Second Crusade was announced by Pope Eugenius III in 1145 and popularized by the famed scholar Bernard of Clairvaux.

factum

During the Crusades, monks brought chess to Europe from Syria. They made changes to the game to reflect their devotion to Mary. In Syria, the figure who followed the King was the Minister. In the Crusaders' version of the game, this figure could move in any direction—becoming the most powerful piece of the game—and was renamed the Queen or the Virgin.

As the soldiers marched into battle, they may have prayed the Salve Regina: "Hail Holy Queen, Mother of Mercy, our life, our sweetness, and our hope. To you do we cry, poor banished children of Eve, to you do we send up our sighs, mourning and weeping in this valley of tears. Turn then, most gracious advocate, your eyes of mercy toward us; and after this our exile, show us the blessed fruit of your womb, Jesus. O clement, O loving, O sweet Virgin Mary."

During the medieval period, the Virgin Mary was not only present in the minds and hearts of the Crusaders. Her influence permeated the hearts of the majority of medieval Christians, and their love for her was intimate, earthly, and sometimes romanticized.

It was during the medieval period that ancient Eastern practices of devotion to Mary were expressed through artwork, architecture, and writings, leaving us with a rich tapestry of insights into Marian devotion, and into her role as intercessor, guide, and mother.

Chapter 10

Toppling Mary: The Reformation

Some modern Protestants believe that the original reformers, especially Martin Luther, rejected all of the more ancient teachings associated with the Virgin Mary, especially the invocation of her prayers and the belief that she was ever-virgin. But most of the reformers had a fairly complicated relationship with Mary. This chapter explores the ways that different reformers viewed the Virgin Mary and also considers the gradual decline of Marian devotion within Protestantism, as well as the faint glimmers of a contemporary Marian revival.

The Rise of Protestantism

In our day, modern Protestants often define themselves in terms of doctrines that have a specifically anti-Catholic slant. The very term "Protestant" speaks to the reality that this movement was sparked by a protest that was originally related to some medieval Catholic abuses such as the widespread practice of selling indulgences. Indulgences were passes that, for a fee, guaranteed the buyer the right to be spared time in purgatory.

The sale of indulgences was not only viewed as spiritually beneficial to the purchaser, but was also a great fundraiser for the Roman Catholic Church. Reformer Martin Luther was especially appalled by the sale of the Peter Indulgence, the profits of which funded the Roman Catholic Church's completion of the construction of Saint Peter's Basilica in Rome.

discussion question

What does *sola fida, sola gratia, et sola scriptura* mean?
One of Luther's most famous Latin sayings related to his convictions about salvation and theology is *sola fida, sola gratia, et sola scriptura*. This saying can be translated as "by faith alone, by grace alone, and by Scripture alone." This conviction is one of the central creeds of many Protestant Churches.

Protestants have also pointed to the concern that was foremost on Martin Luther's mind—anxiety related to his own salvation. As Luther studied the Bible, he became increasingly convinced that salvation came through "grace alone and faith alone," and not from purchasing indulgences from the Church. This newfound conviction brought him profound inner peace and courage, as well as the desire to share this good news with others.

Luther was a professor at a university in the German town of Wittenberg. Many students responded enthusiastically to his teachings about the sufficiency of faith, grace, and Scripture for salvation. Much of what he taught, however, grew out of a personal reaction to a particular context and time in the history of the Roman Catholic Church.

Tumultuous Times

It is nearly impossible to understand Martin Luther's drive to challenge the Roman Catholic Church without considering the historical times in which he lived. Luther lived in Germany in the sixteenth century. As the son of a father who had worked his way out of the peasant stock and owned a mine, Luther's parents expected much of him and encouraged him to study hard. He completed his bachelor's degree in one year, went on to receive his master's degree, and then proceeded to study law. In 1505, he found himself in the midst of a raging storm. After lightning nearly struck him, he prayed to Saint Anna (the mother of Mary) to save him. He promised her that if he survived the storm he would become a monk.

A Nagging Question

Martin Luther survived the storm and kept his promise to Saint Anna by becoming an Augustinian monk. Although he devoted himself to the prayerful monastic life, he found that all of his work brought him no peace. A question that had plagued him before he joined the monastery continued to haunt him within the walls of the cloister. How was he to know that he was going to be saved? How much work did he have to do to be accepted by God, who in Luther's eyes (and perhaps the eyes of many of his contemporaries) was a righteous judge who looked upon all of his efforts with a disapproving frown? The harder Luther worked, the more aware he became of his own sins. As he grappled with his many sins, God's love seemed increasingly far away.

The Vicar General of the German Augustinians, John Staupitz, instructed Luther to commit himself to academic work as a way to busy his mind and to keep from falling into the trap of endless ponderings. Luther was ordained a priest, began teaching theology at the University of Wittenberg, and went on to receive a second bachelor's degree in Biblical Studies. Eventually, he received a doctorate of theology from the University of Wittenberg.

factum

During Luther's years in the monastery, he became so obsessed with the idea of trying to be perfect that the Vicar General of the German Augustinians, John Staupitz, encouraged him to focus on the love of Christ, and to study the Scriptures.

A Way Out?

As Luther immersed himself in the Scriptures, he discovered that according to Paul from the book of Romans, salvation was not dependant on works but on the grace of God, which was accomplished through Christ's death on the cross. This insight brought much-needed clarity to Luther's life. Just as he found liberation through his study of the Scriptures, he sought to liberate others. Luther's formula appealed to many, and his influence was widely felt both by his fans and by his enemies.

Christendom Cracked

On October 31, 1517, Luther nailed his *95 Theses* to the door of a Catholic church in Wittenberg. This document made multiple accusations against the Church, but Luther's central objections were related to the sale of indulgences and a teaching that is often referred to as "works based salvation."

Luther's *95 Theses* are not only significant from a theological perspective, but also from a historical perspective, because the *95 Theses* were subsequently published and distributed all over Europe (tens of thousands of copies were generated). This was made possible by the advent of the printing press in the 1450s.

The Roman Catholic Church did not take Luther's views as constructive criticism, which is what Luther might have hoped would be the reaction to his work. In 1520, a papal bull (official statement) of excommunication was issued against Luther, which Luther publicly burned along with a stack of church books.

fallacy

It is a fallacy that the Roman Catholic and Eastern Orthodox Churches teach that salvation is through works alone. Neither church endorses faith alone, but both believe that while faith is the central component of salvation, faith without works is dead (James 2:14). Both churches emphasize that while we are ultimately saved through faith, authentic faith is always connected to works.

The Diet of Worms

Ultimately, Luther was brought before the Diet of Worms, a council in which he was to deny or affirm his previous writings. His books were laid out on a table and he was asked if he had written them all. He said yes and was then asked if he still believed all the things that had been written. He asked for time to think and pray about it, and this request was granted.

Eventually, Luther apologized for the harsh tone of some of his writing (especially the writing that criticized specific individuals), but he refused to repudiate his work. He felt that to deny those statements would be tantamount to encouraging abuses to continue. "Here I stand," Luther is reported to have said. "I can do no other. God help me, amen." Many contemporary scholars question whether these words were actually said or are merely part of the tradition. No official documents from the Diet of Worms actually contain this quotation.

Outlawing Luther

In 1521, the "Edict of Worms" was issued by Holy Roman Emperor Charles V, officially banning Luther's writings and claiming that Luther was an outlaw. According to the "Edict of Worms," anyone was welcome to kill Luther without legal ramifications.

Although Luther was promised safe passage to and from the Diet of Worms, many believed that he would be arrested and possibly taken prisoner on his way home from the council. Because of this, Luther's ally, Prince Frederick, arranged to have him secretly snatched by his envoys and taken to the Wartburg palace. There, Luther began work on his famous German translation of the Bible.

Luther's writings (although officially banned) continued to attract widespread popular support. By the time he died in 1546, he was still calling for reform within the Church, yet the seeds of Lutheranism had already been planted in the hearts of some of his followers. While he was still alive, some Christians who believed in his famous formula *sola gratia, sola fida et sola scriptura* began calling themselves Lutherans.

Martin Luther and Mary

The earliest Protestant Churches retained many of the beliefs and practices of the Roman Catholic Church. As the years progressed, however, these churches resembled Roman Catholicism less and less. Few people recognize how significant Marian devotion was to many of the reformers, although the reformers were generally cautious in their Mariology.

Luther was outspoken in his concerns about some of the excessive forms of Marian devotion, and was especially appalled by some practices that he saw as being on the level of folk piety—he did not like to see the Virgin Mary equated with God. Sometimes, Luther made the common mistake of lumping together practices that were accepted on the level of popular practice with actual dogma of the Roman Catholic Church.

factum

Luther did not intend to start a new church, but rather to bring about reform within the Roman Catholic Church. Although passionate about taking a stance against the abuses he experienced, he was deeply conflicted over the possibility of schism. His excommunication indeed did bring about an era of schism in which Protestant churches broke apart from each other.

Praying to Mary

Although early in his ministry he sometimes seemed to invoke the prayers of the Virgin Mary in a public way, over time Luther became increasingly wary of the practice of invoking the prayers of the saints. He was especially uncomfortable (as many Protestants are to this day) with the idea of Mary as a mediator or intercessor. As Luther's ministry evolved, he came to distrust the practice of invoking the prayers of the saints. His caution, however, did not suppress his belief that the departed saints do continually pray for those on earth and that Mary, especially, prays for the Church.

Luther also offered some cautions related to the saying of the Hail Mary. While he believed that this prayer could be useful for believers who wanted to meditate on Mary's faith, he was concerned that those who didn't believe in God might say the "Hail Mary" in a way that was spiritually dangerous. He was troubled that some people would pray to Mary instead of Christ.

Luther's Catholic Convictions

Luther did, however, believe in most official Roman Catholic teachings related to the Virgin Mary, especially her ever-virginity and her Immaculate Conception, although the latter was not officially proclaimed as dogma by the Roman Catholic Church until 1854. Although Luther called this doctrine a "sweet and pious belief" and embraced it on a personal level, he did not believe that the

Immaculate Conception should be forced upon believers because he did not see sufficient Biblical evidence to support it.

fallacy

It is fallacy to believe that the Immaculate Conception refers to Jesus' birth from a virgin. The Immaculate Conception is a view held by the Roman Catholic Church that Mary was conceived without the original stain of sin which had been passed on to every person since the fall in the Garden of Eden.

Luther also believed in the ancient Christian idea that Mary was the spiritual mother of the Church. And he believed that Mary was a wonderful person to meditate on and emulate, especially because of her extreme humility and obedience to the will of God.

According to Martin Luther, not only was devotion to Mary a spiritually helpful practice, but it was an almost intrinsic aspect of healthy spirituality. According to a sermon he gave on September 1, 1522, "the veneration of Mary is inscribed in the very depths of the human heart."

Ulrich Zwingli

Although he came before Luther, the Swiss reformer, Ulrich Zwingli (1484–1531) often takes a back seat in discussions about the Reformation, perhaps because he did not have the same commanding personality as Luther. But while Luther was studying the Scriptures in Germany and coming to the conclusions that would ultimately cause him to be excommunicated, Ulrich Zwingli, a Catholic pastor in Switzerland, was also troubled by abuses within the Roman Catholic Church and was personally engaging the Scriptures. Both men began to call for reform within the Catholic Church.

Devotion to Mary

Some theologians say that Zwingli was the most devoted to Mary of all the reformers. It is certainly the case that the first wave of reformers, including Zwingli and Martin Luther, were far more Marian in their personal devotions and sermons than the second wave of Reformers, including John Calvin.

Zwingli had a very particular devotion to the Virgin Mary, and he was concerned that people knew about it, especially because his calls for reform may have caused some to think that he held positions that he did not. On September 17, 1518, he sent a sermon he'd written to his brothers with a note attached that said, "If you are told that I despise God or his Mother, or that I falsify God's teaching, do not believe it."

Like Luther, Zwingli felt that a measure of reverence for Mary was intrinsic to Christian piety. Many people may be surprised to discover that Zwingli held the conviction that good Christians would be in the habit of reciting the Hail Mary, although he, like Luther, he would have only been familiar with the first, Biblical portion of this prayer, "Hail Mary, full of grace, blessed art thou among women and blessed is the fruit of thy womb, Jesus." He would not have been familiar with the later addition, "Holy Mary, Mother of God, pray for us now and at the hour of our deaths. Amen."

discussion question

Did Zwingli ask for Mary's intercessions?
Zwingli was not comfortable with the idea of asking for Mary's intercessions. Because of this, he said that the Hail Mary was merely a greeting and a praise, but not a prayer—as prayers generally contained petitions. Still, from Zwingli's perspective, the Hail Mary offered a valuable means of contemplation.

Zwingli often spoke of Mary when he commented on the Bible. This was especially the case between 1516 and 1518 when he served as a chaplain at the monastery. During these years, one of his primary responsibilities was to offer sermons to flocks of pilgrims who came to venerate a statue of the Virgin Mary. Mary would have naturally been on the minds of these pilgrims and she was certainly part of the equation in Zwingli's thinking.

Like Luther, Zwingli held to the the ever-virginity of Mary. He was also comfortable with the title Theotokos, as a term for describing the Virgin Mary's unique role in the history of salvation.

Zwingli also often referred to Mary as Immaculate. He believed that she occupied a special place among the saints because the weakness toward sin was not passed on to her through her parents, Joachim and Anna, as it had been passed down to every single human being since the Fall. Zwingli was, however, concerned about the widespread practice of asking the saints, and particularly Mary, for prayers. He did not feel that this was an appropriate way to pray.

Contemplating Mary

Zwingli did encourage contemplation of Mary, especially contemplation of her heart. He believed that the practice of meditating on her heart was rooted in Luke 2:51. According to this passage, when Mary was pregnant with Jesus she pondered all things in her heart and kept them. Because of this, Zwingli felt that it was a fruitful project to contemplate Mary's heart, which was so full of God's intention for the world. Like Luther, Zwingli felt that Mary's witness was also to be contemplated. But Zwingli was always careful to make clear that Mary never intended to draw attention to herself. Her value was directly related to her relationship with her son and her obedience to God. According to Zwingli, Mary was not just a great example in her faithfulness, but also in the struggles she faced. He stated, "therefore may you, with your poverty and your weariness, find an example in her: this misery that is so well known to humans must be borne, since the holy Mother of God was not sheltered from it."

John Calvin

French-born Swiss reformer John Calvin (1509–1564) participated in the second phase of the Reformation, moving toward a Christianity that was increasingly less Catholic. Of all the reformers, Calvin was perhaps the least effusive about the Virgin Mary, and the most critical toward the Roman Catholic Church.

Protestant Commonalities

There are a few areas, however, in which Calvin shared the convictions of Luther and Zwingli. Calvin firmly believed, for example, in the ever-virginity of Mary. He was familiar with a theory circulating during his time that Mary had other children with Joseph after Jesus was born, but he dismissed this theory as an ancient, recycled heresy, based on the teachings of Helvidius, who lived in the fourth century and provoked the ire of Jerome over the issue of Mary's ever-virginity. Calvin went so far as to say that this ancient heresy had been brought back into fashion by those who speculated upon Scripture in a way that was dangerously imaginative.

factum

Calvin is most well known today for Calvinism, a theory based upon Luther's model related to salvation through faith alone. Calvinists emphasize the grace of God in predestining souls to heaven or hell, teaching that chosen people experience "irresistible grace," which means that they are powerless to turn away from the grace of God once selected to receive it.

For Calvin, whose father suffered for many years under a ban of excommunication from the Roman Catholic Church, it was very important to approach Christian theology with a healthy dose of intellectual sobriety. He derided those who took a more speculative approach to Scripture, reading things into the text that weren't there. According to Calvin, one of the key ways to combat the "terrible confusion" of the Roman Catholic Church of his day was to remain intellectually sober. Calvin also expressed concerns about some of the reformers who seemed to love speculating and coming up with new theories that were not firmly grounded in Scripture.

In light of Calvin's concern for sobriety, it is no surprise that he railed against some of the common practices of his day related to Mary. Like Zwingli, he was firmly opposed to images of Mary. He felt that the excessive Roman Catholic pomp surrounding the Virgin Mary bordered on blasphemy.

He was also opposed to the saying of the Rosary, as well as to the practice of naming churches and chapels after Mary. He was appalled by what he perceived as the increasingly superstitious quality of the Hail Mary, which had mysteriously changed from a mere greeting to a prayer, and was increasingly viewed on the popular level as one of the only ways to attain the grace of God. Calvin was disturbed when he saw people praying the Hail Mary instead of approaching God directly.

The Mirror of Faith

Ironically, as much as Calvin deplored physical images of the Virgin, his chief way of speaking about her involved mental images. Mary was an invaluable example to believers because of the ways in which she represented the epitome of an obedient life of service to God. According to Calvin, Mary had no merits in her own right, but because of her obedience to God, her witness can help the faithful live in a way that is more consistent with Scripture. According to Calvin, "She was a mirror of the faith that we must bring to God."

Calvin expressed the ancient connection between Mary and the Church in a profound way:

"Let us learn from the sole title of mother how useful, indeed necessary, is the knowledge of her, inasmuch as there is no entrance to permanent life unless we are received in the

womb of this mother, and she begets us, and feeds us at her breasts and finally she preserves us and keeps us under her guidance and government . . . it is also to be noted that outside of the womb of this Church one cannot expect forgiveness of sins or any salvation."

Calvin suggests that, like Mary, all believers should be open to receiving the Word of God in their own hearts. Mary is a model, not only of a faithful life that embraces Christ, but also of the Church.

A Marian Revival?

In December 2003, the prominent Evangelical magazine *Christianity Today* featured an article called "The Blessed Evangelical Virgin Mary." This article begins with a striking anecdote from John Knox's book *History of the Reformation in Scotland*. In this story, a young man who had left the Roman Catholic Church was forced to row in a galley ship for nineteen months. Soon after the boat arrived in Nantes, France, an image of the Virgin Mary was brought to those in the ship to kiss. This young man took the image and threw it into the water, saying, "Let our Lady now save herself: she is light enough; let her learn to swim!"

According to the author of the article, Timothy George, this attitude toward Mary often resurfaces in the Evangelical response to Mary. Evangelicals generally have an extreme wariness and instinctive distrust of Marian piety. But George asks the question voiced by many of his contemporaries: "Does Protestantism have a place for the Virgin Mary or, like Knox of the galleys, must we throw her overboard once and for all?"

This question is currently being answered in a variety of ways. On a personal level, many Protestants are slowly warming to the idea of asking for Mary's intercessions, or at least very intentionally contemplating her example.

Princeton theologian Robert Jensen, a Lutheran, and coeditor of the book *Mary, Mother of God* now encourages the practice of praying to Mary in stark contrast to his father, who was a strict Lutheran pastor. According to Jensen, asking for Mary's intercessions does not decrease our focus on God or take away from prayers to God. Instead, this practice is more like asking for the prayers of a deceased friend or family member—these prayers allow for participation in the Communion of Saints and are not a negation of God.

fallacy

It is a fallacy that all Protestant churches reject Mary. The worldwide Anglican Communion (to which the Episcopal Church in the United States belongs) has, in certain quarters, retained some measure of veneration of Mary.

A recent joint commission of Anglicans and Roman Catholics issued a statement that it is officially theologically acceptable within both contexts to ask for the prayers of the Virgin Mary. The statement also clarified that according to Anglican principles of Biblical interpretation, the Immaculate Conception and the Assumption of Mary are not necessarily contrary to Scripture, although concerns were raised about the fact that the Scripture does not explicitly recount these events. Anglicans also expressed some concerns about the ways that these doctrines were proclaimed by popes without a church council.

Increasingly, Protestants are expressing desires to find ways to integrate Mary's witness into their own spirituality. Although many have historically felt that Mary "belonged to the Catholics," more and more churches are now seeking ways to make Mary their own. In a recent article in *U.S. News & World Report* Senior Pastor Mark Roberts stated that the increasingly warm feelings toward Mary within Protestant churches suggests "that the dividing wall between Catholics and Protestants has come down a bit." As this wall comes down, questions about Mary begin to surface, and some Protestants are finding ways to integrate Marian devotions into their own lives.

Chapter 11

Messages from Mary

During the course of the last century, apparitions of the Virgin Mary seem to be increasing in frequency. Apparitions, however, are not a new phenomenon. Reports of apparitions have circulated since at least the first century. Although these apparitions have varied according to the time in which they occurred, certain themes have emerged. This chapter will explore some of the questions surrounding apparitions, as well as some of the universal themes that come through them.

A Global Phenomenon

Often, when we think of apparitions of the Virgin Mary, well-known locations come to mind, such as Fatima or Lourdes. But apparitions of the Virgin Mary are a wider phenomenon than most people realize. The full scope of these apparitions is detailed in Roy Abraham Varghese's book *God-Sent: A History of the Accredited Apparitions of Mary*. Almost every culture in the world has a story to tell of an encounter with the Virgin Mary. Some of these stories seem more credible than others, but each account helps create a more cohesive picture of the phenomenon that is reported to occur around the world.

Vatican Investigations

Before the Enlightenment, apparitions were not subject to scientific investigation. These apparitions were valued, however, because the communities that experienced them firsthand testified to their authenticity and because apparitions cohered with the larger witness of church life and teaching. In the last several hundred years, apparitions have been subject to scientific investigations, and when the scope of the apparitions has warranted it, the Vatican has commissioned investigations.

fallacy

It is a fallacy that the Roman Catholic and Eastern Orthodox Churches embrace apparitions without careful investigation. Apparitions are not necessarily considered valuable publicity for the churches. The most significant apparitions—those that draw the largest crowds and create the greatest followings—tend to be investigated by theologians, civil authorities, and secular medical and scientific professionals.

The Vatican has a policy of investigating only apparitions that have far-reaching effects, such as those at Fatima and Medjugorje (discussed in greater detail in Chapter 13). When the apparitions are smaller in scope, Vatican officials allow local bishops to carry out their own investigations.

The investigations vary from case to case, but they generally employ theologians, scientists, medical professionals, and forensic specialists—particularly when the apparitions involve blood or other bodily fluids.

Scientific Investigations?

To date, scientific evaluation has had only limited use in terms of being able to prove or disprove an apparition, as the actual phenomena transcend the understanding of science. Because the actual apparitions cannot be tested by empirical means, investigations have generally focused on those things which can be studied—in particular the mental health and responsiveness to external stimuli of the people (known as visionaries) who experience the apparitions. During an apparition, visionaries are thought to enter into an ecstatic state and do not respond to pain, heat, or bright lights being flashed in their faces.

When statues have emitted bodily fluids, such as blood, sweat, or tears, scientists have taken samples of these fluids so that they can be identified in the laboratory setting.

A Case Study

The apparitions that occurred in Akita, Japan, began in 1973 and ended in 1981. They were primarily experienced by Sister Agnes Sasagawa, a nun in the convent at the Institute of the Handmaids of the Eucharist. Sister Agnes experienced many unusual phenomena, including the stigmata (meaning that she developed the painful, bleeding wounds of Jesus), as well as the restoration of her hearing, which had been lost shortly before the apparitions began. She also witnessed the statue bleeding, weeping, sweating, and speaking to her on multiple occasions.

This apparition had some unusual elements—for one, the entire nation of Japan was able to view the statue weeping on national

Japanese television. In 1975, the blood, sweat, and tears were sent to professor Eiji Okuhara, a Catholic physician at Akita University's department of biochemistry. When he tested the samples, he determined that the tears and sweat were type AB and the blood was type B. These samples were then sent to a non-Christian forensics specialist named Dr. Kaoru Sagiska, who confirmed professor Okuhara's findings. A later test contradicted the results from the first two examinations, and it was finally concluded that the blood was type O, while the other bodily fluids were types A and AB. (It seems that the earliest tests were flawed because the blood sample had accidentally been contaminated by some of the handlers.)

factum

The Vatican eventually said that the apparition in Akita, Japan, was authentic. In a statement from the Vatican dated June 1988, Joseph Cardinal Ratzinger, now Pope Benedict XVI, stated that the "Akita events and messages were reliable and worthy of belief."

After the samples had been tested and confirmed, the Church brought in a Mariologist from Toyko named Fr. Garcia Evangelista, who was a well-known critic of the apparitions. He developed a highly unconventional theory. He said that the blood, sweat, and tears that flowed from the statue were actually being transferred to the statue through Sister Agnes's ectoplasmic powers (meaning that this holy person could actually weep, bleed, and sweat *through* the statue). Many individuals, including Roy Varghese, felt that there were some significant flaws in Fr. Garcia Evangelista's theory, most notably the fact that Sister Agnes's blood type was B, while the blood, sweat, and tears from the statue were type O, AB, and O, respectively. Fr. Evangelista ultimately admitted that he could not account for the differences in blood type. When he tried to claim that another nun was using her ectoplasmic powers, all the nuns were tested and none were shown to have the same blood type as the samples from the statue.

In 1984, after seven years of investigation, this apparition was deemed to be authentic. The local bishop, Most Reverend John Shojiro Ito, confirmed that the apparition was "of supernatural origin" and officially allowed the diocese to venerate the "Holy Mother of Akita." More than 500 Christians and non-Christians, as well as the Buddhist mayor of the town, also testified to witnessing the weeping statue. These events were also deemed authentic by Vatican authorities.

Evaluating Claims— Psychological Reflections

Often, people are tempted to write off apparitions as "hallucinations." This term, however, is rarely applicable to the accredited apparitions. The apparitions that are deemed authentic tend to have many common elements.

discussion question

What is the difference between an apparition and a hallucination? In most cases, hallucinations are connected to ideas that would already have been in the mind of the person who experienced the hallucination. But with the authentic apparitions, the visionaries often found that they were unable to understand what they had seen, and in many cases, they could not easily convey what they had experienced.

According to Roy Abraham Varghese in his book *God-Sent: A History of the Accredited Apparitions of Mary*, the first element that has been significant from a psychological perspective is that those who experience authentic apparitions are consistently of sound mental health. They demonstrate no more suggestibility than their peers. A person who experiences an apparition is often called a visionary. On the other side of the spectrum are those who experience hallucinations. Hallucinations tend to be experienced by those who have specific mental conditions related to neurosis or psychosis, which predispose them to experience altered states of reality. Hallucinations may also be drug-induced. Visions are also frequently (but not always) experienced by at least a few people, while hallucinations are generally experienced by an individual.

The Making of a Visionary

Certain people are more likely to see the Virgin Mary than others. Poor children, for example, are far more likely to see Mary than adults. Children make for more trustworthy witnesses because they are less successful at deception. Some skeptics, however, claim that children are also more likely to fabricate encounters with the Virgin Mary because of their overactive imaginations.

This theory, however, seems less plausible when one considers the scrutiny that these children often face after experiencing an apparition—in Fatima, a nine-year-old shepherd girl named Lucia Dos Santos was beaten by her mother after describing her encounter with the Virgin Mary. Her mother repeatedly tried to force her to take her story back, but Lucia held to her original account. Later, all three children seers were kidnapped by a local civil administrator. He separated the children and threatened them with death in a red hot frying pan if they did not retract their stories or share their "secrets." All three children endured three days of interrogation and did not alter their stories or surrender their secrets.

During a Vision

During a vision, those who see the Virgin Mary are thought to enter into an ecstatic state where they are unresponsive to external pain or stimuli. Often, their faces radiate peace and joy as they gaze toward a specific location. Witnesses to the apparition who aren't visionaries will not actually see the Virgin Mary, but may be able to observe the progress of the vision through the face of the visionary. They may also experience companion phenomena that are distinct from what the visionaries are seeing, such as the miracle of the sun at Fatima and the lunar miracles at Medjugorje.

Scientists and medical professionals have tested the authenticity of apparitions in ways that may seem barbaric. During the course of an apparition, they have sometimes stabbed the visionaries with needles or knives or attempted to burn them with flame. When the ecstatic state is authentic, the visionaries do not flinch from the pain and their bodies are unable to receive injuries.

Visionaries report lifelong transformation after encounters with the Virgin Mary. Some apparitions recur multiple times and are followed by extreme periods of persecution from local authorities. In some cases, visionaries have suffered martyrdom after experiencing an apparition. Such was the case with the apostle James, who according to Christian tradition, was both the first Christian ever to experience an apparition of the Virgin Mary, and the first apostle to be martyred for the faith.

Evaluating Claims—Theological Reflections

After the cycle of sightings has come to an end (in some cases over 1,000 visitations will occur over the course of several years), the apparitions are investigated. Apparitions are not considered accredited until church authorities have had an opportunity to evaluate them. Some Christians believe that apparitions are demonic. To this concern, writers such as Roy Varghese respond that authentic apparitions cause conversions, something that Satan could not (or would not) do.

A Call to Prayer

In almost every apparition, the faithful are urged to pray more. This call to prayer is often accompanied by warnings about events that might occur if people do not change. In many cases, predictions have come through the apparitions, including predictions of World War II, and of the rise, spread, and eventual collapse of Communism.

symbolism

Many of the contemporary apparitions echo the catastrophes referred to in the Book of Revelation. Although these messages come from a great variety of cultural contexts, apparitions that are deemed authentic generally are theologically consistent, both with one another and with the broader church tradition.

Apparitions in Context

Apparitions have occurred in such locations as India, China, Vietnam, South Korea, Croatia, Russia, and Japan. After these apparitions have occurred, statues and paintings have sometimes been created to commemorate them. These works of art testify to Mary's ability to transcend cultures. She tends to be universally recognizable as the Virgin Mary but is also depicted as a person native to the country and culture in which the apparition occurred. In the statue of Our Lady of LaVang, Vietnam, created in 1798, Mary appears as a Vietnamese woman, holding an Asian infant Christ—both appear in gowns that would be appropriate to Vietnam's culture. In the statue Our Lady of Good Health from India, she and the Christ child wear shimmering gold saris and have distinctly Indian faces. In Our Lady of Akita, in Japan, Mary appears as an elegant Japanese woman.

One of the fascinating aspects of apparition accounts is that Mary most often seems to come in a form and context that will be recognizable to the locals. The messages she gives (as well as the ways in which she communicates them) tend to be ideally suited to the culture in which she appears. This was certainly the case with the recent apparitions in Damascus, Syria, in which a woman began to experience olive oil dripping from her own fingertips (and then her icon of the Virgin Mary began to weep myrrh-scented tears). Olive oil is an ideal conduit for a miracle in the context of the Middle East because in the Christian Middle East, olive oil is associated with sacred rituals, health, and healing.

Each accredited apparition has left a profound mark not only on the individuals who report having witnessed the event but also on the heritage of each nation that includes apparitions in their national history. Mary's ability to be present in a variety of cultures is celebrated in the great variety of international depictions of her.

Comfort and Consolation

The Virgin Mary often seems to come to offer comfort or consolation particularly to the poor and vulnerable. While many of the apparitions include requests or warnings, at least a few of them seem to be connected to the Virgin Mary's desire to bring comfort to those who are in need.

This was particularly the case in apparitions that were reported to occur in Vietnam. Christianity was introduced to what is now Vietnam in 1533. Since then, Christians have suffered much persecution. In the past three centuries, thousands have been martyred for the faith. In 1798, an apparition of the Virgin Mary occurred in LaVang, Vietnam, to a group of Christians who had escaped to the jungles in the mountains. One day, this group was praying the Rosary when a radiant woman appeared to them, flanked by angels and holding the infant Christ in her arms. She assured them of her protection and care.

factum

In the apparition in LaVang, the Virgin Mary is said to have done something quite intriguing. She pointed to several plants and flowers and explained how they could be used medicinally.

There have been numerous "silent apparitions" in which the Virgin Mary has appeared to people, offering healing and hope without saying a word. Her presence in places like Zeitun, Egypt, has been taken as a sign of God's continual love for the people of the world.

Health and Healing Springs

Many who experience apparitions also experience healing. This has been particularly the case in places like Lourdes, France, and in India, where the shrine of Our Lady of Good Health exists to this day. Many apparition sites contain healing springs (this is true of both Lourdes and India) where people can wash themselves and drink of the water as they seek healing.

It is remarkable to consider the vast number of healing springs or ponds associated with the Virgin Mary all over the world, in places such as Vailankanni, India; Lourdes and LaSalette, France; Banneux, Belgium; and many other locations, including the one at the House of Mary in Ephesus, Turkey.

The Virgin Mary is often referred to as Our Lady of Good Health in India because of the continual healing she has brought to people of many faiths beginning with the healing of a boy, who was lame, to whom she appeared personally during the sixteenth century.

Although many seek physical healing when they visit apparition sites, often the healing that they experience is instead emotional or spiritual. Some also report finding strength to endure suffering in their lives as a result of visiting apparition sites.

Pope John Paul II lost his mother at a very early age, and many people have connected his deep devotion to the Virgin Mary to his experience of early loss as a child. This is also the case with the much-loved Saint Thérèse of Lisieux, who became devoted to the Virgin Mary at a young age after her own mother died.

Saint Thérèse of Lisieux came from a very pious Catholic family in which all of the girls were named for the Virgin Mary. Because Thérèse lost her mother at a young age, she experienced intense anxiety, insomnia, and headaches. She suffered from these afflictions for most of her childhood. When she was ten years old, she was praying before a statue of the Virgin Mary and she saw the statue smile at her (this statue had also spoken to her mother twice). From that moment forward, Thérèse reported experiencing a mental wholeness and healing that she had not experienced since her mother's death. This sense of mental wholeness continued for the rest of her short life until her death from tuberculosis at age twenty-four. Although Thérèse did experience feelings of intense darkness and despair near the end of her life, she always said that just beneath that darkness there was great joy.

discussion question

How does one know when healing will occur?
In some cases, healings come as a result of multiple prayers and requests, and in some cases, people pray earnestly for healing and do not receive it. There is no uniform rule for how, when, or if healings will occur.

Warnings

Many of the more recent accounts of apparitions—especially those at Fatima and Medjugorje—have contained dire warnings about things that will come if people do not change their lives and begin to pray. In some apparitions, the Virgin Mary describes the threat of a third world war that could employ germ and biological warfare. She also sometimes describes natural disasters, widespread destruction, and loss of life. Some people have made a connection between the content of her messages and the ways in which she comes to people—often through weeping statues and icons.

factum

In apparitions, the Virgin Mary sometimes expresses motherly frustration and anguish over people's unwillingness to change. She also constantly encourages people to pray, not only for themselves but for all of the people who have no one to pray for them.

During many of these apparitions, the Virgin Mary has said that the end of the world is near and that a period of intense suffering will be followed by a period of relative peace before the return of Christ.

Although some of the messages of the apparitions can be frightening, in most cases, visionaries experience a sense of confidence despite the dire predictions, because they believe that despite difficulties ahead, God will be present with them.

Fatima Predictions

At Fatima, Portugal, the Virgin Mary told three shepherd children that there would be a world catastrophe during the time of Pope Puis XI if people did not repent. During the last year of the reign of Pope Pius XI, World War II began. It was also at Fatima that the Virgin Mary predicted both the rise and fall of Communism in Russia, as well as the spread of Communism to many other parts of the world.

The apparitions that occurred at Hrushiv, Ukraine, in 1914 and 1987 also contained predictions. In these apparitions, the Virgin Mary told a group of villagers that Russia would turn away from God and endure two wars. She also predicted that although the Ukraine would endure hardship for eighty years, it would eventually become an independent state.

An apparition that reportedly occurred in 1830 in Paris, France, also contained a warning of an event that is now well recorded in history books. A postulant of the Sisters of Charity named Catherine Laboure went to bed the night before the feast of Saint Vincent de Paul after swallowing a small fragment of the deceased saint's surplice. Nobody is quite sure why she did this. Perhaps Catherine felt that by swallowing this small fragment, she would be able to draw closer to the saint.

Like many other holy people, Catherine had a lifelong devotion to the Virgin Mary that was most likely connected to her own loss of her mother as child. When she was nine years old and grieving the death of her mother, Catherine held a statue of the Virgin Mary and said, "Now Blessed Mother, you will be my mother."

The night of the Eve of the feast of Saint Vincent De Paul, Catherine woke in the middle of the night to a small child standing near her bed who told her to go to the church because the Virgin Mary was there waiting for her.

discussion question

Do visionaries experience special protection?
In many cases, visionaries do experience protection, such as Catherine Laboure whose convent remained safe despite all of the violence in Paris during the French Revolution.

Catherine dressed quickly, rushing quietly to the church, which was fully illuminated—every candle in the church had been lit as if for midnight mass, but the church was empty. Suddenly, Catherine heard the sound of silk rustling. She looked up and there was the Virgin Mary seated in the chair that belonged to the father director of the monastery.

Coming Sorrows

The Virgin Mary told Catherine that France's throne would come toppling down and that misfortunes were on the way. "Sorrows will befall France," the Virgin Mary said. "The throne will be overturned. The whole world will be plunged into every kind of misery." The Virgin Mary went on to predict that bishops and priests would be killed, and that many monasteries would be attacked, although Catherine's monastery would be protected.

The French Revolution

Just a few days later, the throne of King Charles X was overturned and mass rioting broke out. Churches were desecrated and bishops' palaces were attacked. Although many monasteries and convents were destroyed, Catherine's monastery remained unharmed just as the Virgin Mary had predicted.

Marian Secrets

Some apparitions have also contained "secrets," such as those reported in Fatima. These secrets were statements made by the Virgin Mary during apparitions that are not supposed to be revealed immediately. Although some people are fascinated by the secrets, the phenomenon of secrets is not unusual from a Biblical perspective.

In the Scriptures, Christ often asks people not to speak of his miracles because they are not to be revealed until the appointed time. In essence, he asks direct witnesses to keep secrets on his behalf, just as many of the visionaries (particularly in Fatima and Medjugorje, discussed in detail in Chapter 13) have been asked to guard secrets that Mary has shared with them.

Many of the secrets are actually prophecies that are not supposed to be known until the appointed time. The secrets are often deeply Biblical. When Sister Lucia, one of the visionaries from Fatima, was pressured to reveal a secret from Fatima, she said, "Just read the Gospels and the Book of Revelation. It's all in there."

Sister Lucia's words highlight one of the larger themes of the apparitions: for these spiritual experiences to be deemed authentic, they must be consistent with Scripture. As Pope Benedict XVI said in an interview with Roy Varghese in 1991, "Apparitions are never required for salvation. The Old and New Testament revelations have all that is necessary for salvation." Although the Roman Catholic and Eastern Orthodox Churches have both affirmed that authentic apparitions can aid the faithful, these subjective experiences are never supposed to overshadow the Scriptures or the witness of the Church.

Chapter 12

Ancient Appearances

Apparitions of the Virgin Mary date back to the first century. In the earliest apparitions, Mary often came to offer comfort and consolation. In some cases, she requested that churches be built to commemorate the spot where she appeared. Remarkably, from some of these earliest apparitions, tangible reminders still remain. This chapter will explore a selection of the earliest apparitions.

The First Apparition

After the death of Jesus, his apostles sought to spread the message of the good news all over the world. According to church tradition, the apostle Thomas made it all the way to India, and Saint James (the brother of John) is said to have traveled to Saragossa, Spain.

Around A.D. 40 James had become deeply discouraged. He felt that his mission was not progressing in the way that he'd hoped. One day he was preaching beside the Ebro River when the Virgin Mary, flanked by angels, appeared to him and gave him a statue of herself and a six-foot-tall pillar made of jasper wood. Her gift came with directions as to how the statue and pillar were to be used.

factum

The word *apostle* means "one who is sent." It is particularly used for Jesus' twelve disciples as well as for the seventy who formed the larger circle of coworkers for the Gospels, the good news about Jesus. More generally, it can refer to anyone who has been commissioned to preach the Gospel.

According to James, the Virgin Mary told him, "This place is to be my house, and this image and column shall be the title and altar of the temple you shall build." Shortly after the visitation, James began work on a small chapel in honor of the Virgin Mary.

Like many ancient holy sites, this chapel has been destroyed and rebuilt multiple times throughout the centuries. After almost 2,000 years, the pillar and the statue are still venerated at the Basilica-Cathedral of Our Lady of the Pillar in Zaragoza, Aragon, Spain. Throughout the centuries, this statue and pillar have had multiple healings attributed to them, and they can be visited to this day, although they are not always kept on display.

symbolism

The miracle of James's vision of Mary occupies a special place in the national memory of Spain, and is linked to the discovery of the Americas. The Spanish Feast of El Pilar is commemorated on October 12. It was on this day in 1492 that Christopher Columbus arrived in the New World, after traversing the ocean on his ship, the *Santa Maria*.

While this visitation must have brought James joy and comfort, it probably also brought him dread, as it was through this apparition that the Virgin Mary informed him that God had requested that he return to Jerusalem so that he could become the first martyr for Christ.

Four years later, James was martyred in Jerusalem. His own death is part of a larger trend that continues in our own day—visionaries sometimes suffer terribly for sharing what they've experienced. Some child visionaries have been beaten by their parents, others have been interrogated by church and civil authorities, and still others, like James, discovered through a vision that they would die unjustly.

As you will see as you explore the other apparitions, the Virgin Mary is often reported to leave behind tangible reminders of her visits. Although skeptics might say that these "reminders" could have easily come from other sources, all that we have now (especially in the case of the most ancient apparitions) are the stories that communities tell about how these objects—pillars, statues, and churches—came to them. These stories are valuable, both for what they convey about the communities that guard these reminders as well as for what they convey about beliefs surrounding the Virgin Mary.

Patmos, Greece, A.D. 81

According to tradition, the Book of Revelation was written by Saint John after a series of revelations that occurred on the Island of Patmos in Greece. In one of the visions, Saint John saw a "woman clothed with the son" (Revelation 12) who stood upon the moon and was crowned with twelve stars. The woman was in the process of giving birth to a son who was to rule the nations. As she cried out from the pains of childbirth, a dragon waited nearby to consume the child. After the child was born, however, he was protected by God and enthroned. The woman escaped to the wilderness.

Although this woman is never directly identified as the Virgin Mary, the parallels between this vision and later apparitions are quite strong. Over time, Mary came to be associated with the moon and stars, and this theme has often been incorporated into many artistic representations of her. In icons, her veil is adorned with stars, and in many of the statues and paintings of the Virgin Mary, she stands upon the moon.

Neocaesarea, Asia Minor, A.D. 238

When Saint Gregory the Wonderworker was preaching in Asia Minor, he became confused about the doctrine of the Trinity. One night, Gregory couldn't sleep because he was so anxious about his inability to articulate the theology of the Trinity. At some point during the course of this long, restless night, two beings are reported to have appeared to him. He might not have known who they were, had they not addressed each other by name.

The radiantly beautiful female figure turned to the aged male figure and addressed him as "Saint John the Evangelist." She and he discussed Gregory's dilemma and then she asked Saint John to explain the doctrine of the Trinity to Gregory. Saint John replied that he would certainly comply with the wishes of "The Mother of the Lord."

After Saint John offered a basic explanation, he concluded with these words, "There is therefore nothing created, nothing greater or less in the Trinity . . . The Father has never been without the Son, nor the Son without the Spirit; and the same Trinity is immutable and forever unalterable." The content of this message has been continually affirmed by the Church ever since.

discussion question

How could Gregory be confused about the Trinity?
At the time of Gregory's vision, the full doctrine of the Trinity had not yet been formulated. Many of the definitions and creeds developed slowly over time. Especially tricky were doctrines like the Trinity, which were implicit in Scripture, but could not be properly understood without a good deal of interpretation.

Rome, A.D. 352

Children and peasants are generally more likely to report apparitions than wealthy people. In a few cases, however, wealthy people have encountered the Virgin Mary, particularly those who were generous and seeking guidance as to how to better use their resources for God.

This type of apparition occurred during the fourth century when a wealthy, childless couple in Rome was struggling over how to best use their fortune. They had often prayed to the Virgin Mary for guidance, and on August 4, A.D. 352, she finally appeared to them in response to their multiple requests.

On that day, she instructed them to begin construction on a church located on one of Rome's hills. Just to be clear about exactly which hill and exactly how large she intended the church to be, she promised to send snow to cover the earth on the exact spot where the church was to be built.

August is the hottest time of the year in Rome, so the idea of snow was baffling to this couple. But just as they were receiving the message about the church they were to build, Pope Liberius received a parallel message.

The next morning, Pope Liberius and the wealthy couple were astonished to discover that a portion of Esquiline Hill was blanketed in snow. They had just enough time to measure the space where the church was to be built before the snow melted. Within eight years, the world's largest church devoted to the Virgin Mary, Saint Mary Major, was constructed. This church still stands to this day.

One of the themes of this apparition—that the Virgin Mary is able to cause a reversal of weather patterns, such as snow in the middle of August—is often repeated in the apparitions. Sometimes the miracle is poetically reversed and instead of summer snows, roses bloom in the dead of winter.

Walsingham, England, 1061

Like the apparition in Rome, in Walsingham, England, the Virgin Mary appeared to a wealthy person—in this case, it was a widow named Lady Richeldis de Faverches, who had been praying about how to best use her resources. One night that year, the Virgin Mary came to her with a request: build a mini-replica of the house from Nazareth, where the Annunciation occurred. The Virgin Mary wanted the replica to serve as a reminder to the people that she was available to help them.

According to accounts of these apparitions, the Virgin Mary is often quite detailed in her requests, not leaving much to the imagination of the visionary. In Walsingham, she not only asked Lady Richeldis de Faverches to create the replica, but she also transported the Lady through space and time to her original house in Nazareth so that she could get the measurements exactly correct.

A year after the visitation, the house was completed. A chapel called the Slipper Chapel was also built about a mile away from the house so that pilgrims could leave their shoes behind and travel the last mile without them.

Walsingham became an extremely popular pilgrimage spot during the Middle Ages but was destroyed during the Reformation. Only the Slipper Chapel survived the pillaging.

symbolism

Walsingham, which was once one of the most popular pilgrimage sites in Europe, has attracted the attentions of prominent people. During construction, Edward the Confessor offered the entire country of England to the Virgin Mary as a dowry. After the replica was completed, all of the English kings up to Henry VIII made pilgrimages there.

Many centuries later, when English Catholics were once again permitted to practice their faith in England, the shrine was rededicated to Mary. Presently, a remnant of the original Slipper Chapel shares space with an Anglican shrine for Our Lady of Walsingham. Walsingham is now considered one of Europe's great ecumenical sites.

Czestochawa, Poland, 1382

In Poland there is an icon that is often referred to as the Black Madonna. This icon, which is one of the most famous in the world, is part of a larger school of dark-skinned images of the Virgin Mary and the infant Christ. There are several Black Madonna icons as well as statues that were especially popular during the medieval period in Europe.

The Black Madonna icon in Poland, Our Lady of Czestochawa, is one of the most famous icons in the world. Some even believe that this icon changed the course of history in Poland. According to one church tradition, this image was painted by the apostle Luke. Reportedly, while he was painting it, the Virgin Mary told him many things about the life of Christ, which he ultimately included in his Gospel.

Although one tradition holds that the icon was created by Luke in the first century, the icon seems to have disappeared from the popular eye for a few hundred years, resurfacing in A.D. 326, when it was discovered by Saint Helen in Jerusalem. Saint Helen passed the icon to her son, the Emperor Constantine who was reportedly able to scare off an invading army by placing the icon on the walls of the city. According to accounts of this event, the soldiers took one look at the icon and fled.

factum

Pope John Paul II had a lifelong devotion to the Black Madonna. As a student, he visited this icon and returned again shortly after he became Pope. He loved to mention the miraculous history surrounding the Black Madonna in sermons, and he treasured his own copy of the icon of Our Lady of Czestochawa, which he kept in his private chapel at the Vatican.

After this event, the icon passed through many hands and finally found its way to Poland. In 1382, the Virgin Mary appeared to the man who possessed the icon at the time, Prince Ladislaus of Opolo. During the course of this apparition, the Virgin Mary asked that the icon be placed at a mountaintop monastery, Jasna Gora, located in Czestochowa.

After the icon was moved, many miracles were reported and recorded in a book at the monastery. One of the most remarkable events occurred in 1430, when the Tartars took over the monastery. When one of them attempted to steal the icon, he found that it became heavier and heavier the farther he walked. Finally, in a fit of desperation he took out a knife and slashed the cheeks of the Virgin Mary and threw the icon into a river. Although it was eventually recovered and the slashes were repaired multiple times, the wounds mysteriously continue to be visible.

symbolism

In Sue Monk Kidd's bestseller *The Secret Life of Bees*, a small paper replica of a Black Madonna icon linked a child to the mysteries surrounding her deceased mother. The girl carried the icon to a house inhabited by African American beekeepers who possessed such deep love for this image that they affixed it to all of their honey jars.

Many believe that Our Lady of Czestochowa helped protect Poland during invasions and wars. In 1655, the entire country was taken over by Charles X of Sweden. Only a few Polish soldiers and monks from Jasna Gora were able to fight for resistance. Although they were sorely outnumbered, they successfully resisted the Swedes for forty days, and the Swedish soldiers fled.

On September 14, 1920, the Russian army was preparing to attack Warsaw, but their plans changed when they saw a vision of a woman in the skies over Warsaw. After that frightening experience, they felt they could not invade Warsaw.

During World War II, when Poland was occupied by the Nazis, Hitler demanded an end to all pilgrimages. In a brave show of defiance, nearly half a million Polish people ignored Hitler's orders and visited their precious icon. When Poland was liberated in 1945, one-and-a-half million Polish people visited the shrine to offer their gratitude to Our Lady of Czestochowa for her deliverance and protection. Three years later, when Russia captured Warsaw, 800,000 Polish people again risked their lives, passing the Communist soldiers who patrolled the roads as they made their way to visit the sanctuary at Czestochowa for the Feast of the Assumption.

Kazan, Russia, 1579

Russia treasures a number of ancient icons that may date back to the age of the apostles. Perhaps the most famous of these is called Our Lady of Kazan. According to Church tradition, this icon was brought to Russia from Byzantium around the thirteenth century. Its name comes from city where it was housed, Kazan.

In the thirteenth century, when the city of Kazan was destroyed, the icon disappeared beneath the rubble of a monastery and was lost for almost three hundred years.

In 1579, a nine-year-old girl named Matrona had a vision of the Virgin Mary. In this vision, Mary told Matrona to seek and find the icon. The Virgin Mary told Matrona exactly where to look.

After Matrona witnessed three apparitions, a bishop and several others began digging in the location described to them by Matrona, but they failed in all of their attempts to find the icon.

On July 8, 1579, the authorities finally allowed Matrona to dig. Almost immediately, she found the icon, wrapped in a red cloth. After this discovery, many miracles and healings came to be attributed to the icon. Just as Our Lady of Czestochowa was viewed by the Polish people as a protective icon, Our Lady of Kazan eventually came to be seen as the protector of Russia.

During the Communist revolution on October 13, 1917, the church that housed the icon that Matrona unearthed was destroyed, and the icon disappeared. Perhaps not coincidentally, the reverberations of this day in Russia were felt throughout the world.

factum

In Fatima, Portugal, on October 13, 1917, the miracle of the sun occurred. Through an apparition, the Virgin Mary reported that Russia would spread its errors throughout the world. Many believe that through these apparitions Mary predicted the rise and fall of Communism in Russia.

There are conflicting reports about what happened to the icon of Kazan after the church was destroyed. Some believe that the icon was destroyed, and others say that it was whisked away to safety.

Through a mysterious sequence of events, a valuable copy of Our Lady of Kazan eventually made it to the United States, where the Roman Catholic Church raised more than one million dollars to purchase the icon from a private collector.

The icon was displayed at the New World Exposition in New York in 1964, where thousands kissed and prayed before it. Afterward, it traveled to Fatima and was held by the Blue Army, a Catholic organization that seeks to raise awareness of the Fatima apparitions.

discussion question

How did the Roman Catholic and Eastern Orthodox Churches grow apart?
For the first thousand years of Christianity, the two churches were united. The great schism between them was the result of a growing sense of alienation on both sides. The biggest disagreements between the churches were over the role of the pope and the Western addition of the phrase "and the Son" (*fillioque*) into the Nicene Creed.

In 1993, the icon was presented to Pope John Paul II. For many years, he housed it in his private apartments in the Vatican, although he never wavered in his commitment to return the icon to Russia, hoping that this gesture could be the beginning of healing the rift between the Roman Catholic and Eastern Orthodox Churches.

Tensions in Russia between the Eastern Orthodox and Roman Catholic churches made it difficult for Pope John Paul II to personally return the icon to Patriarch Alexei II. Finally, on August, 30, 2004, Pope John Paul II sent a commission to Russia with the icon, which traveled there in a special jet. The pope sent a statement with the icon that said he had often prayed before that icon for the day that the two churches would again be one.

Patriarch Alexei II thanked the pope for this act of unity, although he also expressed his concern that unification would only be possible if the Roman Catholic Church would make concessions to Eastern Orthodox theological positions. Roman Catholic newspapers have reported that relations between the two churches have warmed slightly since the historic return of the icon.

Guadalupe, Mexico, 1531

During the sixteenth century in Mexico, tensions between the Spanish invaders and local Aztecs were fierce. By 1531, the Aztecs were so outraged by the abuses they experienced that they threatened to kill every Spaniard in the country. Although Spanish missionaries were simultaneously working to bring Catholicism to the native Aztecs, the political tensions between the two groups created an impossible climate for missionary work.

This tense situation set the stage for the most dramatic apparition-related mass conversion in the history of the world. Juan Diego was a fifty-seven-year-old Aztec peasant and a convert to Catholicism. One day while he was walking to Mass, he heard birds singing. The song sounded like it was coming from a nearby hill.

As he drew closer to the hill, the song stopped and he heard a female voice calling to him. "Juan, Juan Diego, Juanito," she said. Juan Diego climbed the hill and saw a stunning fourteen-year-old Aztec girl. Speaking in his own language, she told him that she was the Virgin Mary. She wanted a church to be built on that hill where she stood. She asked Juan Diego to go to Mexico City and inform the bishop of her request.

A Request Denied

Juan Diego went immediately to the bishop to make his request, but the request was denied. Although the Bishop believed that Juan Diego was sincere, he struggled to believe Juan Diego's extraordinary account. Defeated, Juan Diego returned to the Virgin Mary and told her that if she wanted to get her message across, she should have chosen somebody more important to deliver it.

To this, the Virgin Mary replied that she knew what she was doing; she reassured Juan Diego that she wanted him to deliver the message. She urged him to go back and try again with the bishop.

When Juan Diego returned to the bishop, the bishop requested a sign. Juan Diego returned to the Virgin Mary again, who told him to come back at daybreak. When Juan Diego arrived home that day, he discovered that his uncle was fatally ill with a fever. Juan Diego nursed him all night long and through the following day, and he was unable to meet with the Virgin Mary at sunrise.

As Juan Diego rushed into town seeking a priest, he attempted to sneak around the East side of the hill, hoping that he wouldn't be interrupted by the Virgin Mary. Although on other occasions she had appeared on the West side of the hill, she came down the East side of the hill just as he tried to rush by.

When Juan Diego told the Virgin Mary about his uncle, the Virgin Mary said, "Am I not your mother?" Then she told him that his uncle was being healed even as they spoke.

The Virgin Mary spoke many consoling words to Juan Diego. She said, "Hear me, my littlest son: Let nothing discourage you, nothing depress you. Let nothing alter your heart or your countenance. Do not fear any illness, anxiety, or pain. Am I not your mother? Are you not under the protection of my mantle? Am I not your fountain of life? Is there anything else that you need?"

She then asked Juan Diego to climb the hill and pick flowers, and these flowers would be her sign. Juan Diego obediently climbed the hill, although he could not imagine flowers growing during the coldest month of the year. To his astonishment, he found that the hill was covered with Castilian roses.

The Tilma of Guadalupe

Juan Diego picked several roses and carried them back to the Virgin Mary. She took the roses from him and arranged them in his tilma (a cloak made of cactus fibers that was worn by the Aztecs of the time). She handed Juan Diego the roses bundled in the tilma and instructed him to not let anyone other than the bishop see them.

When Juan Diego arrived at the bishop's residence, servants tried to take the tilma from him, but he refused. When he finally met with the bishop, he unrolled the tilma and the roses fell to the floor. Juan Diego was confused and amazed as the bishop and those who surrounded him dropped to their knees before his tilma.

On his tilma, there was a luminescent image of the Virgin Mary appearing as an Aztec, just as she had in the apparitions. Her image also bore a striking resemblance to the woman from Revelation 12. The image on the tilma convinced the bishop that the apparition was authentic.

symbolism

The Tilma of Guadalupe is one of a few images that many Christians believe was actually created by Mary. This image almost perfectly mirrors imagery from Revelation. On the tilma, Mary stands on the moon, and rays of light emanate from her body. Her outer cloak is blue, covered with gold stars—a constant theme in images of Mary.

The bishop immediately traveled with Juan Diego to see the hill where the chapel was to be built, and then the bishop's assistants traveled with Juan to visit his uncle. They found his uncle in perfect health. He explained that the Virgin Mary had also come to him and told him that the image on the tilma was to be called Santa Maria de Guadalupe.

This event transformed the practices of the over 8 million Aztecs who converted to Christianity in the wake of the apparition. According to Roy Abraham Varghese in his book *God-Sent: A History of the Accredited Apparitions of Mary,* one of the descriptions that Mary used for herself in Guadalupe can be translated as "Entirely perfect, holy Mary, who will crush, stamp out, and abolish the stone serpent." This title is sometimes linked to the end of the Aztec practice of sacrificing humans because the Aztecs worshiped a god called Quetzalcoatl, whose name can be translated as "the stone serpent." After the apparitions at Guadalupe, human sacrifices to the stone serpent abruptly (and permanently) halted.

The spiritual dimensions of the apparition, however, are just one aspect of the larger phenomenon. The events that occurred at Guadalupe also have political and social implications: the conversion of the Aztecs saved the lives of thousands of Spaniards, who would have likely been killed had not the Virgin Mary appeared to Juan Diego.

Likewise, some contemporary writers have focused on the way that this apparition marked a Biblical reversal of order—a peasant member of an oppressed people was chosen to bear a message that would change the history of his country, and by extension, the lives and beliefs of millions of Latin Americans. As Megan McKenna wrote in her book *Mary, Shadow of Grace* of Our Lady of Guadalupe, "She is the sister to the poor and the mother of compassion and healing for all those who live on the edges of life . . . She is the symbol of the small of the earth, inconsequential except to God, found with all those who live faithfully in situations of darkness, despair, lack, and need, yet powerful in their very weakness and numbers."

Although historically it has been believed that the tilma was made of cactus fibers, a recent scientific inquiry has cast some doubt on this theory. In 1999, when two fibers of the tilma were tested by Professor John J. Chiment from the Department of Earth and Atmospheric Sciences at Cornell University in Ithaca, New York, he determined that the fibers are not from native cactus plants, nor are they made of wool or cotton. Instead, he believes that they are actually made of hemp, an extremely durable fiber that could account for the long lifespan of the cloak.

To this day, the tilma and image remain intact. Scientists have been unable to identify the source of the pigments in the image. One of the most mysterious aspects of this image is the Virgin Mary's eyes, which reflect the images of three people, as if she is looking at them still—Juan Diego, the bishop and his interpreter. The tilma remains on display at the Basilica of Guadalupe and is visited by five to ten million people annually.

Chapter 13

Modern Sightings

Over the past several hundred years, apparitions of the Virgin Mary have continued to occur, and, according to the late scholar Jaroslav Pelikan, this phenomenon seems to be increasing. The following chapter will explore a wide variety of modern sightings that have spanned the globe and addressed a variety of contemporary concerns: Communism, the rift between the Eastern and Western Churches, and conflicts between believers and secular governments. This chapter will explore some of the most famous and unusual apparitions to date.

Vailankanni, India, Sixteenth Through Seventeenth Centuries

During the sixteenth through seventeenth centuries, the Virgin Mary came to the small Indian town of Vailankanni, and healed a lame boy and a young shepherd boy. When the Virgin Mary appeared with the infant Jesus to the lame boy, the boy was selling buttermilk in the shade of a large banyan tree. The Virgin Mary requested some buttermilk for her baby. When the boy gave her buttermilk, she asked her son to heal him, which he did immediately, although the young boy did not realize what had happened.

She then asked the lame boy to seek out a wealthy Catholic Vailankanni to ask him to build a chapel in the Virgin Mary's honor. The boy said that there was no way he could do this, because he couldn't walk. The Virgin Mary smiled at him and encouraged him to stand up and try. Upon trying, the boy realized that he was able to walk.

At this, the boy leapt for joy and rushed to the village to find the man at the Virgin Mary's request. When he found him, he had no trouble convincing him because the older man had also had a vision of the Virgin Mary the night before in his sleep. In his vision, the Virgin Mary bore exactly the same message that she had given to the little boy who could not walk.

The two returned together to Vailankanni and the older man began construction on a small, thatched church with the assistance of the locals, who were moved by the sight of the lame boy walking. The older man placed a statue of Our Lady of Good Health on the altar.

Matha Kulam

Another young boy also had an encounter with the Virgin Mary. This young boy was a shepherd who was carrying milk to his master's house. On a hot day he took refuge in the shade of a banyan tree beside a pond. While he was resting there a beautiful woman appeared with a child in her arms. She asked him for milk for her baby, and the young shepherd gave it to her immediately. As he did this, a smile spread across the infant's face.

The shepherd then rushed to his master's house with the remaining milk. When he arrived, he tried to explain why his milk pot wasn't full. When the lid was removed, however, he discovered that the pot was full and overflowing. His master was astonished and rushed with him back to the site, falling down on his knees and putting his head to the ground on the spot where the shepherd reported having seen the Virgin and child. This pond is now known as *Matha Kulam*, meaning "Our Lady's Pond." Pilgrims continue to flock there, believing that the waters have miraculous, healing powers.

Our Lady of Good Health

Later in that same century, a Portuguese ship encountered a fierce storm in the Indian Sea. The sailors fell to their knees and prayed that Mary would calm the storm, promising to build a church in her honor if they made it safely ashore. The storm halted immediately, and the tattered ship washed ashore at Vailakanni.

As soon as the sailors set foot on the land, they knelt on the ground and thanked God and the Virgin Mary for their safe journey. When locals saw them kneeling they realized the sailors must be Christians and directed them to the chapel of our Our Lady of Good Health.

The Portuguese began work shortly afterward, constructing a larger brick and mortar church to honor Mary. They placed the statue of Our Lady of Good Health on the altar in the newly built chapel, and they dedicated the church to the Nativity of Our Lady, in honor of the day they washed ashore, September 8—the day of the Nativity of the Virgin Mary.

After Vatican II, Pope John XXIII officially recognized this pilgrimage site as the Lourdes of the East. India is now graced with many shrines to Our Lady of Good Health. Many have reported miraculous healings associated with the shrine and pond. Adjacent to the church is a "museum of offerings" where hundreds of pilgrims have left offerings behind. Presently, thousands of Catholic, Protestants, Hindu, Parsee, and Muslim people visit this basilica daily.

Lourdes, France, 1858

Lourdes is a small town located at the foothills of the Great Pyrenees Mountains in France. A young girl named Bernadette, the oldest of four children, lived with her family in a single room that had once been the town jail.

One day, she, her sister, and a friend went searching for dry wood for her mother. Bernadette's sister and friend crossed a small stream, but Bernadette hesitated at the bank. Suddenly, she heard a loud crashing noise and looked toward a stone grotto where a single bush was waving as if it was a windy day. Then, a golden glow came from the center of the grotto, and a beautiful woman appeared. Although Bernadette was initially terrified, when the woman smiled, her fear vanished.

A Healing Well

Bernadette then experienced multiple visions of Mary. In one of these encounters the Virgin Mary told Bernadette, "Go and drink from the spring and wash yourself there." Bernadette saw no spring, so she got down on her hands and knees and began to dig. Soon, the small hole was filled with water, from which she drank and washed her face. This small pool became a river, and very quickly, people came to believe that this river had healing properties because a man who was going blind regained his vision after submerging his face in the water. Another woman with a paralyzed hand was able to use it completely after immersing it in the water.

Bernadette experienced eighteen apparitions of the Virgin Mary. Word of the apparitions spread, causing concern among local and church authorities. A local doctor subjected Bernadette to a battery of tests. She was repeatedly shown to be of normal mental health. In one of the more humorous incidents related to this apparition, Bernadette's local priest Abbe Peyramale refused to believe in the apparitions and requested a sign. But the Virgin Mary was unwilling to perform this sign for the skeptical priest. When Bernadette reported back to her priest she told him, "She smiled when I told her that you were asking her to work a miracle. I told her to make the rose bush, which she was standing near, bloom; she smiled once more. But she wants a chapel."

When Bernadatte visited the grotto, others would flock there in the hopes of witnessing the visitation. During one apparition, 20,000 people were present. In August 1858, the Emperor of France, Napoleon III, ordered that water be brought from the well to be sprinkled on his two-year-old son who had contracted dangerous sunstroke with the threat of meningitis. When his son was cured, Napoleon III ordered that the barricades be removed from the grotto.

fallacy

It is a fallacy that intellectuals did not recognize the significance of apparitions. In Sigmund Freud's book *The New Introductory Lectures on Psycho-Analysis*, he wrote, "I do not think our cures can compete with those of Lourdes. There are so many more people who believe in the miracle of the Blessed Virgin than the existence of the subconscious."

Lourdes Today

Today, five million pilgrims annually flock to Lourdes, which is called the Capitol of Prayer, seeking healing and spiritual refreshment. The small well that Bernadette uncovered now produces 15,000 gallons of water daily. Many drink from the wells, and over 400,000 visitors annually immerse themselves in the water in a nearby bathhouse.

A recent medical study demonstrated that over 2,500 healings have occurred in Lourdes, although church authorities to date have only officially recognized a small number of cures (about 65). Many more potential healings are currently under investigation, and more than 5,000 people claim to have experienced miracles at Lourdes.

Bernadette eventually joined a convent, although she was sickly for most of her life and died at thirty-five. To this day, her body remains incorrupt. She was canonized a saint on December 8, 1933.

Fatima, Portugal, 1917

The apparitions that occurred in Fatima are the most famous and influential of all known apparitions. Four million pilgrims visit Fatima annually. Like many of the apparitions, these came during a time of local Christian persecution, shortly after the monarchy in Portugal had been overthrown, causing anti-Christian groups to seize power and kill more than 1,700 Roman Catholic priests and monastics. In the wake of this violence, three shepherd children, named Jacinta Marto, Lucia dos Santos, and Francisco Marto experienced some of the most dramatic reported apparitions in history.

These apparitions of Mary were preceded by the appearance of an angel to the three young children telling them to pray this way, "My God, I believe, I adore, I hope and I love you. I ask pardon of you for those who do not believe and do not adore, do not hope, and do not love you." The angel also offered them Holy Communion.

After the angel's visit, the Virgin Mary appeared to the children six times, on the thirteenth day of each month.

Visions

The first apparition occurred when the children were out with their sheep in an area called the Cova da Iria. They saw a bolt of lightning come from the clear blue sky. They ran toward their sheep, and as they did this they saw another flash of light and then a globe of light that landed in a nearby oak tree.

Before their eyes, the Virgin Mary emerged from this globe. She asked the children if they wanted to offer themselves to God and to suffer for Him. They said yes, and she told them that they would suffer much but would be strengthened by the grace of God. She also told them that two of them would be in heaven shortly. The shepherd girl who would be left behind, Lucia, would be responsible for spreading the word about the apparition and spreading devotion to the Lady's Immaculate Heart.

In the next vision, the Virgin Mary offered the children a terrifying glimpse of hell. She told the children that the Lord wanted them to help establish devotion to her Immaculate Heart to bring more souls to salvation. All of this took place during World War I. Mary then told the children that this war would end, but a worse war would later begin. She told them that Russia would spread its errors all over the world and entire nations might be obliterated if it was not consecrated to her Immaculate Heart. Its consecration, however, would lead to "the conversion of Russia."

The next apparition did not occur as planned because the children were kidnapped and held prisoner for three days. They survived and the prison administrator was forced to release them. On August 13, eighteen thousand people witnessed what they interpreted as a sign of God's anger for the kidnapping of the children. They saw lightning and thunder, the sky turned pale, and a yellowish haze hung about. A white cloud hung in an oak tree and transformed into all the colors of the rainbow.

On August 19, the Virgin Mary appeared to the children again and asked them to pray for all those who did not pray, saying that many souls are damned because there is no one to pray for them.

The End of the World?

On October 13, 70,000 people arrived at the Cova. A storm had just swept through Europe the night before. The Virgin Mary told the children that she was "the Lady of the Rosary" and that people must change their lives and not offend the Lord anymore because He was already greatly offended. She stretched her hands toward the sun and rays of light streamed from her fingers and the sun began to spin—the event that is now known as the famous Miracle of the Sun.

discussion question

How do many people interpret the "conversion" Mary spoke of? Although some people have interpreted the "conversion" Mary reportedly spoke of to mean that Russia would become a Catholic country, others have linked this to the fall of atheist Communism and the reemergence of the local churches.

Rays of color streamed from the sun and then the sun seemed to fall from the sky and rush toward the earth. All the onlookers dropped to their knees praying for forgiveness because they thought the world was ending. Just when it seemed the sun was about to collide with the earth, it returned to its place in the sky. While onlookers as far as thirty miles away were witnessing this solar phenomenon, the visionary children were watching scenes from the heavens. They saw Jesus in a red robe blessing the crowds, the infant Jesus with Joseph and Mary, and then Mary in brown robes. This was the final public vision at Fatima.

Sister Lucia

Both Francisco and Jacinta died of influenza. Lucia was later sent to a girls' school run by the sisters of Saint Dorothy. In 1934 she became a nun, after having one more vision of the Virgin Mary and Jesus in 1925. In 1929 the Virgin told Sister Lucia that it was time for the pope to consecrate Russia to his heart.

In 1989, Sister Lucia sent a message to the world to let everyone know that the pope's consecration of Russia had been accepted and that the results of his action would become clear later that year. In late 1989, the Berlin Wall fell. By 1991, Communism had collapsed in Russia. On August 19, 1991, in a Communist coup, Mikhail Gorbachev was captured and held for three days, just as the three visionary children at Fatima had been held for three days. This all occurred on the same day as the delayed fourth apparition at Fatima. The coup ultimately failed and Gorbachev was set free on August 22, which is also the Roman Catholic feast of the Queenship of Mary.

Zeitun, Egypt, 1968

Zeitun is a district of Cairo, Egypt. St. Mary's Church is said to be located right along the path traveled by Joseph, Mary, and Jesus when they journeyed into Egypt to avoid King Herod's wrath. In 1918, at a time when the shrine marking this spot (which had been torn down and rebuilt many times through history) had completely vanished, a wealthy Coptic Christian family owned the property. A member of the family had a vision of the Virgin Mary in which she told them that this location was important to her, and if they would built a church there, many special blessings would come fifty years after the church was built. The family donated the property to the Coptic Orthodox Church, and church authorities constructed a church according to the lady's request.

The Lady on the Dome

Exactly fifty years later on April 2, 1968, Muslim workers noticed a luminescent woman walking back and forth on a dome of the church. These men thought she was a nun who was about to jump off the roof. One of them pointed a finger at her to try to get her to stop. His finger had been riddled with gangrene and was going to be amputated. According to accounts of this unusual event, his finger was healed within the day.

Many gathered to watch the woman walking on the roof of the church, observing her until she vanished. She was seen again over the church seven days later. From that time forward, she reappeared multiple times until May 2, 1971. Many who witnessed these visions reported miraculous healings. Crowds occasionally swelled to as many as 250,000 people from many backgrounds, including Muslims, Jews, Catholics, Orthodox Christians, and Protestants. Occasionally she would bow to the crowd or bless them.

symbolism

A few times, in Zeitun, Egypt, the apparition of Mary was reported to have appeared holding an olive branch. This is appropriate because the name of the town, Zeitun, means "olive" in Arabic.

Other unusual phenomena accompanied her appearances; sometimes incense would come from the church domes into the crowd and occasionally dovelike creatures would take flight around her.

The Official Statement

The Coptic Pope, Kyrillos VI, appointed a committee of high-ranking priests and bishops to investigate these phenomena, and on May 4 issued a statement recognizing the legitimacy of the apparitions. In it, he wrote:

"Thousands of people from different denominations and religions, Egyptians and foreign visitors, clergy and scientists, from different classes and professions, all observed the apparitions. The description of each apparition as of the time, location, and configuration was identically witnessed by all people, which makes this apparition unique and sublime.

Two important aspects accompanied these apparitions: The first is an incredible revival of the faith in God, the other world, and the saints, leading to repentance and conversion of many who strayed away from the faith. The second are the numerous miracles of healing which were verified by many physicians to be miraculous in nature."

The apparitions were also confirmed by Fr. Henry Ayrout, a Jesuit priest, Rev. Dr. Ibrahim Said of the Protestant Evangelical Ministries, and authorities from the General Information and

Complaints department of Zetiun. They were also witnessed by a group of Catholic nuns, who sent a report to the Vatican. Pope Paul VI then sent an envoy, whose members also witnessed the apparitions.

Damascus, Syria, 1982–1990

Many of the places where apparitions occur have historical and spiritual significance. This is certainly the case with Damascus, Syria. When Saint Paul was approaching Damascus, he was blinded for three days after seeing a heavenly light (Acts 9:3).

It was also in Damascus that a young, nominally religious couple named Myrna (a variation of Mary) and Nicholas were married in 1982. In that same year, Nicholas's sister Layla became very sick. While Myrna was praying for her, Myrna's fingers started to drip with olive oil. Another woman who was praying with Myrna suggested that Myrna anoint her sister-in-law with the oil. As soon as Myrna did this, her sister-in-law was healed.

A Weeping Icon

On November 27, 1982, Myrna's icon of the Virgin Mary, called Our Lady of Soufanieh, began to exude large quantities of olive oil. This oil was subsequently tested and found to be chemically pure. While praying for discernment with family members, Myrna suddenly could not hear anyone around her. She heard a voice calling, telling her to not be afraid, but to open the doors so that all could see.

On December 15, 1982, Myrna was led to her rooftop garden by an invisible being. There, she saw the Virgin Mary shining as if she were covered with diamonds. Myrna ran away in terror, but was helped by a priest who had experience with supernatural events. Three days later she was again led up to her rooftop garden, this time accompanied by her husband and several friends. She saw a globe of light on the highest point in a nearby tree. A woman emerged from the globe and approached Myrna by climbing over a "bridge of light" to her. The Virgin Mary encouraged her to spread the good news about Mary's son—a particularly challenging task in the largely Muslim Middle East. Mary also said, "Love one another. I am not asking for money to give to churches, nor for money to distribute to the poor. I am asking for love."

discussion question

What is the significance of olive oil?
Within Middle Eastern cultures olive oil is considered to be useful for many purposes beyond cooking. Not only is it used in religious services for anointing, but it is also used in the blessing of homes, and for family folk cures. Within theses cultures, olive oil signifies healing, peace, wholeness, and life.

The Virgin appeared many more times and continued to convey messages. Over 100,000 people came to see the oil flowing from the icon and from Myrna, and many reported healings. Again, both Eastern Orthodox and Roman Catholic church officials conducted investigations and agreed that these sightings were authentic.

In 1984, two years after the first apparition, Myrna experienced three days of painful blindness (just as Saint Paul had experienced almost two thousand years before in that same city). Her eyes exuded oil for all three days. On Holy Friday of that year, Myrna experienced the stigmata (the painful, bleeding wounds of Christ), including wounds from Christ's thorny crown. After four hours the wounds began to close and heal on their own.

Healing the Rift

On August 4, 1984, Myrna heard the words of Jesus at the end of Mass, as she went into ecstasy. She was reportedly told by Jesus that anyone who divides the church or rejoices in the divisions is guilty of sin. To this day, Myrna, is devoted to struggling to heal the historic divisions between the Eastern Orthodox and Roman Catholic

Churches. She is no stranger to this painful separation, because she is a Melkite Catholic and her husband is Eastern Orthodox.

factum

> Many copies of the icon of Our Lady of Soufanieh have been anointed by the olive oil tears from Myrna's icon. Of these, more than one hundred have been reported to weep.

Medjugorje, Bosnia, 1981 to the Present, and Rwanda

Like the warnings reported in France in which the Virgin Mary predicted the French Revolution, warnings have more recently occurred in Rwanda and in Medjugorje, Bosnia-Herzegovenia. In the early eighties in Rwanda, visionaries were warned that rivers would fill with blood, and that the visionaries should flee to safety. During the devastating civil war in Rwanda, more than a million people were killed, and the rivers became clogged with dead bodies just as the Virgin Mary had predicted.

In Medjugorje, the Virgin Mary focused on the theme of peace. In one of the Virgin Mary's messages at Medjugorje, she said, "Peace. Peace. Peace. Be reconciled with one another."

Parallels Between Fatima and Medjugorje

Some theologians have seen parallels between the apparitions at Fatima and the apparitions at Medjugorje. Both series of apparitions contained warnings and secrets. Some have even said that the apparitions at Medjugorje are a continuation and fulfillment of the apparitions that began in Fatima.

Like Fatima, in Medjugorje there have been multiple reports of "miracles of the sun" in which the sun has become a spinning disk during the visions. Many people have reported miraculous healings, and hundreds of thousands (some estimate millions) of people have converted to Christianity as a result of these apparitions. Upon returning home from Medjugorje, some pilgrims have reported that metal beads on their rosaries turned to gold.

Some have also made a connection between the apparitions at Medjugorje and Fatima because of issues related to Communism. In Fatima, many believe that the rise, spread, and fall of Communism was predicted. In Medjugorje, some have suggested the widespread effects of the apparitions in Bosnia-Herzegovenia, a Communist country, seemed to indicate the continual demise of Communism around the world.

discussion question

How common are reports of sightings of the Virgin Mary?
During the past twenty years, there have been more than 2,000 claims of Mary sightings. Of these, only 65 have won the status of "accredited apparitions" by the Roman Catholic Church.

Some believe that Medjugorje was supernaturally protected during the war in Yugoslavia. Medjugorje was located in the center of the Republic of Bosnia-Herzegovinia, where some of the most intense battles raged. Though great bloodshed broke out in the surrounding area, the village of Medjugorje remained virtually unharmed. Strangely, only one air raid was attempted on Medjugorje, and the few bombs that were dropped did little damage.

On November 9, 1992, *The Wall Street Journal* reported, "The war has enhanced Medjugorje's fame as an oasis of peace and mystery." The same article quoted Dragan Kozina, the town's mayor, as saying, "You have to believe that either we are very lucky, or that someone is protecting us."

Chapter 14

Mary in Catholic Thought

When many people think of the Virgin Mary, they associate her with the doctrines and devotions of the Roman Catholic Church. Marian theology has evolved slowly, taking on different meanings and emphasis through the centuries. This chapter will explore the history and practical applications of Roman Catholic doctrines associated with the Virgin Mary, including that of the Immaculate Conception.

The Immaculate Conception

One of the most significant Roman Catholic dogmas associated with the Virgin Mary is the belief that at her conception, the stain of original sin that had been passed down to every living person since the fall of Adam and Eve was not passed on to her.

Although the dogma of the Immaculate Conception was not officially proclaimed until December 8, 1854, there were many precursors to this historic event. The Immaculate Conception is rooted in a particular understanding of the fall of man in Genesis and its consequences, articulated by influential theologians such as Saint Augustine and Ambrose of Milan.

Ambrose, for example, was particularly interested in the passage from Psalm 51:5: "Behold I was brought forth in iniquity and in sin did my mother conceive me," and sought to articulate the way Mary was set apart from this cycle of sin. Augustine, on the other hand, emphasized a passage in the book of Romans 5, which emphasizes the radical difference between those "in Adam" and those "in Christ." Augustine wrote about how deeply sin has infected and corrupted those who have not been reborn to a new humanity "in Christ."

factum

Christian theologians have likened Mary to the Ark of the Covenant in the Old Testament. For them, Mary's purity was vitally important. She had to be a pure vessel, because otherwise she might be destroyed as was Uzzah, who accidentally touched the Ark of the Covenant in which God dwelled (1 Samuel 6:6–7).

Because of the belief that Mary needed to be a completely pure vessel to bear God in her womb, it has been long understood in the West that Mary was the singular exception to the rule of sin being passed down through the human generations since Adam.

On December 18, 1439, an official statement was made about the Immaculate Conception at the Council of Basel. According to this statement, the doctrine of the Immaculate Conception was consistent with the teachings of the worship of the Church, the Holy Scriptures, and reason, and should be proclaimed universally. This council also condemned anyone who spoke against the Immaculate Conception.

This council was never viewed as universally authoritative, however, because other council statements related to the authority of the pope were condemned by the Church. Although there were questions surrounding these statements and this council, by the end of the fifteenth century, the Immaculate Conception had gained widespread popular acceptance. Some even used the statements from this council to condemn those who spoke against the Immaculate Conception, saying that although there was once a time when the issue could be debated, those debates ceased with the Council of Basel.

Apparitions Related to the Immaculate Conception

During the next three centuries, belief in the Immaculate Conception was widespread, if not completely universal in the West. A few decades before the dogma was officially proclaimed in 1854, an apparition was reported in France that some have interpreted as foreshadowing this official pronouncement.

The Miraculous Medal

In 1830, a postulant at a Paris convent for Our Sisters of Charity named Catherine Laboure had a vision of the Virgin Mary. In this vision, the Virgin Mary wore a long white silk gown and stood upon a globe. Near her chest, she held a golden ball, and each of her fingers had three jeweled, luminescent rings upon them. The Virgin Mary explained that that light was a demonstration of the graces that would come to all who asked for them. Some of the jewels on Mary's fingers were darkened, and Mary explained that these were symbolic of the graces that people forgot to ask for. On the ground near her feet was a green and yellow snake.

As Catherine watched, Mary seemed to turn around. Catherine then saw a large *M* surmounted by a cross. Two hearts were beneath the cross, one wrapped in thorns, the other pierced by a sword. A large oval surrounded Mary and she was encircled by these words, which were written in gold: "O Mary, conceived without sin, pray for us who have recourse to thee."

The Virgin Mary instructed Catherine to have this image printed as a medal, and the image of the "Miraculous Medal" was born. These medals were extremely popular in Catherine's day—more than fifty thousand were given out in 1832 and 1833 and millions more each year after that. The medals were taken by missionaries to other countries, and the apparition gained global recognition. Over one billion miraculous medals have now been distributed. These medals are commonly associated with miraculous healings and cures. During the apparition, the Virgin Mary said of the Miraculous Medal that, "Those who wear it will receive great graces; abundant graces will be given to those who have confidence."

Pope Pius IX

The widespread popularity of this image may have helped pave the way for the dogma that was proclaimed by Pope Pius IX twenty-four years after the apparition. Pope Pius, who believed that the Virgin had healed him from epilepsy when he was a child, had a lifelong personal devotion to her. His papacy was set against the backdrop of the Enlightenment. During this period, the church was in an increasingly vulnerable position, because more and more people were buying into the ideas of the Enlightenment, which championed science and reason over religion. Pope Pius felt that he might be able to counteract some of this mentality by demonstrating the power of the Virgin within the Roman Catholic Church.

When Pope Pius began to consider proclaiming the Immaculate Conception as dogma, he met with a team of theologians who offered overwhelming (although not universal) support for endorsing the dogma. Pius then contacted several bishops, nine-tenths of whom agreed that he should proclaim the Immaculate Conception as dogma. His actual proclamation took place against a distressing backdrop—Italian nationalists threatened the Church: Massini and Garibaldi were preparing to attack Rome.

factum

During the French Revolution, numerous ancient statues of the Virgin Mary were destroyed, and revolutionaries put up a statue called the "Goddess of Reason" in Notre Dame. The revolutionaries also sang a mock Ave Maria to the allegorical figure Marianne, "Hail Marianne, full of strength, the people are with thee, blessed is the fruit of thy womb, the Republic."

On the day of the Feast of the Immaculate Conception, December 8, 1854, Pope Pius IX read *Ineffabilis Deus*, through tears:

"The Doctrine holds that the blessed Virgin Mary, at the first instant of her conception, by singular privilege and grace of the omnipotent God, in consideration of the merits of Jesus Christ, the savior of mankind, was preserved free from the stain of original sin from the moment of her conception, has been revealed by God and is to be firmly and constantly believed by all the faithful."

Differences of Opinion

Although the Immaculate Conception had been a popular belief among many Western Christians many centuries before the dogma was officially proclaimed, there had always been those in the West who opposed the doctrine, such as Thomas Aquinas, Anselm of Canterbury, and Saint Bernard of Clairvaux.

183

Bernard of Clairvaux was concerned that the doctrine of the Immaculate Conception made it seem as though Mary had no need of a savior herself. His reasoning went something like this: if she was born without the stain of sin and if she never sinned during her earthy life, why would she be in need of a redeemer?

Those who were uncomfortable with the idea of the Immaculate Conception had two major objections. Some objected to the Augustinian idea that all conception was evil, based on Psalm 51, which reads "In sin did my mother conceive me." Some simply objected to this seemingly negative view of sexual intercourse. Still others felt uncomfortable with the way this dogma seemed to separate Mary from the rest of humanity.

When the dogma of the Immaculate Conception was proclaimed, many of these old objections resurfaced, along with some new ones. In particular, Anglicans and Eastern Orthodox expressed concerns about how the dogma was proclaimed. These churches felt that the pope seemed to be acting too much in isolation. Perhaps they sensed what was to come: later that same century at the First Vatican Council in 1869–70, the doctrine of Papal Infallibility was officially proclaimed. This doctrine is quite foreign to the understanding of papal primacy and church authority that developed in the Christian East.

In her book *In Search of Mary,* Sally Cunneen highlights a fascinating aspect of the proclamation of this dogma: the proclamation was both preceded and followed by apparitions that seemed to echo the underlying themes of this teaching.

Four years after Pope Pius IX proclaimed the dogma of the Immaculate Conception, a young girl named Bernadette Soubirous experienced several apparitions of the Virgin Mary. When Bernadette asked the woman who she was, the woman spread her arms in a way that would have been recognizable to Bernadette as her pose upon the Miraculous Medal. The Virgin Mary responded, "I am the Immaculate Conception."

Vatican II

Vatican II was a council that began on October 11, 1962. At this council, religious officials attempted to remain faithful to the ancient heritage of the Roman Catholic Church while also bringing a renewal of church life. Vatican II was infused with a desire to return to some of the original Scriptural and patristic understandings of the faith, while helping the Church to remain relevant to the modern world.

Changes Resulting from Vatican II

Most people who lived through Vatican II are most familiar with the ways in which the Catholic worship experience was transformed as a result of the council. The services were no longer in Latin, but instead used the language of the locals (the vernacular). The priest no longer served facing the altar, but instead faced the people. In many cases, statues were removed from churches or placed in less conspicuous locations in an effort to appease Protestants.

symbolism

The day Vatican II opened, October 11, 1962, was the day dedicated to the motherhood of the Virgin Mary (before the introduction of a revised liturgical calendar). The council closed on December 8, the Feast of the Immaculate Conception.

Vatican II also represented a shift from the more rigid scholastic thought that had dominated official church theology since the Council of Trent to a more Biblical and patristic form of exegesis, meaning that the Church's revised interpretation of the Bible would be based more on the writings and beliefs of the fathers of the Christian Church. Vatican II encouraged lay ministry, the self-organization of convents, and an increasingly strong desire to reach out to "the separated brethren"— Protestant and Eastern Orthodox Christians.

One of the most significant debates related to Mary from this Council revolved around the question of how teachings about Mary would be incorporated into the documents from the council. Some of the more "progressive" theologians argued that the statements about Mary should be included as one chapter in the larger context of all of the writings from the Council, while some of the more traditional Catholics had hoped that the writings related to Mary would be preserved as a separate document.

These more traditional Catholics feared that if the teachings about Mary were not kept separate, they might be reduced or minimized. Those who felt that Mary should occupy a chapter of the larger collection of statements instead of an entire document felt that it was more appropriate to place Mary in the context of the larger church. The vote between these two groups was extremely close: 1,114 people were in favor of including the documents related to Mary in the larger body of work, while 1,074 wished to keep documents related to Mary separate. So the decision was made to include the writings about Mary as the final chapter of the council's constitution.

factum

Each side of the Vatican II discussion posed the argument in terms of "what Our Lady would want." Those desiring a separate document insisted, "Our Lady would like a separate document" while those who pushed for including Mary as one chapter in the set of documents stated, "Our Lady would prefer to be treated within the entire context of the Church."

The decisions that resulted from Vatican II about Mary were extremely deliberate in their wording. There was a conscious effort to minimize "past excesses" while also avoiding the error of being too narrow-minded in statements surrounding Mary.

Statements were made about Mary's role in the Church and her role in the history of salvation. Mary was called a "helper." Controversial titles such as Advocate and Mediator were carefully qualified; Mary could be called by those titles only when they were being used in a minimalist sense, which would imply that Mary shares in these ministries of Christ because of her relationship with him.

The Wake of Vatican II

Many theologians feel that Vatican II produced significant documents related to Mary, which brought helpful clarity and nuance to discussion about Mary in the Catholic Church. At the same time, in the wake of Vatican II, the role of the Virgin Mary has often been downplayed. Charlene Spretnak, in her book *Missing Mary*, describes the aftermath of the council, in which statues disappeared, rosary use in the parishes became more infrequent, and certain novenas for the Virgin Mary were no longer said. In Spretnak's opinion, one result of Vatican II is that there is now an entire generation of American Catholics who have not experienced the full scope of Marian devotion that would have been a staple of their parents' and grandparents' spirituality.

John Paul II

Although in the years since Vatican II many liturgical practices associated with the Virgin Mary have become less popular, there are still many Catholics who have a deep love for her and devotion to her. During this past century, Marian shrines have become extremely popular. Some people believe that there is something of a Marian revival going on, both within and outside the Catholic Church.

One of most prominent figures from modern times who held a deep and unwavering devotion to the Virgin Mary was Pope John Paul II. His lifelong devotion to her may have been fueled by the loss of his own mother when he was only eight years old. His mother, whom he had once described as "the soul of the house," adored him and had always felt that he would one day be a priest and a great man.

Pope John Paul II (whose birth name was Karol Wojtyla) always carried the memory of his mother with him, and even as an adult, when he traveled to faraway pilgrimage sites, he carried with him a photo of his mother holding him as a young child. After his mother died, his father took him to one of Poland's famous Marian shrines, Kalwaria, near Wadowice, Poland. It was most likely on this pilgrimage that he was able to transform some of his grief into a deep love for the Virgin Mary.

A Tragic Childhood

Although Karol Wojtyla's father devoted himself to caring for his young son, their lives were marked with tragedy. When Karol Wojtyla was twelve years old, his only brother died of scarlet fever. When he was twenty, his father died. Karol was deeply grieved that he had not been able to be present with his mother or father when they died. After his father died, he knelt by his body and prayed for twelve hours.

symbolism

The phrase *Totus Tuus* originated with Saint Louis-Marie Grignion de Montfort in the eighteenth century. Saint Louis-Marie Grignion de Montfort advocated utter devotion (almost slavery) to Mary, which was intended to symbolize complete surrender to the will of God through Marian devotion.

All of these factors may have contributed to Karol's devotion to Mary. By the time he was fifteen years old, he was leading a large society in his hometown which was dedicated to the Virgin. Later, when he was a young priest, he made a special place for Mary in his soul. When he became an archbishop he included a large *M* in his coat of arms, a symbol of Mary. When Pope John Paul II was newly elected as pope, he made an unusual request for his papal coat of arms. He asked for a gold cross with a blue Marian background as well as a large *M* for Mary. Although he was told that this request was quite unusual he was ultimately allowed to wear this coat of arms.

The papal slogan he selected for his papacy, *Totus Tuus* or "My whole self is Yours," also reflected his deep love for the Virgin Mary.

An Assassination Attempt

In 1981, when Pope John Paul II was riding in his Jeep through Saint Peter's Square to greet people, a Turkish man named Mehmet Ali Agca shot him. As he was rushed to the hospital, he cried out to the Virgin Mary to save his life. After his condition was stable, the pope made a television broadcast in which he thanked everyone for their prayers. He also attributed his survival directly to the intercessions of the Virgin Mary, taking note of the fact that the assassination attempt occurred on the anniversary of the apparitions at Fatima. During his convalescence, he read through all of the documents associated with the apparitions at Fatima. After recovering from the assassination attempt, the pope went to the prison cell of Mehmet Ali Agca and offered him forgiveness.

A year later, John Paul II made a pilgrimage to Fatima to deposit the fragments of the bullet that nearly took his life into the crown of a statue of Our Lady of Fatima. While there, a priest lunged at him with a knife, but the priest was stopped before any harm was done.

The Pope of Many Pilgrimages

Pope John Paul II wrote beautifully about the Virgin Mary; his *Book of Mary* is a compilation of his many writings on Mary. One of the most beautiful quotes from the book comes from a section near the beginning. On October 6, 1976, he wrote:

> *"This woman of faith, Mary of Nazareth, the Mother of God, has been given to us as a model of our pilgrimage of faith. From Mary, we learn to surrender to God's will in all things. From Mary we learn to trust even when all hope seems gone. From Mary we learn to love Christ, her Son and the Son of God. For Mary is not only the Mother of God, she is the Mother of the Church as well."*

During Pope John Paul II's papacy, he made many journeys to Marian shrines. Whenever he was back in Poland, he visited the famous icon of the Virgin Mary located there, called Our Lady of Czestochowa. During his papacy, John Paul II was also responsible for creating an additional set of five mysteries, called the Mysteries of Light, which were added to the rosary.

Titles Associated with Mary

There are many titles associated with the Virgin Mary that have sometimes been used within the Catholic context as a way of understanding Mary. These terms are not considered formal dogma, but are suggestive of the unique nature of Mary's role in the world.

None of these terms are used universally, and they can be confusing when taken out of context. While some Catholics have pushed for these terms to be used more, or even to be proclaimed as dogma, there are still others who warn that terms like Mediatrix and Coredemptrix are likely to cause unnecessary confusion and should only be used with great caution, if at all.

Mediatrix

One of the most ancient of these terms is *Mediatrix*, which is the Latin feminine form of the word *Mediator.* This term is used to describe the mediating role the Virgin Mary has as the bridge between heaven and earth. This term is quite ancient and even shows up in the fourth-century writings of Saint Ephrem of Syria, who says, "With the mediator, you are the mediatrix of the entire world."

factum

It has been said that Mary is the Mediatrix because it was through her very body that the savior entered the world—in this way, she played an active, mediating role in the drama of redemption.

Applying the title Mediatrix to the Virgin Mary has been a source of controversy because, according to Scripture, there is only "one mediator between God and men, the man Christ Jesus" (1 Timothy 2:5). Many people feel that it is scandalous to confer a title on the Virgin Mary that seems to be reserved for Christ alone.

Those in the Roman Catholic Church who support the use of this title for the Virgin Mary feel that it is useful because it demonstrates the Virgin Mary's role, as she intercedes on behalf of humanity before the face of God. Some have even said that at the wedding at Cana when she pleaded with her son to turn water into wine, she was serving as a Mediatrix. This belief is expressed by Dwight Longenecker in the book he coauthored with David Gustafson, called *Mary: A Catholic Evangelical Debate.* Longenecker also makes the point that all Christians are called to a ministry of mediation and reconciliation.

As Christians pray before God for others and seek to bring knowledge of God into the world, they participate in a ministry that is something like Mary's. In this line of reasoning, Mary serves as the ultimate example of a ministry to which all Christians are called.

Advocate

The title Advocate is closely linked with the title Mediatrix. From a Biblical perspective, Jesus is the Advocate. His role as Advocate, however, does not diminish the idea that all Christians can have a ministry of advocacy.

This term implies that Mary, like a lawyer, stands up for people and makes a defense for them before God. This defense takes the form of fervent prayers. For some, this title is problematic because it hints of the notion that the Virgin Mary is compassionate while Jesus is merely a judge. Certainly, a balanced Biblical view of Jesus would see him as both compassionate advocate and judge, while Mary is never associated with judgment.

Coredemptrix

The term *Coredemptrix*, meaning that Mary participates in the redemption of humanity through her intercessions and cooperation with God, is perhaps the most controversial because Christians believe that Christ is the exclusive Redeemer. For those who embrace this term, however, calling the Virgin Mary Coredemptrix does not take away from Christ's redemptive work. Instead, the term highlights the fact that Mary, by being the first Christian and saying yes to God in such a way that redemption became possible, participated in God's plan of salvation.

Many Christians believe that Mary's openness and obedience to God continues, and that her participation in the salvation of the world is ongoing. Some interpret her apparitions as an expression of her continual desire to convince lost sheep of the importance of Jesus' message and to make her son known in this world.

From Title to Dogma

Some Catholics would like the titles of *Coredemptrix* and *Mediatrix* to be proclaimed as dogma. Supporters of these titles feel that they contribute to a more robust view of Mary, suggestive of her continual quest to reconcile humanity with God.

There are many, however, who don't want these titles to become dogma. In particular, Pope Benedict is opposed to Coredemptrix because he feels that it has the potential to create unnecessary confusion. These disagreements highlight the sometimes delicate process of articulating Christian teaching, as theologians attempt to bring clarity without confusion and fullness without excess in the Catholic Church.

Chapter 15
Mary in Popular Culture

Mary occupies a unique place in popular culture. She is an object of loyal devotion and of occasional artistic deprecation. In some cases, these strange manifestations seem to be largely harmless, while in others the Virgin Mary is exploited for commercial use in a way that is offensive to believers. This chapter dives into the more curious (and in some cases, disconcerting) manifestations of the Virgin Mary in popular culture, as well as the attempts of many of the faithful to protect her image when they feel it has been tainted.

The Power of Images

Who could forget the photographs taken during the terrorist attacks that occurred on September 11, 2001? Some of the most heartbreaking images were taken of people jumping from the windows of the smoldering Twin Towers, hands clasped as they fell to their deaths. These images express the reality of what happened that day in a way that words cannot, capturing the fear, desperation, and agony experienced by so many.

The images from September 11 were so powerful that many people sat before their televisions day after day in a sort of trance, repeatedly watching footage of the planes crashing into the World Trade Center towers, trying to piece together some semblance of order from all of these images. Even now, when people think of this day, they likely think not so much in words but in images. Long after the event, images remain crisp while words blur and become foggy in memory.

Images have also occupied a prominent place within many religions, including Christianity. Images of the Virgin Mary have been especially potent, not just for the way they express the traditional Christian teaching of the Incarnation, but also for the messages they convey about motherhood, femininity, and God.

symbolism

During the Christmas season of 1995, the U.S. Postal Service printed 700 million stamps bearing an image of the Virgin and Child created by Giotto di Bondone, a painter in Florence, Italy, in the fourteenth century. Although these stamps were scheduled to be replaced with angel stamps, they have been brought back due to popular demand.

In a more specific way, images are often viewed as synonymous with the Roman Catholic or Eastern Orthodox Churches. Sometimes, when people want to attack these churches or the ideas they represent, they vandalize statues or deface icons. This approach is not unlike burning flags to protest American policies.

Some critics believe that some pop-culture icons exploit images of the Virgin Mary in a way that is not only distasteful but also destructive. Some Christians might even believe that some cases of tainting Mary's image have a diabolical character because they only serve to distract people from more central Christian realities. You may discern for yourself how these images might be interpreted in light of larger cultural and spiritual realities.

Sacred or Profane?

Increasingly, we are assaulted by a barrage of images everywhere we go—billboards are plastered with scantily clad women, and the Nike and Starbucks logos are so widely recognizable that the companies don't even need words for promotion. Images are sometimes used to stir emotions and sell products. When the Virgin Mary is used as a marketing tool, this practice is sometimes viewed as disrespectful by religious people.

For this reason, the Christian response to these particular manifestations of Mary's image has often been one of skeptical wariness, if not outright condemnation. It's important to realize, however, that at least a few of the individuals who will be discussed in this chapter seem to be sincere. They don't necessarily recognize the negative impacts of their statements or art. Still, many of them have experienced a great backlash of criticism from those within and outside of Christianity who resent these depictions.

Mary in Modern Art

In an opening scene of a *Simpsons* episode, Bart writes on a chalkboard over and over, "I will not create art from dung." Bart's penance on the TV show was directly related to an exhibit that had opened at the Brooklyn Museum of Art in 1999. This exhibit was called

"Sensations: Young British Artists from the Saatchi Collection" and featured the work of a variety of edgy artists. One of these, Chris Ofili, created a painting of the Virgin Mary that was dappled with elephant manure and encircled by pornographic images.

The Holy Virgin Mary was the most infamous and hotly contested piece in the exhibit, attracting over 300,000 people who needed to see this image for themselves. The image also generated a passionate response from the religious communities in New York City.

The Holy Virgin Mary

The Holy Virgin Mary contained a large Black Madonna who was surrounded with disembodied pornographic images. The painting was also created using elephant manure, a substance that the artist used frequently in his work. Supporters of Chris Ofili's art said that in the African culture from which Ofili drew his inspiration, dung and urine don't have the same negative connotation that Americans attach to them. These claims, however, did nothing to curb the backlash against the exhibit. New York's mayor at the time, Rudolph Giuliani, described it as "very sick stuff."

Even before the exhibit opened there were protests. One self-described artist stood in front of the museum, throwing manure at the museum's façade. When the police took him away, he explained that he was "expressing himself creatively," and that the painting of the Virgin Mary was just a form of Catholic-bashing.

Giuliani threatened to take away the city's funding of the museum for the month, and also expressed a desire to pull its lease. Like many of the opponents of the exhibit, he was particularity appalled by the image of the Virgin Mary. According to Giuliani, his position was not related to censorship but was primarily focused on concerns that public funds should be used appropriately. According to Giuliani, "art" that was deeply offensive to a large portion of the tax-paying public was not a proper use of funds. The case eventually went to court and the judge ruled in favor of the museum because of the First Amendment.

discussion question

Was the reaction in New York to Chris Ofili's work unique?
No. The Tate Gallery in London garnered a similar response to the one experienced in New York City when it awarded Chris Ofili the prestigious Turner Prize in 1989. One protestor left a large heap of manure on the front steps of the museum, along with a sign that said, "Modern Art is a heap of . . . ."

Neither the manure-slinging man nor Giuliani was successful in preventing the exhibit from opening. After the manure incident, the Brooklyn Museum of Art realized that more attacks were likely, so they covered the image with Plexiglass. The Plexiglass did not, however, deter a retired English teacher named Dennis Heiner who showed up at the exhibit with a tube of white paint. As he approached the image of the Virgin Mary, he leaned against a wall, pretending to be ill. He then snuck behind the Plexiglass and made a line of white paint all down the Virgin's face and body. He quickly spread the white paint with his hands all over the painting, effectively concealing the image.

When he was caught, he made no attempt to escape. When a security guard asked him why he had defaced the painting, he quietly responded, "It's blasphemous." Heiner was later charged with second-degree criminal mischief and a $250 fine. The verdict was seen as quite lenient by the arts community.

In the years since, Chris Ofili has toned down his work a bit. In an interview with *The New York Magazine*, Ofili told a reporter, "At the time, I felt quite vulnerable. I didn't really know what the American rules are. I didn't know how extreme things could get." When *The New York Times* interviewed Ofili, he refused to describe his inspiration or give any interpretation of the work, because he felt that viewers should interpret it for themselves.

Marian Kitsch

In recent years, there has been an overwhelming amount of products associated with the Virgin Mary. Some of these products are sold at tacky trinket stands in places like Lourdes where millions of pilgrims flock each year. At Lourdes, one can buy bright pink rosaries and velvet images of Christ. Online, one can purchase a variety of other items, from tasteful to tacky, and from reverent to flippant.

Printed Devotion

One of the more recent items associated with the Virgin Mary that is turning some heads and turning a significant profit is T-shirts that read "Mary is my homegirl." These T-shirts are being produced by Teenage Millionaire, a California-based clothing company. According to the company, these T-shirts are one of their bestsellers. Young Catholics and Protestants have been attracted to these T-shirts as a way to witness their love and admiration for Mary. There is, as one might imagine, a companion T-shirt that says "Jesus is my homeboy" on it.

Some skeptics have expressed concerns that these T-shirts (along with a the slew of other Mary products being marketed) are disrespectful because they present these spiritual figures in a way that is perhaps too lighthearted, or that is meant to be taken ironically. The "Mary is my homegirl" T-shirts, do, however, witness to increasingly widespread enthusiasm surrounding the Virgin Mary in our society. These T-shirts also garnered popular attention when they were mentioned on the hit TV show *Gilmore Girls*.

The "Holy" Sandwich

Sometimes Mary pops up in unusual places. In 1994, one of the most unusual Marian "manifestations" was claimed. This time, the face of the Virgin Mary appeared in the burn marks on a grilled cheese sandwich. According to Diana Duyser, a 52-year-old woman living in Hollywood, Florida, she had taken one bite of her grilled cheese sandwich, and then she noticed the face of the Virgin Mary staring back up at her. She was alarmed and called her husband into the room to see the image on the sandwich.

Duyser then put the sandwich in a clear plastic box and placed it beside her bed. She kept it for ten years, and she reports that it did not mold or crumble at all during the decade. According to Duyser, she sincerely believes that the image on her sandwich is that of Mary, the Mother of God. She was not, however, averse to making a profit off the sandwich. According to Duyser the sandwich brought her significant good luck and fortune, including winnings of $70,000 at several nearby casinos.

After ten years, Duyser decided that it was time to share her sandwich with the world and she posted an ad for it on eBay, with a starting bid of $3,000. While the sandwich was for sale, more than 1,700,000 people visited the site, and many of them placed joke bids, along with joke items that followed the theme of the sandwich. The price of the sandwich rose and rose to $99.9 million and then finally began to decrease, because so many of the bids were fake.

factum

eBay initially pulled the Virgin Mary sandwich from the site because they don't sell hoax items. Eventually, however, eBay allowed it to be sold because Duyser did intend to hand over the sandwich to the highest bidder. She wrote on online request that all hoax bids be stopped. She also cautioned potential buyers that the sandwich "was not for consumption."

In the end, an online casino called GoldenPalaceCasino.com purchased the sandwich for $28,000 The CEO of the online casino said that they intend to use the sandwich to raise money for charity. As to why they were so eager to acquire the sandwich, their spokesperson Monty Kerr was quoted in the *Miami Herald* saying, "It's a part of pop culture that is immediately and widely recognizable. We knew right away that we wanted to have it."

Mary in Popular Music

The pop star Madonna won her fame, in part, by exploiting the connections between her birth name, which is Madonna (given to her by her Italian immigrant parents), and the actual Virgin Mary.

Madonna was raised in a large, devout Catholic family located in a suburb of Detroit. For much of her childhood, she attended Catholic schools. Her mother died of breast cancer when Madonna was only five years old. Some have speculated that the trauma of Madonna's childhood loss permeates her music through her use of Mary imagery. Many of her videos also use religious imagery such as rosaries and crosses. These potent Catholic symbols are very likely drawn from Madonna's childhood experience in a devout family as well as her years in parochial schools.

symbolism

The Virgin Mary has not only been the subject of songs by Madonna. She has also been the subject of a dazzling number of more reverent songs such as the Beatles' ballad "Let It Be."

Madonna must have sensed early on that her name was powerful. During the course of her career, she has often drawn on Christian and Marian themes and used them to shock and attract crowds. Madonna's use of religious imagery, however, has not always worked to improve her image. In the eighties, she lost a Pepsi sponsorship when she released the controversial hit song "Like a Prayer" in which she drew connections between prayer and sexuality. The music video for the song, which featured burning crosses and Madonna wearing provocative clothing, added to the controversy.

Madonna might have gained popularity in part because society is so full of conflicted feelings about the Virgin Mary and about sexuality. Madonna tapped into the public's general interest in the Virgin Mary when she named her 1990 album *The Immaculate Collection*. The album's colors of blue and gold resonate with some of the colors used in traditional images of the Virgin Mary. Madonna also named her daughter Lourdes, after the apparition site in France.

Mary in Literature

The Virgin Mary continually surfaces in contemporary literature. The Virgin Mary has inspired the poetry of Gerald Manley Hopkins and Rainer Maria Rilke, and she has even been indirectly referred to in Garrison Keillor's fictional *Lake Wobegon*, in which the town's Catholic church is named Our Lady of Perpetual Responsibility. The Virgin Mary has also taken a prominent role in the writings of Canadian poet and novelist Margaret Atwood.

Sue Monk Kidd

Perhaps one of the most gripping and vivid contemporary depictions of the Virgin Mary in literature appears in Sue Monk Kidd's *The Secret Life of Bees*. Although the Mariology expressed in Kidd's book might be seen as excessive, Kidd powerfully expresses the universal longing for a mother that so often motivates Marian devotion. Kidd's main character, Lilly, accidentally caused her mother's death when she was a small child, and this loss shaped her life. Ultimately Lilly finds solace in the Virgin Mary.

After Lilly runs away from her abusive father in search of the truth about her mother, she finds her way to the bright pink home of the Calendar sisters. The Calendar sisters are three African American beekeeping sisters named May, June, and August, who expose Lilly to their folk religion, which finds its heart in devotion to the Black Madonna. The women venerate a large black wooden statue of a woman who was once part of a boat's masthead. The statue is adorned in chains, and Lilly is startled by this until one of the Calendar sister explains to her that the Virgin Mary is adorned with chains not because she wears them, but because she breaks them.

In *The Secret Life of Bees* the Virgin Mary is clearly associated with the universal longing for a mother as well as the widely held belief that the Virgin Mary identifies with the oppressed, crossing racial and social lines as Lily did when she went to live with the Calendar sisters during the era of the civil rights movement in the South. Sue Monk Kidd writes in *The Secret Life of Bees:*

> *"She is a muscle of love, this Mary. I feel her in unexpected moments, her Assumption into heaven happening in places inside me. She will suddenly rise, and when she does, she does not go up, up into the sky but further and further inside me. August said she goes into the holes life has gauged for us."*

Margaret Atwood

For Margaret Atwood and many contemporary women, Mary is increasingly considered an empowered woman who actively engages the questions of life, while being wearied (as contemporary women so often are) by the demands that love puts upon her. Sally Cunneen offers fascinating insights into Atwood's writing in Cunneen's book *In Search of Mary*.

Cunneen describes one scene from Atwood's book *Cat's Eye*, in which the author depicts a strikingly contemporary image of Mary. Atwood describes a painting of the Virgin Mary with the head of a lioness, dressed in the traditional blue and white. She is dressed in an overcoat and is carrying heavy bags of groceries from which several items have fallen.

This depiction captures a fierce side of Mary that seems somewhat unusual to most people. It also captures a weary Mary that seems very believable considering the depth of her active love and the ways in which she was called by God to suffer for it. The lioness image is based on some traditional images that have portrayed

Christ as a lion. This image of Christ as a lion parallels C. S. Lewis's *Chronicles of Narnia* where Aslan the lion is a Christ figure.

factum

The Virgin Mary has been the subject of the poetry of Gerard Manley Hopkins. In his poem "The Blessed Virgin Compared to the Air We Breathe," he writes, "She, wild web, wondrous robe, Mantles the guilty globe . . . Men are meant to share her life as life does air."

According to the narrator in the Atwood story, "My Virgin Mary is fierce, alert to danger, wild. She stares levelly out at the viewer with her yellow lion's eyes. A gnawed bone lies at her feet." One can easily imagine why a less-tame, but still accessible, Mary would appeal to contemporary women.

Chicago Oil Spot

In 2005, a young woman named Obdulia Delgado was driving on one of Chicago's major freeways when she saw what she believed to be a figure of the Virgin Mary in an oil spot in an underpass. She was so astonished that she could barely drive, and many frustrated people honked at her as she slowed down to examine the figure. Delgado reported that she had been praying to the Virgin for assistance, which was in part why she found this figure so astonishing.

Word spread quickly, and many came to view the mysterious oil spot. Some left candles and flowers and prayed the rosary there, while others were skeptical, saying that the oil spot looked more like a pawn in a chess game than the Virgin Mary.

The city decided to treat the oil spot as they would any roadside memorial. They barricaded the area so that the image (which was accompanied by the phrase "Go Cubs" written in a graffiti tag beside it) would remain protected. Some people drew parallels between the event that was occurring in Chicago that day and the event that was occurring that same day in Rome, as the new pope was being selected.

Most people in society don't know quite how to feel about bizarre manifestations like the Virgin Mary oil spot or the face on the grilled cheese sandwich. There are many skeptics, but it is also striking that those who experience these manifestations directly often seem to be genuine in their responses.

All of these manifestations of the Virgin Mary offer different glimpses into the way that society views her. Just beneath the surface, emotions about Mary run deep. Some individuals are willing be arrested as they protest art that they perceive as disrespectful, while others will gather at a freeway underpass, light votive candles, and pray the rosary before an oil spot that loosely resembles Mary. Still others have found effective ways to tap into the passion surrounding Mary, to mingle the sacred and profane in ways that attract crowds and turn profits.

The Marian manifestations in popular culture witness to the reality that emotions surrounding Mary run deep. Images of her continue to be powerful, both for those who create them through art and literature, and for those who encounter them. In an age in which people are bombarded with images and often experience sensory overload, it is interesting to see how powerful images of Mary remain. Just as images spoke to those in the early church and to those in the medieval villages, images of Mary continue to resonate in our day.

Chapter 16
Praying with Mary

Some of the most ancient icons of Mary show her with her arms raised in prayer. According to the book of Acts, Mary prayed with the disciples while waiting for the Holy Spirit to come (Acts 1:14–2:1). These images express Mary's role as intercessor. This chapter will explore ways in which Christians have prayed with Mary through the centuries, as well as offering some practical suggestions for making space for Mary within our own homes.

The Meaning of Marian Prayers

Some of the controversies and questions surrounding Marian prayers were explored in Chapter 10. The most important thing to remember in relation to Marian prayers, however, is that all prayers to Mary find their end in Christ. Mary is never meant to be the end, but a means to an end.

The tradition of asking Mary to intercede for Christians is ancient, dating back to at least the fourth century. The idea of asking for the intercessions of those who have gone before is closely related to the belief in the Resurrection of the dead. Christians believe that Christ died and rose again, and that those who believe in him also continue to live, even after they have died. Because of this belief in the ongoing life of those who have died in the earthly sense, many Christians have embraced the idea that the departed in Christ can continue to pray for those on earth.

factum

Mahatma Gandhi, on observing Marian devotion, said: "The feeling has since then been growing on me, that all this kneeling and prayer could not be mere superstition; the devout souls kneeling before the Virgin could not be worshiping mere marble. I had the impression that I felt then that by this worship they were not detracting from, but adding to, the glory of God."

The intercessions of Mary are closely connected to this belief. Just as Mary was the link between heaven and earth when she lived on this earth, Christians have historically believed that Mary continues to help us. Mary's prayers have been invoked by millions of people around the world who seek her assistance in every kind of difficulty.

Mary's prayers have been requested by sailors at sea, couples struggling with infertility, soldiers heading into battle, farmers sowing their fields, and parents who grieve the loss of a child. Just as little children run to their mother when they are afraid, for centuries, Christians have invoked Mary's prayers. Some have even felt that Mary was more available and accessible than Christ, although the idea of seeking the intercessions of Mary instead of the intercessions of Christ was officially censured at Vatican II in which the pope said, "Mary is not happy when she is placed above her son."

Though the intercessions of Mary are never supposed to replace intercessions to Christ or God the Father, but only to be one piece of the entire fabric of a life of prayer, many ascribe miraculous events in their own lives directly to her, and have found comfort, solace, and strength in Mary's witness and her continual prayers.

Ancient Prayers

Marian devotion is quite ancient—one of the oldest frescos in the Catacombs is of the Virgin Mary and dates back to about the second century. The oldest known prayer to Mary, the Sub Tuum Praesidium, dates back to the third or early fourth century. By the fifth century, Christians described special Marian "graces." One such Christian was the historian Sozomen, who described the apparently miraculous events that occurred in the famous Anastasia Chapel in Constantinople (present-day Istanbul).

Sozomen described a divine power that seemed to manifest itself in this church. This power helped cure illnesses and brought relief from afflictions to members of this community. Sozomen wrote, "The power was attributed to Mary, the Mother of God, the Holy Virgin, for she does manifest herself in this way."

Sozomen's statement suggests that the events that occurred at this church were not entirely unique but were related to a broader phenomenon that he may have already been familiar with. His statement seems to parallel the reports of healings and transformed lives that are associated with apparition sites.

Saint Gregory of Nazianzus

It seems appropriate that the events described by Sozomen would occur at the Anastasia Chapel in Constantinople, because Saint Gregory of Nazianzus preached in this chapel.

discussion question

Was Saint Gregory open about his Marian devotion?
Yes. Saint Gregory was quite bold in his devotion to the Virgin Mary. In A.D. 379, he said, "If anyone does not accept the holy Mary as Theotokos, he is without the Godhead."

Saint Gregory was devoted to the Virgin Mary, and he did not shy away from mentioning her in his sermons, even early on in his career. During Saint Gregory's first year preaching in Constantinople in A.D. 379, he publicly called the Virgin Mary Theotokos, long before the Council at Ephesus had officially used this title to describe her. Saint Gregory also believed fervently that Mary responded to prayers and that healings could be attributed to her.

The conviction that Mary continually prays for those who seek her intercessions has been passed on from century to century, crossing ethnic and cultural lines, and finding different expressions within a variety of communities around the world.

Making Space for Mary

Saint John of the Cross said, "If you meet the Virgin on the road, invite her into your house. She bears the word of God." Increasingly, people are seeking ways to bring Mary into their lives and into their homes. There are many small ways to create space for Mary in one's home.

House Blessings

The Catholic, Eastern Orthodox, and many Protestant Churches have retained the ancient tradition of house blessings. House blessings are usually done by a parish priest who walks through a house with the family, sprinkling holy water throughout while praying for those who live in the house as well as for all of the family's loved ones.

The ancient ritual of house blessing is based on the idea that physical spaces can be transformed by prayer, meaning that a house of brick or wood can become a holy space through the prayer-infused sprinkling of water. Christians have also found intentional ways of inviting Mary to dwell in their homes.

Prayer Corners

In Eastern Orthodox communities, the most common way to create space for the saints inside of the home is by creating a prayer corner. Prayer corners do not always have to be literally located in corners, although many families do place them in a corner of their home. Traditionally, icon corners have been placed on a wall that faces east because Christians have historically prayed facing eastward—in the direction of the rising sun. Praying eastward is one more way in which the Church has integrated the natural rhythms of the earth into its prayers.

Icon corners vary from home to home. Some families will have an entire wall of images that are significant to them, while others will have very basic icon corners. The most basic family icon corners include icons of Christ, the Virgin Mary, and the saints for which each of the family members are named.

Prayer corners are often lit by small oil lamps called lampadas. Traditionally, these lamps are filled with olive oil because olive oil burns clean and is frequently used for liturgical purposes in the Church—baptisms, Chrismations (or Confirmations in the West), as well as anointing for healing.

Many Orthodox families keep their lampadas burning at all times as a way of remembering that God is always present, along with the unseen communion of saints, and that we are called to keep watch for the coming of the Lord. The lampadas that burn in the homes of many Orthodox bring to mind the ten virgins from Matthew 25:7, who must keep their wicks trimmed and their lamps full of oil in anticipation of the coming of the Bridegroom. These simple lampadas require only a minimal amount of care, but the very act of trimming the wicks and keeping the oil full can serve as a physical reminder of the continual sense of watchfulness that permeates a Christian's life of faith.

factum

Some families that keep their lampadas burning at all times put a small amount of water in the bottom of the lamps as a precautionary measure. Should the lampada run out of oil, this water can prevent a fire.

By creating icon corners, families are able to set aside a small sanctuary within their home. Many families place the icon corners in their dining rooms, saying prayer before meals while facing the icons. The icon corner serves as a constant reminder of unchanging heavenly realities, helping to transform the home from a mere dwelling place to a place of holiness, hospitality, and peace.

Mary Gardens

After inviting Mary into our homes, we might also consider inviting her into our yards. Gardens are particularly appropriate places for remembering God because according to the book of Genesis, the world began in a garden.

The Garden of Eden was originally a place of peace and harmony between man and woman, animals, and every type of plant. Many gardeners say that working in the soil is a spiritual experience for them. By helping to nurture and order the natural world, we are able to participate in the living memory of that very first garden.

symbolism

The early Church Fathers made a connection between Eden and Mary. Saint John Chrysostom wrote about a parallel between the soil of Eden, which blossomed without any seed, and Mary, who gave birth without the seed of man. According to Saint John Chrysostom, in Hebrew Eden means "Virgin Soil."

Before Christianity, the attributes of different plants were connected to particular pagan gods and goddesses. Plants were used for healing and medicinal purposes. Later, during the medieval period, plants continued to be used in similar ways. However, the healing and health that came from them became separated from their earlier associations with pagan deities, and came to be increasingly associated with the Virgin Mary.

Renaming the Flowers

When devotion to Mary was widespread, hundreds of flowers were renamed for her, each calling to mind a particular event, story, or characteristic. Marigolds were known as Mary's Gold, periwinkles were called Virgin Flower, forget-me-nots were called eyes of Mary, and bluebells of Scotland were called Our Lady's Thimble. During the Reformation many of these flowers lost their Marian folk names. Currently, flowers like "lady's slipper" are rooted in Marian devotion, but the flowers have become separated from their history.

One flower has a particularly interesting reason for its name. It is called milk thistle because of a legend that the white spots on its leaves were caused when the Virgin Mary dripped a little of her breast milk upon the plant. The naming of this flower suggests that Christians weren't afraid of Mary's earthiness.

According to the English writer Hepworth Dixon, the connection between Mary and flowers is quite strong. He writes, "We have made her the patroness of all our flowers. The Virgin is our Rose of Sharon, our Lily of the Valley. The poetry no less than the piety of Europe has ascribed to her the whole bloom and coloring of the fields and hedges."

Mary as a Garden

The Virgin Mary is not only historically and spiritually connected to individual breeds of flowers, she is also occasionally thought of as a garden. A particularly strong association was made between her and the garden mentioned in the Song of Solomon, "A garden enclosed is my sister, my spouse; a spring shut up a fountain enclosed" (Song of Solomon 4:12).

This garden imagery referred to Mary's ever-virginity. According to Roman Catholic and Eastern Orthodox tradition, her womb opened only once to bring Christ into the world. Because of this, medieval artistic renderings of the Virgin Mary show her in enclosed gardens, surrounded by many of the flowers that were associated with her attributes.

factum

According to one Apocryphal legend, after the Virgin Mary was assumed into heaven her tomb was found empty but flush with roses and lilies in full bloom. To this day, the Assumption Lily, native to Japan and China, is so named because these lilies bloom in mid-August, around the time when the Assumption is celebrated.

According to another legend, when the three magi came to the cave bearing gifts for the infant Christ, they discovered chrysanthemums blooming just beside the cave's opening. They picked a bouquet of them and presented them to the new mother with their gold, frankincense, and myrrh.

The tradition of Mary gardens is quite ancient. In the fourth century, Saint Benedict had a rosary, or a monastic rose garden. A few centuries later, in the seventh century, the Irish patron saint of gardening, Saint Fiacre, cared for a Marian garden dedicated to Mary that surrounded the small chapel and hospice for the poor and infirm. From the ninth century we have detailed records of "Assumption bundles," which were assorted flowers and plants that were taken to the church on the Feast of Assumption to be blessed, and then brought home.

The First Mary Garden

The first record of a garden that was actually referred to by the title "Mary Garden" is located in a fifteenth-century monastic accounting record from Norwich priory, England, which details the purchase of plants for a Mary Garden.

discussion question

What was the first flower named for Mary?
The earliest record of a flower named after Mary is Seint Mary Gouldes, or marigold, which was included in a recipe of a plant-based medication used for treating illness.

The connection between the Virgin Mary and flowers seemed to grow with time. According to records from the thirteenth century, Saint Francis of Assisi was extremely careful when walking because he didn't want to step on any flowers—for him, each of them represented the Virgin Mary, and he couldn't bear to stomp on her image.

By the fifteenth century, the Flemish and French *Book of Hours* included images of symbolic flowers associated with the Virgin Mary. Medieval artistic depictions of Mary show her surrounded by plants and animals, as well as many of the flowers that were symbolically associated with her.

In the twelfth and thirteenth centuries, the Christian mystic Hildegard of Bingen wrote beautifully about the Virgin Mary and flowers, "O Branch, God foresaw your flowering on the first day of his creation. You are the shining lily. You point before all creation where God fixes his gaze."

Mary Gardens Today

In recent years, some Americans have sought to revive the tradition of creating Mary Gardens. In 1951 John Stokes Jr. and the late Edward A. G. McTague were inspired to start a nonprofit organization called Mary's Gardens of Philadelphia after reading an article about a Mary Garden at Saint Joseph's Church in Woods Hole, Cape Cod, Massachusetts, which was originally planted in 1932 by Frances Crane Lillie around a statue of the Virgin Mary.

factum

Traditional paintings of the Annunciation from Florence often show the angel Gabriel presenting a lily to the Virgin Mary. Paintings from Siena do not use the lily imagery because Siena was historically the rival of Florence. In paintings from Siena, the angel Gabriel offers Mary an olive branch instead.

Mary's Gardens of Philadelphia, Pennsylvania, has been operating since its inception. This organization is dedicated to researching the vast, international varieties of plants with Marian associations, as well as helping to distribute information about the history of Mary Gardens. It is also committed to providing a wealth of practical information for those seeking to create their own Mary Gardens. Visit Mary's Gardens of Philadelphia online at *www.mgardens.org*.

Creating Your Own Mary Garden

Mary gardens are extremely versatile. They can be created in yards, on porches in small planters, or on windowsills. They are usually made up of at least a few varieties of flowers that have historical associations with the Virgin Mary, and in most cases, the flowers surround a small stone, wood, or ceramic statue of Mary. Some Mary gardens incorporate fragrant herbs that would have been used in medieval monastic gardens, while others incorporate small pools.

symbolism

Those who pray the rosary in their Mary Gardens use the white flowers for meditating upon the joyful mysteries, the purple and red flowers for meditating upon the sorrowful mysteries, and the gold and yellow flowers for meditating upon the glorious mysteries.

Three ideal flowers to incorporate into a Mary garden are roses, lilies, and irises. Each of these has symbolic ties to the Virgin Mary. Of all flowers, roses are the most closely linked to the Virgin Mary. She has dozens of titles directly linked to roses, and the image on the Tilma of Guadalupe was reportedly created through the Virgin Mary's careful arrangement of Castilian roses on Juan Diego's cloak.

These gardens offer a quiet place for peaceful reflection and prayer. Those who tend Mary Gardens feel that the work of nurturing the gardens helps them to remain attentive to the mysteries of faith. Some people even pray the rosary using the flowers in their gardens instead of rosary beads.

There are Mary Gardens located at the National Shrine of the Immaculate Conception in Washington, D.C., as well as at the University of Dayton in Ohio. There are also Mary Gardens located at some monasteries in America, as well as at several Catholic parishes. They provide a wonderful opportunity for education and spiritual growth within a community.

Mary and the Hour of Death

Many prayers make a connection between the Virgin Mary and death. The Gospel of John places the Virgin Mary at the cross with Mary (the wife of Cleopas) and Mary Magdalene. Mary's placement at the cross where her son died has also been a common theme in Western art, especially much-loved images of the Pieta, which show the Virgin Mary with a look of anguished sorrow on her face while holding Christ in her arms just after he died.

A Unique Experience of Grief

Because many believe that the Virgin Mary witnessed her son's death on the cross, it has been widely believed that her experience gave her unique insights into the experience of grief, loss, and death. Her presence at the cross has given Christians reason to turn to her both when facing the loss of a loved one and at their own final hour. This is especially true for parents who have lost a child, who have sometimes found strength and solace in the example of the Virgin Mary.

The famous philosopher Søren Kierkegaard wrote about the Virgin Mary in his journal. In one passage he described how both Christ and Mary had to suffer in Christ's death. According to Kierkegaard, the sword that was to pierce Mary's heart in the Gospels was not just related to her experience of watching her son die, but was also related to her son's experience of feeling abandoned by God when he was on the cross. According to Kierkegaard, the sword could be connected to the words Christ said from the cross, "My God, My God why have you forsaken me" (Matthew 27:46).

This feeling of being utterly abandoned by God was clearly experienced by Christ, and may have been experienced by his mother as well. Certainly this feeling is common among those who grieve the loss of a loved one.

Nightfall

According to Church tradition, there is a connection between Mary, Saint Simeon (who, as noted in Chapter 8, prophesied to Mary that a sword would pierce her heart), and the hour of death. Evening prayers in both Eastern and Western churches often quote the words Simeon spoke just after the infant Christ was brought to the Temple for dedication, "Lord you have now set your servant free to go in peace as you have promised, for my eyes have seen the Savior of the world a light to the gentiles and the glory of your people, Israel." This statement was not connected to Simeon leaving the temple so much as it was to Simeon leaving this world. According to a prophecy he would not die until his own eyes had seen the Savior. The placement of this passage in the Western Compline services and the Eastern Orthodox Vespers service draws a connection between nightfall and death.

factum

The ancient Christians believed that every night was a trial run for their own deaths, and that the darkness of night represented the fearfulness of the unknown and death.

Christians have held the belief that each night is a practice run for the final laying down of arms, in which we die in this world and wake in the next. Christians have also often referred to faithfully departed as those who "have fallen asleep."

This idea serves as a reminder that death is more like sleep than a final condition. Within the Eastern Church, the feast of the Dormition, the Virgin Mary's "falling asleep," is celebrated on August 15. (This is another name for the feast more commonly called the Assumption in the West.)

The Rosary and the Hour of Death

The connection between Mary and the hour of death is also made explicit through the rosary. The last line of the rosary prayer is, "Holy Virgin Mary, Pray for us sinners, now and at the Hour of our deaths." This section of the rosary was added later to the original, Scriptural portion of prayer. This change probably occurred during the eleventh century, a time when infant mortality was high and lives were shorter. Death was an ever-present reality, and the need to incorporate petitions related to that unavoidable reality would have been great.

Even in our day, when death seems more far off, these words allow a person who prays the rosary to retain a continual attitude of prayer and to remember that life can end at any moment. As this awareness grows, so does one's sense of needing mercy. The Virgin Mary has been closely associated with mercy through the ages, and this association is particularly clear at the hour of death.

Chapter 17

Special Devotions

For many Christians, the idea of praying to Mary might sound inappropriate at best, and idolatrous at worst. However, for millions of Christians around the world, prayers to and with Mary have been an integral part of faith. Some Christians believe that honoring Mary is an essential component of honoring Christ. This chapter will explore the ways that Christians have integrated Marian prayers into their own lives, as well as discuss some of the dilemmas that surround these types of prayers.

To Christ Through Mary

One of the guiding principles of Marian prayers is that they must always find their end in Christ. The Virgin Mary was never intended to be an end herself, but only a path to God. From time to time, concerns have been expressed that some faithful members of the Church have become too focused in praying to Mary and neglected the larger, spiritual picture. The entire context of worship, which is profoundly focused on the person of Christ and his role in the Trinity, in both the Roman Catholic and Eastern Orthodox Churches can help direct the focus of believers and clarify any confusion surrounding Marian prayer.

Complicated Prayer

One of the difficulties some have with idea of praying to Mary is related to the word *pray*. In contemporary usage, the word *pray* is almost always related to intercessions before God. However, if you've ever read Shakespeare, you've probably noticed that *pray* was once used differently as a synonym for *ask*. Similarly, some of the older texts can also be confusing in their use of the word *worship*. An example of this can be found in the marriage service in the old 1692 *Anglican Book of Common Prayer*. After the bride and groom exchanged their vows and as the rings were exchanged, the man would say, "With my body I thee worship." This statement expressed a pledge of honor and love rather than the kind of adoration which is due to God alone.

factum

Writer Jack Kerouac expressed his faith in Mary's prayers in a letter sent in 1963. "I had some stunning thoughts last night . . . as a result of praying to Saint Mary to intercede for me to make me stop being a maniacal drunkard," Kerouac wrote. "So far, every prayer addressed to the Holy Mother has been answered."

All Marian prayer finds its end in Christ. Throughout the centuries, there have been times when Marian prayer became especially pronounced because of historical circumstances. For example, Marian devotion was emphasized within the Roman Catholic Church during the seventeenth century when a distortion about Christ (that he was harsh and impossible to please) caused people to be afraid to pray to him.

One priest, Saint Louis de Mountfort, wanted to help his people learn to pray again, and he encouraged them to pray to Christ through Mary. At this time, especially, Mary seemed more accessible to some people than God. Rather than entirely halting their prayers, these people prayed through Mary to Christ.

Contemporary Devotion

Recently the Virgin Mary has become a subject of popular discussion. With the ever-increasing phenomenon of apparitions of Mary, many modern-day Christians have begun to reconsider her role in their own spirituality. Those who have developed a devotion to Mary testify that this devotion helps deepen, rather than distract from, their own relationship with Christ.

There has always been an important distinction (made in both the Roman Catholic and Eastern Orthodox Churches) between the type of honor given to Mary and the saints, and the honor that is reserved for God alone. In Greek, there are different words for the different types of honor:

- *Latria*
- *Dulia*
- *Hyperdulia*

Latria is the type of worship reserved for God alone, whereas *dulia* implies merely service and reverence. *Hyperdulia*, which is reserved for Mary, is an intensified form of *dulia*, which is commonly used to refer to all the saints.

The following methods of praying to and with Mary must be understood within these contexts. As the Protestant reformer Martin

Luther said, "Mary doesn't ask that we come to her, but through her, to Jesus."

Pilgrimages

When Americans think of the term *pilgrim* they may think of the Mayflower and the Puritans. But historically, pilgrimages were not so much about escaping one's present circumstance as they were about growing spiritually and drawing closer to the past events that continue to shape the lives of the faithful. The pilgrimage concept is prominent in almost every world religion, including Christianity, Judaism, Islam, Hinduism, and Buddhism. Recently, as a response to readers' desires to travel in a more spiritually meaningful way, the online multi-faith publication *Beliefnet* began offering sacred tours to many different parts of the world.

One of the most popular pilgrimage sites continues to be the Holy Land, especially for Jews, Christians, and Muslims. This region has been much loved by pilgrims for millennia. Rich and poor, young and old, and healthy and sick have traveled great distances to walk in the footsteps of their spiritual ancestors.

fallacy

It is fallacy to believe that pilgrimages have only become popular in recent times. Pilgrimages to the Holy Land have been so common historically that by the fourth century, Saint Jerome wrote that so many pilgrims were pouring into the Holy Land that it felt almost as if the entire world were visiting.

In some cases, pilgrimages were very strenuous. The hardships along the way, however, only bolstered the spiritual value of the pilgrimage in the minds of the faithful. Some believed that by taking a difficult earthly journey to a faraway holy site, they were helping ease their transition into the next world. Three of the most popular ancient pilgrimage sites were Jerusalem, Rome, and Santiago de Compostela in Spain (because this city was believed to house the tomb of Saint James the apostle).

Pilgrimages continued to be popular through the eighteenth century, although during the Reformation some of the important European shrines, such as the House of Nazareth in Walsingham, were destroyed. When Catholics were again allowed to worship in England in 1827, much of Walsingham was restored, and an Anglican chapel was built on the site. Walsingham is now considered one of Europe's great ecumenical centers, and it continues to draw pilgrims.

Pilgrimages Today

Recently, pilgrimages have become increasingly common, and much of the current popularity is related to the widespread reports about apparitions of the Virgin Mary and healings associated with the places where she is reported to have appeared.

Marian shrines are visited by people of a wide variety of religious traditions. In some countries, such as Turkey (for a discussion of Mary's House at Ephesus, see Chapter 18) and India, shrines to Mary serve as a bridge between diverse cultures and religions that honor Mary. There are also special organizations that plan "interfaith" pilgrimages for those who would like to come into contact with Marian devotion outside of the boundaries of their own religion.

Seeking Mary

The increasing amount of media attention devoted to the apparitions of the Virgin Mary has helped the global community become aware of some of the most significant Marian shrines. Lourdes, France; Fatima, Portugal; and Vailankanni, India, continue to be popular Marian pilgrimage sites.

Appendix C contains a listing of many popular Marian pilgrimage sites. Also included is guidance about how to plan for a pilgrimage, times of year to visit, and general tips for those who are making a pilgrimage for the first time. If you are intrigued by a pilgrimage site that is not listed in the appendix, consider doing a simple search on the Internet. Most Marian pilgrimage sites have a wealth of online information devoted to them.

Dedications

Many Protestant denominations do not baptize infants. Some of these churches, however, devote services to the "dedication" of infants from the community to God. This idea echoes the Biblical story of Christ being dedicated in the temple as an infant (Luke 2:22–23). Within Christian tradition, it is also believed that the Virgin Mary was brought to the temple and dedicated as an infant.

factum

Even kings went on pilgrimages as a way to prepare for battle or to repent after they had ordered killings. After Thomas Becket, Archbishop of Canterbury, was murdered in Great Britain, Henry II took a pilgrimage as a penance.

This basic premise is helpful when we consider the practice that has been widespread in the Roman Catholic and Eastern Orthodox Churches of dedicating churches and monasteries to the prayers and memories of holy people.

The earliest examples of these dedications are shrines set up over the tombs of martyrs in the times when the imperial Roman authorities persecuted Christians. Even to this day, churches are often dedicated to a saint whose relics are placed within it.

That said, there was always a clear distinction made between the dedication of the church and the one to whom sacrifice was being made in the temple—sacrifice the Eucharist may be offered on behalf of many people, but it is offered only to God and never to a saint. Many times, people, and even whole nations, have been consecrated to the Virgin Mary. Correctly understood, all consecrations have their end in Jesus. Dedicating people or countries to Mary was seen as a way of placing them in the hands of God.

The Rosary

Saying the rosary is primarily a Catholic practice, although some Anglicans, Methodists, and Lutherans have been known to use the rosary as a way of integrating Marian prayer into their lives and contemplating different events from the life of Jesus. Although the practice of praying with beads or stones is quite ancient and is present in many religions, it has a unique role within Christianity.

Early Marian Prayer

Within Christianity, prayers to Mary have existed since at least the second century, and many of the earliest churches were dedicated to the Virgin Mary. The oldest known Marian prayer dates back to at least the fourth century and is still often sung in conjunction with bedtime prayer (the Compline service) in the Eastern Orthodox Church. This prayer is preserved in Greek on a piece of papyrus. The words of this prayer are: "Beneath your compassion, we take refuge, Mother of God. Do not reject our prayer in our necessities, but deliver us from harm, O pure and blessed One."

The rosary may be loosely related to the ancient Jesus Prayer, which is still used widely in the Eastern Orthodox Church. This kind of prayer became popular in early desert monasticism, and was explicitly mentioned by the fifth century when Diodochos of Photiki taught that repeating this prayer could lead to inner stillness.

In its most popular form, the words of the Jesus Prayer are: "Lord Jesus Christ, Son of God, have mercy on me, a sinner." Especially within monastic practice, a small prayer bracelet has been used for keeping count of prayers. This simple prayer is intended to be repeated over and over until it permeates all of life's decisions, thoughts, and actions.

The Origins of the Rosary

According to one legend, the rosary in its present form may have originated with Saint Dominic de Guzman (1170–1221), the founder of the Dominican Order. This legend states that Saint Dominic's devotion to the rosary began as the result of a series of revelations from the Virgin Mary in which she revealed the rosary to him.

This pious legend, however, seems to have little basis in historical fact. The story originated with a Dominican named Alain de la Roche abound two hundred years after Saint Dominic's death. Although the practice of saying the rosary dates back to at least the ninth century, the present form of the rosary dates back to the fifteenth century. In 1562, Pope Pius V issued an official statement about the rosary, in which he detailed the fifteen mysteries that are to meditated upon as a person repeats the prayers of the rosary.

symbolism

According to one medieval legend, as a young monk said Hail Marys, the Virgin Mary was seen taking rosebuds from his lips. She then arranged the rosebuds into a garland and placed them upon her head. *Rosary* means garland or bouquet of roses.

Many believe that saying the rosary will bring them special protection. When the atomic bomb exploded in Hiroshima, Japan, there was a house located just eight blocks (one kilometer) from the spot where the bomb exploded. All of the other houses and buildings in the area were obliterated, and the church that was attached to the house was destroyed. The house, however, survived, along with the eight German Jesuit priests who lived there and prayed the rosary each day. Many scientists continue to be puzzled by the fact that not only did these men survive with only minor injuries, but they all lived many more years without developing radiation sickness or loss of hearing as a result of the exposure.

How the Rosary Works

The rosary is a chain, much like a necklace, of about fifty beads with a crucifix on the end. The beads are broken into sections of ten beads each that are called decades. The decades are separated by larger beads. Each decade corresponds to a different event in the life of Christ, which is taken from the Gospel accounts. Many Roman Catholics believe that the rosary helps them to draw close to Christ and Mary and to enter into the central events in the life of Christ—to effectively integrate these pivotal moments into their own lives.

factum

> The expression "knock on wood" can be traced back to some of the more ancient, primitive rosaries, which used wooden beads. During anxious times, Christians would knock their wooden beads together. Many cultures have "worry beads," which are typically used for non-religious purposes, as a way to keep the hands occupied in times of anxiety.

Saying the Rosary

The first step in saying the rosary is to say the Apostles' Creed, a statement of faith that originated as a baptismal formula in ancient times. Then, for each special bead separating the decades, the Lord's Prayer is said, followed by ten recitations of the Hail Mary (one for each bead in the decade). Then, at the end of each decade, the mystery from the life of Christ is meditated upon. There are four different sets of mysteries that have been prescribed by popes to correspond with different days of the week. Each mystery corresponds to a different phase of Jesus' life. The first set of mysteries is related to the very beginning of Jesus' earthly life. It includes:

- The Annunciation
- The Visitation of Mary with Elizabeth

- The Nativity of Jesus
- The Presentation of Christ in the Temple
- The Finding of Jesus in the Temple

The second set of mysteries is related to Jesus' public ministry. This set includes:

- Jesus' Baptism
- Jesus' First Miracle at Cana
- Jesus' Teaching Related to Repentance and the Kingdom
- The Transfiguration
- The Last Supper

The third set of mysteries is called the Sorrowful Mysteries. It includes:

- Jesus' Agony in the Gethsemane
- The Scourging of Jesus
- The Crowning of Jesus with Thorns
- Jesus' Carrying of the Cross
- The Crucifixion and Death of Jesus

The fourth set is referred to as the Glorious Mysteries. It includes:

- Jesus' Resurrection
- Jesus' Ascension
- The Coming of the Holy Spirit at Pentecost
- Mary's Assumption into Heaven
- The Coronation of Mary and Glory of All the Saints

In 2002, Pope John Paul II proposed an additional, fifth set of "Luminous Mysteries" for the rosary. This set includes:

- The Baptism of the Lord

- The Wedding at Cana
- The Proclamation of the Kingdom of God
- The Transfiguration
- The Institution of the Eucharist

Of these mysteries, some who pray the rosary may simplify their daily prayer by just selecting five mysteries for meditation. Different sets of mysteries may also be prescribed for different days.

discussion question

What is the Hail Mary based on?
The Hail Mary is based on the words from the Annunciation (Luke 1:26–38): "Hail Mary, full of grace, the Lord is with you. Blessed art thou among women, and blessed is the fruit of thy womb, Jesus. Holy Mary, Mother of God, pray for us sinners now and at the hour of our death."

According to Roman Catholic teaching, it is extremely important to pray the rosary in a way that is consistent, intentional, prayerful, and meditative. According to Pope Paul IV, if Catholics do not take time to ponder each mystery with awe, the rosary loses much of its power. It becomes "a body without a soul" and "a mechanical repetition of formulas, counter to the warning of Christ, who said, 'in praying do not heap up empty phrases as the Gentiles do; for they think that they will win a hearing by their many words'" (Pope Paul IV, *Marialis Cultus* 47, citing Matthew 6:7).

Scapulars

Scapulars originated as aprons worn by medieval monks. They were basically large swaths of cloth with a hole for the head, used to protect the monastic habit while the monk was doing manual labor. While scapulars originally had a largely practical function, over time various spiritual meanings became attached to them. In some Roman Catholic orders, they are now considered the most spiritually significant part of the monastic habit.

Saint Simon Stock

One of the traditions associated with the brown scapular of Our Lady of Mount Carmel involves a thirteenth-century saint, Saint Simon Stock, who asked for the Virgin Mary to intercede for his order. According to the story, the Virgin Mary appeared to him in Cambridge, England, on July 16, 1251, with the scapular and offered these words, "Take, beloved son, this scapular of thy order as a badge of my confraternity and for thee and all Carmelites a special sign of grace; whoever dies in this garment will not suffer everlasting fire. It is a sign of salvation, a safeguard in dangers, a pledge of peace of the covenant."

Power and Use of Scapulars

It is a fallacy to ascribe magical powers to scapulars, rosaries, or any other sacred object. Likewise, it is against official Roman Catholic Church doctrine to believe that wearing a brown scapular is a "ticket to heaven." Instead, the scapular is considered a way of dedicating oneself to Jesus and Mary and asking for the ongoing prayers of the Virgin Mary while wearing the scapular. There is an important distinction between magical and sacramental—a sacramental object possesses no power of its own, but is effective through participation in the mystery of Christ.

Scapulars are no longer reserved exclusively for monastic use. Catholics can now obtain smaller versions of the original scapulars. These modified versions look like two strips of cloth that hang over the shoulders with a small square pendant attached on each end. Scapulars are generally connected to specific monastic orders, with lay use being restricted to those associated with that order in a formal way. Those who wear them should be sensitive to the particular intentions of the community in which the particular scapular evolved.

The Use of Scapulars

In lay use, scapulars are to be warn inconspicuously under one's clothing and are often (but not always) made of wool. Laypeople must have their scapulars blessed by their priest, who will pray over the scapular and over the person who is to wear it. This service of dedication is known as the investment. Over time, scapulars wear out and can eventually be replaced with a silver pendant that has the face of Christ on one side and the face of the Virgin Mary on the other.

The scapular plays a significant role in the life of the person who wears it. If an unmarried person wears a scapular, they are expected to remain chaste. Of course, this is the case for all unmarried Catholics, but those who wear a scapular have a special level of accountability because of what they are wearing. The scapular serves as a reminder to continually strive to live a faithful life and to persevere until the end. Many who wear the scapular believe that it is a helpful reminder of God's loving care and protection, as well as a concrete way to remember that the Virgin Mary continually intercedes for them.

A Word for Protestants

Many of these devotional practices may seem foreign if you are not from a Roman Catholic or Orthodox background. Although Mary is an integral part of the worship and prayer life of these churches, the intercessions of the saints make up a small (but significant) portion of the whole spiritual life.

Especially for those who are not raised in these churches but come to them later in life, the veneration of Mary can be a great struggle. As prominent Roman Catholic writer Fr. Richard John Neuhaus wrote in a forward to the book *Mary: A Catholic-Evangelical Debate*, "For many of us who entered into full communion with the Catholic Church later in life, Marian doctrine and devotion was at one time a problem. I daresay that for most of us, and certainly for me, Marian doctrine and devotion has become an exciting and never-ending discovery of deeper dimensions of Christian fidelity."

Many who find their way into the Roman Catholic and Eastern Orthodox Churches later in life find that encountering Mary is a long process that continually calls them to leave behind their own contemporary assumptions about her and to grow and transform as they come to know Mary as she has been loved through the ages.

Pope Paul IV wrote, "When the liturgy turns its gaze either to the primitive Church or to the Church of our day it always finds Mary. In the primitive Church she is seen praying with the apostles; in our own day, she is actively present and the Church desires to live the mystery of Christ with her" (from his statement, *Marialis Cultus*, 1974).

This ancient Christian belief that Mary is present in the Church both yesterday and today is demonstrated through the ongoing devotional practices associated with her. Contemporary Christians, however, may be tempted to dismiss many of these more ancient practices as superfluous, belonging to another place and time. But it is best to retain a respectful silence until one has the opportunity to grasp the deeper idea behind the practice. C. S. Lewis described the temptation to dismiss the beliefs and practices from other times as "chronological snobbery."

Especially within the ever-evolving Christian world, we may be inclined to think in terms of an ongoing revelation where the faithful are always growing closer to the truth. We may imagine that from our place in history we know more than those who went before us. But according to Lewis, this kind of thinking is a grave error. While it can be equally dangerous to believe the opposite fallacy—that all that is ancient is somehow right or superior—it is certainly wise to listen to the voices of those who have gone before us and to see if their experiences might speak to and enrich our own spiritual lives. This is especially important when we think about how Christians in earlier times expressed their faith and their devotion to the saints.

Chapter 18
Mary and Islam

Some people are surprised to discover that the Virgin Mary is esteemed within Islam. One of the longest chapters of the Muslim Holy Book, the Koran, is devoted to Mary (Miriam, or *Maryam* in Arabic). For centuries, Muslims have visited Marian shrines, witnessed apparitions, and named their female children after Maryam, who, according to the Koran, achieved a level of perfection that no other woman attained.

Common Ground

In our day it is increasingly important to find common ground on which people from a variety of religious traditions can communicate. This is a particularly urgent concern in light of the current tensions between Christianity and Islam. It is often a struggle to find a common language and terminology between the two religions, but many scholars believe that the common ground can be found through Mary, who is loved and venerated within both religions, although many aspects of devotion to Mary in Islam do not parallel the way she is venerated within Christianity.

factum

There are currently about one billion professed Muslims in the world who adhere to the teachings and ritual observances set forth in their sacred book, the Koran, and elucidated by their prophet, Muhammad. They refer to God as Allah and reject the Christian understanding of the Trinity.

Islam was founded on the Arabian Peninsula during the seventh century and is based on the revelations of Allah to Muhammad. The Prophet Muhammad taught that Islam was the final religion, building upon and perfecting the teachings of the prophets who went before: Abraham, Moses, and Jesus.

This common story begins to diverge when Abraham becomes the father of two sons, Ishmael and Isaac. One of the most heartbreaking and beautiful stories in the Jewish and Christian tradition is the story of Abraham, who (according to the Old Testament) was told to sacrifice his son Isaac, whom he dearly loved. In the Old Testament account, Abraham and Isaac travel to Moriah for the sacrifice.

Isaac carries wood on his back and notes with some concern that they've got the wood, they've got the fire, but "where is the lamb for the offering?" You can almost hear Abraham sigh when he replies, "God himself will provide a lamb." In the end, God does just as Abraham has promised, but not in the way that Abraham had imagined—he prevents Abraham from killing Isaac and he provides a ram caught in a nearby thicket instead.

The Koran does not explicitly state which son was to be sacrificed, but according to most Islamic commentators, it is Ishmael, Abraham's son by Hagar, who is chosen for the sacrifice. Just as Abraham lowers the dagger to sacrifice Ishmael, the dagger turns to wax in his hand, and God prevents the sacrifice. Like the Old Testament account, God provides a ram in Ishmael's stead.

According to Islamic belief, Ishmael went on to become "the Father of all Arabs," the first Prophet to preach and write of the one true God, and the first to practice his prayers in a worthy manner. Ishmael's prominent status within Islam is especially interesting because the Old Testament account doesn't offer too many details about what ultimately happened to Ishmael after he and Hagar were sent away.

discussion question

What ultimately happened to Ishmael?
According to Genesis 21:18 when Sarah mistreats Hagar and Hagar departs for the first time, God tells Hagar that Ishmael will be the father of a great nation. When Abraham dies, Ishmael returns and reports that he has become the father of twelve sons who reside east and north of Egypt. This geographical location is in present-day Saudi Arabia.

While most countries have a significant Muslim presence, many of the countries of Western Europe have been experiencing particularly rapid growth in their Muslim populations. Muslims make up a majority of the population of the Middle East, North Africa, and Indonesia. Because of the increasingly large Muslim population worldwide, it is helpful to have at least a working understanding of this global religion.

Mary in the Koran

According to Islamic belief, the Koran is the word of God, revealed to Muhammad through a series of visitations from the Angel Jibreel (or Gabriel), which took place over a period of twenty-three years. Muhammad memorized many of these revelations and they were subsequently written down by his successors: Abu Bakr, Omar, and Othman. Islamic teachers have taught that the complete Koran existed in heaven before the Angel Jibreel revealed it to Muhammad. The Koran was completed by A.D. 656.

Even the original story of how Islam was founded holds within it some fascinating parallels between the Virgin Mary and Muhammad. According to Islamic thought, both Muhammad and the Virgin Mary were visited by the Angel Gabriel. Both were told that they would become bearers of the word of God, responsible for bringing messages of great significance into the world. Within Islam, Christ is viewed as both prophet and messenger, but not as the Son of God.

One of the most significant differences between Christian and Islamic teachings on the persons of Mary and Jesus are related to the Christian title Theotokos, or Mother of God, which is a term never used in Islam because Muslims do not believe that Jesus was God incarnate. Another significant difference is that Muslims do not believe that Jesus was actually crucified, only that he appeared to be crucified. Islam also objects to the use of religious imagery, so the portrayal of the Virgin Mary in icons has been rejected by Islamic teachers.

This initial parallel between the two accounts may help clarify why Mary holds a significant position within Islam. Many scholars have noted that the portrait of Mary in the Koran is more vibrant and detailed than the portraits in the Gospels. No other woman in the Koran has an entire chapter named after her, not even two extremely significant women—Eve, who is considered within Islam,

Judaism, and Christianity to be "the mother of all living" (Genesis 3:20), or Hagar, the mother of Ishmael, who was to become "the Father of all Arabs." The Virgin Mary offers a pivotal position in the text, and many references are made about her and her life.

symbolism

The word *Islam* means "submission," and Muslims are those who submit to God. Mary is praised within the Koran for her obedience to God. It may be through Mary's perfect obedience that she is seen as a model of submission.

According to the Koran, Mary's perfection began from the moment of her conception. Although this idea seems to echo the Roman Catholic Dogma of the Immaculate Conception, it should be noted that Muslims to do not believe in the Immaculate Conception. They do not ascribe to the same perspective on Original Sin, although they, like the Catholics and Eastern Orthodox do believe that Mary's special grace began at her conception.

The Koran also supports the idea of the virgin birth of Christ, and offers some details about Mary's early life that are not mentioned in the Gospels but clearly parallel some of the details given in some of the extra-Biblical texts.

Some Christian scholars have said that the contrast between the Gospels and the Koran is that the Koran seems to exalt Mary, while the New Testament is generally restrained in its attitude toward Mary. This may be reflective of the intention of the Gospel writers to emphasize the life and teachings of Jesus.

According to Christian belief, the central moment in the life of Mary occurred at the Annunciation, when she said "yes" to God. This moment is significant enough that it also occupies a prominent space in the Koran, which offers many parallel events with variations on the details from Luke's Gospel.

The Annunciation in the Koran

The Koran, like the Gospel of Luke, portrays Mary as fearful when the angel initially comes to her. Both accounts show the angel offering comfort and reassurance. In the Koran the angel says, "I am but a messenger, come from thy Lord to give thee a boy most pure" (19:19).

Like the Gospel accounts of the Annunciation, Mary responds with uncertainty, "How shall I have a son whom no mortal has touched, neither have I been unchaste?"

The angel's response both parallels and diverges from the Gospel accounts. "Even so thy Lord has said: Easy it is for me; and that we may appoint him as a sign unto men and a mercy from us; it is a thing decreed" (19:21).

The angel's response is especially interesting, because it shows where Muslim and Christian thought diverge in relation to Jesus. In Luke's Gospel, Mary is told that the Holy Spirit will overshadow her and she shall conceive the son of God. This statement is never made in the Koran. This significant omission speaks to the different views between Islam and Christianity about the person of Jesus.

The House of Imran

The House of Imran is a traditional title for one of the surahs, or books, of the Koran. It is named after Mary's father, Imran, whose name can be translated into English as John. This might be a little confusing for English speakers who are used to referring to Mary's father as Joachim, if they speak of him at all.

This chapter offers some fascinating ideas about Mary's conception and early childhood. Some Christian scholars have suggested that it may have been influenced by some of the extra-Biblical stories of Jesus' life that were common at the time. There is some evidence that suggests Muhammad had contact with Christians who would have been familiar with this kind of material. Like the Koran, many of these accounts give an exuberant, detailed account of Mary's conception and early childhood.

factum

Muslims sometimes refer to Christians and Jews as "People of the Book." This statement affirms the common heritage of these three faiths, which all claim fidelity to the God who spoke to Abraham and Moses.

In this surah, when Mary's mother Anna conceived a child, Anna responded with great joy. When she dedicated her child to Allah, she must have imagined that he was to be a boy and that he had a bright future ahead of him as a religious teacher or scholar. But when the child was born, she was shocked to see that she had given birth to a baby girl. Anna expresses her disappointment but then goes on to say that "Allah knows best," and commends her child, as well as her child's future offspring to Allah's protection.

According to the Koran, Allah honors Anna's unusual request, and allows Mary to be raised in the temple and fed by angels. Mary is given to the care of Zachariah. Zachariah is also mentioned in the Gospels as the husband of Elizabeth, and as a priest.

As Mary matures in age, she also matures in virtue. When Zachariah comes to visit her in the temple, he is consistently surprised to see that food has been miraculously provided for Mary. This miraculous provision possibly echoes Old Testament stories about "manna from heaven" and further sets Mary apart as one who is special in the eyes of Allah.

Mary among the Shiites

The Shiite branch of Islam is the second largest. According to the Shiites, Mary is more than a holy woman. Shiite belief has created some interesting parallels between Mary and Fatima (who was the daughter of the Prophet Muhammad). Although the Koran denies that Jesus was crucified, Fatima's two sons were assassinated. Both

Mary and Fatima are considered "suffering mothers." Also, just as Islamic belief puts forth the idea that Jesus was born of a virgin, within the Koran, Fatima, the wife of Ali, is also a virgin when she conceives her two sons. Another interesting parallel between Fatima and Mary is that within this tradition, Fatima comes over time to be viewed as "the protector of the persecuted."

Mary among the Sufis

Sufism is commonly considered the "mystical path" of Islam. Within Sufism, there is strong emphasis both on contemplation and action. One of the accounts of Mary from the Koran offers a text that seems to express something valuable about Sufism. In this text, Mary goes to a far-off place to give birth. While she is lamenting her condition, Allah instructs her to shake a palm tree so that ripe figs will fall to the ground for her.

Some have interpreted this passage to mean that not only must we pray, but we must be active as well. This idea is very much relevant to Sufism. Within Sufism, Mary is a model of the contemplative and active life. As George H. Tavard wrote in *The Thousand Faces of the Virgin Mary,* this passage is "an invitation to work actively rather than just wait for Allah to do something. Thus Miriam [which is Mary's name in the Koran] is a model of obedience and action in the service of Allah, no less than of faith, prayer and contemplation." According to Tavard, in Mary, the Sufis find inspiration, because her life was a clear expression of both obedience and action.

Healing Fountains

Another area of common ground between historical Judaism, Christianity and Islam is the ways in which all three religions "of the Book" relate to water. All three share a sensitivity to the theological significance of water, and water has been present in many significant rituals belonging to each of these religions.

They all teach that water was one of the principal elements in the creation of the world. All three understood that both life and death come through water and that we are inextricably dependant upon God (or Allah) to provide water for us.

Water in Judaism

Within Judaism, water is present in many rituals, most notably the purifying ritual bath called the mikvah, which is prescribed for women seven days after menstruation. The waters used in the mikvah must come from a natural, free-flowing source and must not have been carried by human hands. Women immerse themselves in the Mikvah not only to become ritually pure, but also as way of being spiritually renewed and cleansed before they return to their husbands, following a period of about two weeks of abstinence.

Within Judaism, hands are ritually washed as part of preparation for the Shabbat, or "Sabbath" meal, which begins at sundown on Friday. Within Christianity, water plays an equally profound role. Christians are initiated into the faith by immersing themselves (or being sprinkled by) the waters of baptism, which also offer cleansing and renewal. Clergy in the Roman Catholic, Eastern Orthodox, and Anglican Churches ritually wash their hands before they consecrate the Eucharist.

symbolism

Within Christianity, water is deeply connected with Christ, who walked on water, promised to the woman at the well that he contained "the living waters," and when, according to Christian teaching, he was stretched upon the cross and a sword pierced his side, both blood and water flowed from him.

Water in Islam

Within Islam, water is also of central importance—offering life, sustenance, and purification. According to the Koran, water existed before heaven or earth (this belief brings to mind the Genesis account where the Spirit of God hovers over the water at the creation of the world).

The Koran recognizes the essential value of water for life and the way our relationship to water reminds us of our utter dependence upon the mercy of God. According to the Koran, "He sends down saving rain, for them, when they have lost all hope and spreads abroad his mercy" (Al-Furqan 25:48).

Ritual Cleansing

Within Islam, water is not only considered a principal element of life but is also an essential aspect of ritual purity. Within observant Islam, the faithful pray at five appointed times daily. Each call to prayer begins with a ritual washing, as described in the Koran, "O you who believe, when you rise to pray, wash your faces and your hands as far as the elbow, wipe your heads, and your feet to the ankle. If you are polluted cleanse yourselves . . . God does not wish to burden you but desires to purify you" (Al-Mai'dah 5:6).

Within Islam, a person who does not cleanse himself before prayer will have their prayers rejected. Like the Jewish prescription of a very specific natural source of water for the mikvah, Muslim teaching is specific about what water is acceptable for use in pre-prayer cleansing.

factum

Suitable water for cleansing before Muslim prayer must be pure (meaning that it can not be mixed with any other substances). Water from both moving sources such as rain, taps, streams, rivers, and still sources like lakes and ponds, may be used for ritual cleansing.

Because water holds such a significant place in all three religions, it is not surprising that within Islam, there is a connection between the Virgin Mary (or Miriam as she is referred to in the

Koran) and water. According to the Koran, while Mary was in labor she took refuge under a palm tree and said, "Ah! Would that I had died before this! Would that I had been a thing forgotten and out of sight!" but a voice called to her from beneath the palm tree, "Do not anguish, for the Lord your God has created a rivulet beneath you, and shake toward yourself the trunk of the palm tree. It will let fall ripe dates upon you" (19:23–25).

This passage, which states that there will be a "rivulet" beneath her, is interesting in light of the role of water in stories about Mary. In another place in the Koran, it says that Jesus is born from the "waters of Mary." This is an allusion to the central role of water in birth.

According to the Christian tradition, Mary was at a well when the angel appeared to her. Also notable is the fact that many Marian shrines around the world contain water or wells that many believe contain healing properties. Because Mary holds a special place within Islam, Muslims often visit Marian shrines and drink of the wells. This is especially the case at the House of Mary in Ephesus, Turkey, a site that is arguably more often visited by Muslims than Christians.

The House of Mary

In Ephesus, Turkey, there is a small stone structure set high on a hill. This small structure is believed to be the place where Mary lived her final earthly days with the Apostle John. This tradition is partially based on the account from the Gospels when Jesus calls out to John from the cross to ask him to care for his mother. Christian tradition has taken these words to mean that John quite literally took Mary into his own home and cared for her until her dying day.

According to Christian tradition, John traveled to Ephesus after the death of Christ. It was very likely in this place that he made his home. Also, some say that the first known church dedicated to the Virgin Mary was located in Ephesus, and during the first few centuries of Christianity, churches were only named after saints in cities where that saint had personally resided. It is also notable that the most significant church council related to the title of the Virgin Mary was held at Ephesus in 431, where the name Theotokos was formally recognized as a proper way to refer to the Virgin Mary and to preserve the practice of venerating her.

Rediscovering the House of Mary

Another interesting story related to this house is that some Roman Catholic priests were led to this very site (which was then in ruins) through the revelations of a German Roman Catholic nun, Sister Catherine Anne Emmerich, who both experienced the stigmata and reported having visions of the Virgin Mary in which the exact location of the house at Ephesus was described. When the priests followed the directions set forth by the Roman Catholic nun, they quickly discovered a small stone building in the exact location and formation she had described.

discussion question

Do both Muslims and Christians use the term *pilgrimage* to mean the same thing?
Although in this book the term *pilgrimage* is used, Muslims reserve that word for the great hajj—the journey to Mecca. They generally wouldn't feel comfortable with the more general definition of *pilgrimage* used here.

This house has been preserved and is currently under the care of the Franciscans, a Roman Catholic order, and it receives more than a half a million visitors annually. Many of these visitors are Muslim, who come to the shrine to pray and to drink from the well there, which many believe contains healing properties.

Christian and Muslim Pilgrimage

Pilgrims often like to leave something of themselves behind at holy pilgrimage sites to show that they have visited a place personally.

In many cases, pilgrims will leave behind a small swath of cloth. At the House of Mary, though, there is no place to attach pieces of cloth, so thousands of pieces of chewing gum have been left behind by those who have prayed at the well.

The House of Mary in Ephesus is a very tangible reminder that Mary plays an important role in both Christianity and Islam. Not only do more Muslims visit this holy site than any other religious group, there is also a small chapel that is part of the house and is reserved for Muslim prayer.

The image of Christians and Muslims praying beside each other at this holy site has profound implications for those who only see the areas where Islam and Christianity diverge, who focus on the very real tensions between the two religions without taking note of the authentic common ground. If there is any common ground within Christianity and Islam, a place of peace and prayer amid the tensions of our modern world it is most likely to be found in Ephesus, in the house where the Virgin Mary lived as a faithful model for both religions.

Important Distinctions

Although much has been made of similarities between Marian thought within Christianity and Islam, it is important to note that there are significant differences. Earlier in this chapter it was mentioned that the Muslims do not believe in the Immaculate Conception. This difference means that Muslims have a radically different view of the fall that occurred in the Garden of Eden. They do not share the Roman Catholic perspective that sin was passed on to all through conception but that the Virgin Mary was the exception to this rule. Likewise, within Islam, the Virgin Mary was never viewed as "a second Eve" as she often is in the writings of the church fathers.

It is also important to realize that although the Koran does teach that the Virgin Mary was a virgin, her virginal conception is viewed as just one of the miracles associated with her. There is no special spiritual significance attached to the fact that she was a virgin.

factum

Because of the idea of total dedication to God, celibacy has often been understood as a "foretaste of the kingdom" within Christian tradition. Islam (and most forms of Judaism as well) does not share this perspective and has no special theology surrounding celibacy.

It is also important to realize that the Virgin Mary is just one among many models of female holiness within Islam. Most of the models of female holiness were not celibate but married, such as the Prophet Muhammad's first wife Khadija, his daughter Fatima, and Asiya (who was the wife of the pharaoh in the story of Moses). Of these women, only one of them was unmarried.

Although the Virgin Mary is seen as a model within Islam, Fatima, Muhammad's daughter, is sometimes viewed as "the greater Mary." Some Christian commentators, however, have noted with interest that some of the most significant apparitions of the Virgin Mary of all time occurred at Fatima, Portugal, a name that is especially significant to Muslims. Likewise, Fatima is sometimes referred to as the Mother of Sorrows, a name that has also been ascribed to the Virgin Mary within Catholicism, because she is viewed as the patron saint of all who grieve.

Although it is valuable to explore the common ground between Christianity and Islam, a respectful dialogue between the two religions requires an honest assessment of the distinctions between Christianity and Islam. Some important differences exist in the way Mary is venerated in each tradition. Nevertheless, a common respect for Mary may well be an important bridge between the world's two largest religions.

Chapter 19

Mary and the Goddess

Although the Virgin Mary was never considered a goddess in the Eastern or Western Churches, her image reflects many of the goddesses from ancient religions. If the Virgin Mary seems similar to these goddesses, it is because within Christianity there are elements borrowed from ancient religions. This chapter will explore the similarities, as well as the differences, between the Virgin Mary and a variety of goddesses from ancient religions.

Baptizing the Goddess?

Historically, there has been some tension between ancient pagan religions and Christianity, and this surfaces in certain legends about the Virgin Mary. These legends, whether they are historically accurate or not, offer an interesting glimpse into the mindset of the early Christians, who responded to the interplay between Mary and the goddesses with a good deal of caution. In most of these tales, Christianity proclaims itself to be the fulfillment of everything that was good about the earlier pagan beliefs.

Christian Parallels

Although Christianity was built on the foundation of Judaism, it was not isolated from ancient pagan beliefs or the ideas of the ancient philosophers. There are many parallels between Christianity and other, more ancient religions. One way these parallels come out is through iconography. Christian iconography has many stylistic parallels, both in Roman (pre-Christian) Egypt, in the neighboring religions of the Ancient Near East, and in Hinduism and Buddhism. The way Christianity adapted these and other forms of religious art, teaching, and practice is significant and speaks also to what is unique within Christianity.

discussion question

Where does the term *pagan* come from?
The term *pagan* refers to the people of the countryside. Historically, Christianity spread more quickly through the cities and towns, and took longer to permeate the rural areas. The religion of the country dwellers was called *paganism*—a loose term that denotes a wide variety of natural religious practices.

Many historians have pointed to a resemblance between the Virgin Mary shown in Eastern Orthodox iconography and the ancient goddess Isis. Likewise, even today, some Greek churches have icons of the ancient philosophers just inside the front entrance of their churches. According to Greek belief, the teachings of these philosophers helped prepare the minds of the people to receive Christianity.

One of the ancient legends about the Virgin Mary vividly expresses the tension between pagan religion and Christian belief. This legend is related to the Greek peninsula called Mount Athos, or the Holy Mountain. Mount Athos is a secluded, forested place where over 3,000 monks reside in twenty large monasteries.

Although Mount Athos is now seen as a great Christian center of monasticism, it was not always specifically Christian, but it was historically viewed as a deeply spiritual place. One of the great authors of Greek mythology, Homer, mentioned this mountain in his writings as one of the dwelling places of the Greek gods Zeus and Apollo before they moved to Mount Olympus.

According to this legend, because of the sacred history associated with Mount Athos, pagan hermits once inhabited the local caves. In A.D. 49 the Virgin Mary was sailing to visit her friend Lazarus, when her boat lost course. She was divinely led to a safe bay of Mount Athos. As she approached the mountain she looked up and according to legend, said, "This mountain is holy ground. Let this be my portion. Let me here remain."

As she stepped onto shore, a thunderous crash shook the mountain and the statues from the old pagan shrines toppled over. One of the statues declared that he was a false idol. According to this legend, the Virgin Mary then baptized the pagan hermits living on the mountain. Thus began the Christian history of Mount Athos, although Mount Athos did not become a well-known monastic site until many centuries later.

The Holy Mountain has since become the greatest monastic center in the Eastern Christian world. According to legend, the Virgin Mary was the last woman to ever set foot on the mountain. To this day, women are not allowed to visit the monasteries on Mount Athos, although they are welcome to visit sister monasteries located nearby.

factum

Just as the story of Mount Athos describes a loud thundering sound that caused the statues to topple, there is a well-documented earthquake that took place in Northern Greece in A.D. 49, the same year that, according to legend, the Virgin Mary visited Athos.

Architecture and Integration

Monasteries, churches, and shrines to Mary are often built on sites that were once central within ancient religions. This desire to build on the literal foundations of other religions expresses the ways in which Christianity sought to integrate those elements of the more ancient religions that were compatible with Christianity.

By building churches, shrines, or monasteries on these ancient holy sites, the Church was able to "baptize" certain elements of these ancient religions, as well as provide a bridge and a sense of continuity between the two religions.

One of the most interesting examples of a Christian church being built on a site that was already viewed as sacred within the minds of the local people occurred in Mexico during the visitations of Our Lady of Guadalupe. According to reports of this apparition, when the Virgin Mary appeared to Juan Diego, she requested that a church be built on a hill that was viewed as one of the dwelling places of an ancient Aztec goddess.

Another place where a similar phenomenon occurred was in the ancient city of Ephesus, Turkey. Ephesus was one of the ancient centers of worship of the goddess Diana, but it ultimately became a significant city for Christianity as well.

The New Testament book of Ephesians was written as a letter to the Christians dwelling there. Christianity had had a rocky start in Ephesus, however, because of the prominence of the goddess Diana in that location. When Paul preached in Ephesus, the metal workers who created statues of Diana heckled him, because they feared that if he brought Christianity to Ephesus, they would lose their livelihoods. Ultimately, their worst fears were realized, as Ephesus eventually became home to many Christians.

The temple dedicated to Diana was destroyed in about A.D. 400. Soon afterward, a new church was built in Ephesus, which was the first church dedicated to the Virgin Mary. When the Council at Ephesus declared in A.D. 431 that it would be right and proper to call the Virgin Mary Theotokos, those in the streets responded with enthusiasm. Just as they had once marched through the streets singing the praises of Diana, they now shouted, "Praised be the Theotokos."

The title Theotokos, which can be translated as "God-bearer" or "The One Who Gave Birth to God" connected Mary to the divine in a unique way. Yet, it was also at this council that official statements were made about how Mary was supposed to be viewed—with great respect, love, and reverence, but not as an object of worship.

Parallels Between Mary and the Goddesses

Although she was not to be worshiped as a goddess, there are some strong parallels between Mary and some of the ancient goddesses. In many ways, the Virgin Mary fits the type of woman who is described in the tales of the ancient goddesses. Many of them are referred to as *parthenos*, which means "virgin." Many of these *parthenos* goddesses give birth to a child who is to suffer. Like Mary, they are impregnated by a divine being (or they become pregnant within themselves using their own supernatural powers). These goddesses are often shown holding this sacrificial child, an image that is certainly familiar to those who have seen icons or statues of the Virgin Mary holding her infant Christ, who is destined to suffer for the whole world.

One of the images of the ancient goddess Isis seems to express this particularly well. The poet Lucius Apuleius's fictional story *The Golden Ass* includes the story of an apparition of Isis. In this story, a young man in distress runs to the seashore, prays to Isis, and falls asleep. While he is sleeping, he sees a gloriously beautiful woman rising from the sea before him with stars and a moon on her cloak. The woman begins to speak to him, telling him that she is the mother of all, and the queen of the dead and the immortals. She says that she is known by many names but her true name is Queen Isis and that she has come in response to his prayers. In this passage, the parallels between the Virgin Mary and the goddess Isis are startling.

In many depictions of the Virgin Mary, she has stars on her cloak, is often called Our Lady of the Sea, and is invoked to protect sailors. In this passage, Isis comes in response to intercessions, just as Mary is reported to sometimes come to those who seek her support in times of distress. The symbolism of the moon on Isis's cloak also speaks to the parallels between Isis and Mary—as Mary is also associated with the moon. In the Tilma of Guadalupe and the image of the woman from Revelations 12, she is shown standing upon the moon; and at the apparitions that occurred at Fatima and Medjugorje, lunar miracles are reported to have occurred.

Archetype of the Eternal Feminine

The renowned psychologist Carl Jung often talked about the archetypes that appear in the collective unconscious. Some have applied his "archetype of the eternal feminine" to the Virgin Mary in light of the psychological parallels between her role within Christianity and the role goddesses played in other religious contexts.

The Virgin Mary brought a female face to the Christian discussion of the divine. Although she was not a goddess, her exalted role within Christianity may have helped those who worked closely with the earth or worshipped goddesses to feel more at home within Christianity.

Another connection between Christianity and paganism is related to the dating of the great Christian feasts—Christmas and Easter. These holy days were set on days that had a universal cosmological significance and would have held a special meaning for the ancient pagans.

Christmas is commemorated just after the winter solstice, which is the darkest day of the year. As the hours of daylight begin to increase again, so also the light that comes into the world in Jesus begins our shift out of darkness. Similarly, the ancient formula for determining the time of Easter is to celebrate it on the first Sunday after the first full moon following the vernal (spring) equinox. At this time, spring is in full bloom, and life comes to reign again upon the earth.

symbolism

These lines from an ancient Celtic folk prayer offer a glimpse into how Christian symbols are mingled with the natural world through Mary: "The Virgin most excellent of face, Jesus more surpassing white than the snow, She like the moon rising over the hills, He like the sun on the peaks of the mountains."

These Christian feasts follow the natural rhythms of the earth. They suggest an earthly element in Christianity that is often obscured in the modern, post-industrial world. This earthly element of spirituality also offers a hint of why the worship of feminine goddesses might have held such an appeal in the ancient world and in the modern world as well, as many begin to hunger for a closer connection to the earth.

Because women were able to give birth and their menstrual patterns followed the cycles of the moon, ancient cultures naturally drew connections between motherhood and the earth. The soil, especially, was often equated with fertility. Just as women were able to weather seasons and bring life into the world, the soil was valued because of its ability to nurture seeds and bring life to fruition.

Black Madonnas

Some of the images that most directly connect the Virgin Mary to the soil are the Black Madonna images. Sometimes when the term

Black Madonna is used, people think of the famed Polish icon of the Virgin Mary (detailed in Chapter 12) that has become black through years of exposure to soot and the elements.

However the Black Madonna does not only describe a single icon but an entire school of imagery that encompasses many icons and statues of the Virgin Mary and child. All of them have dark skin.

While it used to be widely believed that these images had darkened (like the Polish icon) because of exposure to the elements, it now seems likely that many of the images were created dark to begin with for very specific reasons that would have expressed something unique about Mary.

factum

In the Middle Ages, many people came to revere the Black Madonna images for their miraculous powers. Some communities even decided to paint their statues black in the hopes that they could attract more miracles to their own communities.

The Black Madonna statues became especially prominent during the Middle Ages. Some of the most beautiful and poignant of them are located in France and can be viewed to this day.

Many of these statues have special legends associated with them. One of the most common is that they were often found in natural settings, sometimes in caves, sometimes near rivers where they might been seen as providing safety for those crossing over the waters. When Christians found these small statues, they would often attempt to carry them to suitable places for building a church. As soon as the Christians turned away from the statues of the Black Madonnas, however, the statues would disappear and would be later found back in their original locations. This disappearing act would be repeated multiple times until the Christians would finally resign themselves to the fact that statues could not be moved. Ultimately, these Christians were forced to build small chapels around the statues in their natural habitats.

discussion question

How are Black Madonna statues similar to Eastern icons?
Black Madonna statues share many qualities with Eastern icons. In them, the Virgin Mary holds the infant Christ and seems to be gazing out from behind him with a look of timeless compassion. She does not smile, but she does not weep, either. Like her image in icons, she seems to be beyond emotions and sentimentality. Her gaze is steady and unrelenting.

The Meaning of the Black Madonna

The darkness of the Virgin Mary's skin has had many different meanings attached to it throughout the years. While some say that the darkness of her skin is merely a result of exposure to the elements, others suggest that the darkness of her skin is suggestive of her ability to identify with many different ethnic groups—this belief would certainly echo many of the apparitions in which Mary was reported to have appeared in familiar guise, with a face and dress recognizable to the local people. This can be seen, for example, in the case in Guadalupe when she appeared to an Aztec as an Aztec.

Still others point to a relationship between the color of the Virgin Mary's skin and the color of the soil. This idea finds echoes in both Christian and pagan belief. The Virgin Mary was often linked to soil and gardens both in the Eastern Church and in the medieval period. The darker skin on some images of Mary may also reflect her Middle Eastern heritage.

In the fourth century, Saint Ephrem the Syrian said that Mary was the soil on which Christ the sun could shine on the world and humanity. This image expressed how she, rooted in the earth as all humans are, was illuminated by her encounter with Christ.

Mingling Legends

Increasingly, as devotion to Mary grew, some of the properties that people once ascribed to pagan goddesses began to be connected to the Virgin Mary. It is also likely that in cultures where pagan beliefs were deeply rooted in the local people, legends surrounding Mary may have mingled with pagan beliefs. This mingling was a continual source of concern for the Church, as it tried to cleanse the beliefs that were incompatible with Christianity while still meeting the needs of those who required a bridge between their pagan beliefs and Christianity.

symbolism

The Black Madonna imagery would have been easily understood within the pagan context, where black was connected to fertility and life while white was connected to death. This symbolic color scheme was an exact reversal of the symbolism widely held among medieval Christians, in which black symbolized death and white symbolized life.

As Christianity spread throughout Europe, petitions that would have once been directed at gods or goddesses sometimes were redirected toward the Virgin Mary. Myths and legends about gods and goddesses that would have once captivated the hearts of the local people were replaced by legends and stories about Mary and the saints.

One of these stories, in particular, would have helped draw a connection between Mary and the fecundity of the earth. This legend was connected to the story of Joseph, Mary, and Jesus' journey into Egypt.

According to the Biblical account, the Holy Family had to flee Bethlehem because of the "slaughter of the innocents" in which

King Herod sought to kill Jesus by sending soldiers to kill every male child in the region who was two years old or under. The Holy Family fled in order to protect Jesus, but it was most likely a perilous, frightening journey for them.

According to one of the medieval tales related to this journey, as the Holy Family passed one Egyptian farmer's field, Mary made the entire crop grow instantly. She did this both to bless the farmer, but also to confuse the soldiers who might have been pursuing her. Should the soldiers come by the farmer's field and ask him if he'd seen the Holy Family pass by, he could report, quite honestly, that he'd only seen the Holy Family just when he'd planted his field.

Gnosticism and Femininity

Gnosticism was a term used to describe a popular teaching within some early Christian circles. According to this teaching, which was ultimately condemned by the church, spirit and matter were utterly separated from each other. The Gnostics viewed the body as evil and the spirit as good and pure.

Although the Christian Church officially condemned Gnosticism, it is interesting to consider certain tendencies within Gnosticism in relation to the ways the Gnostics viewed femininity. Like Saint Paul who said that within Christ there was "no separation of Male and Female," the Gnostics took this idea to dramatic extremes, believing that as women became holy they became "like men."

This idea was related to the overarching belief that gender did not matter. The Gnostics thought that men were naturally more tied to the spiritual world while women were more linked to the physical world because of their menstrual cycle and the ability to give birth. Within this context, both men and women had to abandon their physical selves in order to become fully spiritual beings.

These views are interesting to consider in light of the Virgin Mary, because she was so fully feminine. She is not glorified for being "like a man" but for doing the thing that only women can do—giving birth to a child. Her greatness was directly connected to her femininity.

What's Different about the Virgin Mary?

One of the ancient dilemmas associated with the Virgin Mary has to do with the ways in which some cultures may have viewed her as a goddess. While this view is not compatible with official Christian teaching, the parallels between the Virgin Mary and some of the ancient goddess are strong enough that one can easily imagine the ways in which people may have conflated the Virgin Mary with some of the ancient goddesses.

But Mary's life can easily be separated from that of a goddess because she was never viewed as powerful, apart from her relationship with Christ. All of her strength and goodness came from her loving obedience to God, the way in which she let herself become a vessel of grace.

Mary is also distinct from the goddesses because all of her life pointed to someone else—to helping the story of her son come to fruition in the world. Her life was deeply rooted in both earthly and heavenly realities. She struggled in the way that all humans do, while remaining chiefly concerned with the purposes of God on this earth.

The Virgin Mary's ability to embrace the divine allowed her to become more and more like God, to be transformed by grace, while still remaining rooted in this earth—still connected to the soil from which she was formed.

factum

The fourteenth-century Saint Catherine of Siena said, "God Speaks: You see the gentle loving word born in a stable while Mary was on a journey, to show you, a pilgrim, how you should be constantly reborn in the stable of self-knowledge. There, by grace, you will find me birthed within your own soul."

Mary's human life helps her to be a bridge between earth and heaven, helping all of humanity to see what is possible.

The popular author Kathleen Norris has slowly grown in devotion to Mary. According to Norris, all humans are called, like Mary, "To give birth to God in the this world."

This process of giving birth to the word of God offers many opportunities for fear. Even Mary was afraid, according to the Annunciation account in Luke. Mary's fear, as well as the angel's need to offer her reassurances, shows how fully human she was. If Mary was like the soil that God could shine upon, she was like all of humanity, rooted in the earth, as vulnerable as all living creatures are.

The apocryphal texts are also wonderful sources of very human details about Mary. Even if many elements of these texts are of dubious historical accuracy, they serve to humanize the Virgin Mary, showing that even her humanity was exalted through her perfect obedience to God.

Many examples of this are seen in the Protoevangelium of James. One can see Mary's humanity in the story in which Joachim and Anna consider sending her to live in the temple when she turns two, but they reconsider because of their fears that Mary would be sad without them. Like any toddler, Mary would grieve the loss of her parents, even though she was called to a life of special holiness.

factum

Many people believe that Mary's strength as an intercessor is directly related to her experience of being fully human. As the popular writer Jack Kerouac wrote in a letter to a friend, " . . . every prayer addressed to the Holy Mother has been answered . . . But I do want to point out that the reason I think she intercedes so well for us, is because she too is a human being."

One can also see how fully human the Virgin Mary was in relation to the priest Zachariah, who realized when she turned twelve that he was going to have to send her out of the temple because she would soon begin to menstruate. The Virgin Mary was human in every way. What sets the Virgin Mary apart from the rest of humanity are the choices she made—choices to live fully for God in every situation, to say yes to God in such a fully surrendered way that she could become a fully human "God-bearer" for the rest of humanity.

Chapter 20

Mary as Bridge Builder

There is perhaps no person in the history of the world who has served as a bridge between more cultures, peoples, and faiths than Mary. Mary's ability to connect diverse peoples and cultures is rooted in her openness to the divine—it was in her womb that heaven and earth met, mingled, and produced the person of Christ. People from many cultures report that Mary has appeared to them, offering warnings, reassurance and guidance. And for millions, both within and outside of Christianity, Mary has become the ultimate example of a woman exalted, of a fresh beginning for a weary world.

Heaven and Earth

Visitors to Orthodox Churches are often struck by something that appears strange upon first glance. Many of them have a large fresco of the Virgin Mary above the altar. Some may wonder why the Virgin appears so large and central, occupying such a prominent place.

Mary's place in the iconographic scheme is significant, and her prominence has little to do with her personal merit. When one examines the painted wall more closely, one can see that above her is Christ. She stands with her arms raised in prayer as an image of the Church ready to receive God incarnate. She represents a bridge between heaven and earth.

Just as the marriage of two people contains the mysterious ability to create an entire new being through their shared love, in Mary's womb, heaven and earth were able to come together and create the person of Christ.

It was in this role, when Mary served as the bridge between heaven and earth, that she served in her most cosmic and transformative capacity, offering her earthly self in service to the Divine and giving birth to infinite possibility.

Old and New

Christianity grew out of Judaism, but from very early on, also understood itself as something different, something new—the fulfillment of what had come before. So the task of the first Christians was essentially to find a way to integrate the Old Testament Scriptures into their lives in light of the Resurrection and to differentiate themselves appropriately from those in the Jewish community, who did not believe that Jesus was the Messiah.

Scholar and historian Jaroslav Pelikan points to the role Mary played in this process. In his book *Mary Through the Ages,* he wrote: "Because Mary was . . . 'Of the House and lineage of David,' she represented an unbreakable link between Jewish and Christian history, between the First Covenant *within* which she was born and the Second Covenant *to* which she gave birth."

factum

In contemporary times, people often view obedience as a passive willingness to comply with another's wishes. But the roots of the word imply action, not passivity. The Latin root of the word is *ob audire*, which means "to hearken to." This a form of active listening that requires an alert, attentive response. This type of obedience typifies Mary.

Mary's role as bridge between the Old and New Testaments is also expressed in her lineage. It is widely believed that she, like her husband Joseph, was a descendant of King David. A recently published book called *Mary's Message to the World* offers an interesting anecdote. The book features a woman named Annie, who experienced multiple visions of the Virgin Mary. When she first encountered Mary she said, "You can't appear to me because I'm not Catholic." The Virgin Mary replied, "Nor am I."

It may not be something one thinks about everyday, but Mary was raised Jewish, not Christian. She was spiritually and culturally deeply connected to Judaism.

According to extra-Biblical accounts, Mary was raised in the temple and very much lived according to the laws of Judaism, or the Old Covenant. Yet she was chosen, in a sense, to give birth to the person who was to become the New Covenant. As much as her life, her lineage, and her spiritual witness expressed her heritage and past, her willingness to become Theotokos or to become "the one who gave birth to the one who was God," helped her to bridge the gap between the Old and New Covenants.

Rich and Poor

Mary is known and loved by rich and poor alike. For almost 2,000 years, both have traveled rocky paths to make pilgrimages to her. Statues and images of her have adorned the homes and gardens of both the rich and the poor, and in every class of humanity, people of great resources and those of few, have looked up to her as an example of a faithful, attentive, transfigured life.

Mary is also a bridge between the rich and the poor in light of the ways in which she has appeared through visions. While it is true that she most often appears to the poor, in some cases, she has appeared to both the rich and the poor, instructing them to work together to accomplish God's purpose.

It might be suggested that Mary has always recognized what each person might have to offer. In many cases with the wealthy, she has viewed them as capable for helping to erect churches or shrines or to donate property to the faithful (as occurred on the property that was graced by the Holy Family in Zeitun, Egypt). In those lacking material resources, she may have seen an openness that she couldn't always expect in the wealthy.

Mary's Role

The Virgin's role, as a poor peasant from Nazareth who was chosen by God to become the bearer of the divine and to be remembered with love and reverence in all of the subsequent ages, also serves to remind us of another way in which she brings together the rich and the poor, that is, by clearly asserting that through her, the earthly orders and classes are subject to reversal. All that is seen as great in our world may not be seen as so great in the next, just as Christ said that the first on this earth shall be last and the last on this earth shall be first (Mark 10:31).

It is through Mary that we can see how God reverses the world order—those of few resources receive the wealth of revelation, those who are poor in this world become teachers to the rich, and all of this is demonstrated by the first peasant who lives this reversal in her own life—becoming powerful through humility, and strong in her weakness.

symbolism

> The Virgin Mary illustrates the reversal of the classes when she sings her song, the Magnificat, in which she says that God has put down the mighty from the thrones and exalted those of low degree, that he has filled the hungry with good things, and the rich he has sent empty away (Luke 1:53).

Guadalupe

The Virgin Mary's apparitions at Guadalupe also speak to her recognition of the infinite value of people who lack material resources and are seen as powerless in the eyes of the world. It was there that the Virgin Mary appeared to Juan Diego, a peasant who was from one of the lowest classes in Mexico, an Aztec living in an occupied country, in a position of powerlessness.

After he took her message that the Virgin Mary wanted a church to be built the local bishop and was turned away, he returned to the Virgin and told her that if she really wanted the church to be built, then she should select a more important person to deliver the message.

But at this, the Virgin Mary offered Juan Diego the ultimate affirmation, telling him that it was he she chose. Her complete belief in him despite his powerless position in his own society offers hints of the ways in which the kingdom of God reverses earthly orders—the powerless can become powerful, those of low status, like the Virgin Mary, can be exalted for generations to come.

The message of Guadalupe has become central to Mexican identity, not only because the Virgin Mary's appearances sparked the conversion of nine million Aztecs but also because of the person she selected. Her choice of Juan Diego conveys the important message to anyone who feels slighted by society that they, too, can have a profound influence, and that their life is of infinite value. They, too, can become bearers of the word through their loving, attentive, and active obedience to God.

Women in the Church

For many women throughout Christian history, Mary's presence in the church, represented by icons or statues, affirmed their own unique Christian vocation. These representations made clear that church is a place for men and women equally. Some say that women play an insignificant role in the Bible, but this is not the case.

Even in the Genesis account, it is Eve who first tastes the forbidden fruit and in so doing changes the world. In the New Testament, Mary is chosen as the gate to paradise, the anti-Eve. Christ's death is witnessed by women, and it is the myrrh-bearing women who go to the tomb to anoint Jesus' body while everyone else sleeps. It is these women who are the first to witness the miracle of the Resurrection, and these women who, like Mary, become bearers of the message.

Mary's significant placement in the liturgy of the Church also speaks to her role among believers. Every commemoration and image of her speaks to the ongoing memory of the Church that women shape the world in small and large ways.

Islam and Christianity

As discussed in Chapter 18, there has perhaps been no time in history when the bridge between Christianity and Islam has been more important, especially in light of ongoing conflict between historically Christian and Muslim nations. As the memories of the Cold War dissipate, many political commentators have warned about a "clash of civilizations" which could turn into the greatest conflict the world has ever known.

Added to these concerns is the frightening lack of knowledge the Western world has about Islam, a religion that many believe to be the fastest growing in the world, claiming nearly one billion members. Just as Islam was able to gain dominion over the great Christian city of Constantinople, Islam is also growing in popularity and prominence in the historically Christian countries in Western Europe. Over the last century, Islam has also gained many new members in the United States, particularly within some African American communities.

In light of these developments, it is increasingly important that Christians and Muslims seek out ways to better understand each other. The Virgin Mary provides one such helpful bridge between the two religions.

There is a beautiful Muslim saying by Abu al-Qasim ibn 'Asakir which captures Islamic love for Mary:

> *"Mary said, 'In those days I was pregnant with Jesus, whenever there was someone in my house speaking with me, I would hear Jesus praising God inside me. Whenever I was alone and there was no one with me, I would converse with him and he with me, while he was still in my womb."*

Many of the Marian apparitions and miracles have been experienced by Muslims, who already have within their holy book, the Koran, as well as within the lived practice of their religion, a deep and abiding love for the Virgin Mary. According to some reports from the apparitions at Medjugorje, a few of the visionaries were shocked when they asked Mary who the holiest local person was and she named a local Muslim woman.

Religious Dialogue

For religious dialogue to be fruitful, it must be based on knowledge as well as upon a desire to see and affirm all that is good beyond one's own particular context. This is an increasingly manageable task when one recognizes similar elements between different religions, without minimizing genuine differences.

In the Bible, Mary says, "Henceforth all generations shall call me blessed." The Koran opens a section with the words, "Commemorate Mary in the Book." This statement speaks to Mary's very distinct position within Islam.

Within Islam, Mary has been viewed for centuries as one of the most perfect women. Like Christianity, Islam heartily affirms the value of submission and surrender to God. This is part of why the Virgin Mary is viewed as a model of faith.

symbolism

There is an ancient Persian expression that goes, "Paradise is at the feet of the mothers." This saying is a reminder of the value of motherhood in the Muslim context.

The role of the Virgin Mary in Islam is quite notable for its practical implications as well. Because both Christianity and Islam deeply revere the Virgin Mary, members of both religions flock to Marian shrines to pray. It is quite remarkable against the current backdrop of hostility between these two religions that at certain holy sites such as the House of Mary in Ephesus and the healing pond in India, Muslims and Christians flock to both sites and pray peacefully beside each other (although not with each other). This model of peaceful surrender to God, despite significant religious, historical, and cultural divisions, remains a way out of the danger of increasing conflict and war under the guise of religion.

Nations Around the World

Within the last decade, Western Europe has sought to unify diverse currencies and cultures through the use of the Euro. This unified currency has simplified the rather complicated situation that previously existed because of the way so many little countries were packed so closely together, all using different currencies.

If there was a universally recognizable symbol that could link diverse countries it would most likely be the Virgin Mary, who remains central to many cultures around the world, most notably Latin American cultures such as Mexico, Spain, and Portugal. Within these contexts, the Virgin Mary is as central to their identities as their own national flags. The widespread immigration of Latinos to the United States has also brought the Virgin Mary into the wider attention of the public sphere.

Because the experience of apparitions of the Virgin Mary is shared by almost all of the nations around the world, the Virgin Mary has become for many a unifying symbol. Just as through her person she was able to bring about a unity between heaven and earth, many see in her the hope of peace between nations because she is shared by so many countries around the world. In each context, her appearances have been culturally appropriate to the people who have witnessed her appearance, yet there have also been striking universal themes that have emerged from these visitations, most notably her warnings as well as her exhortation to pray and to work for peace. In one of her visitations she was reported to have said, "Do not pray for peace unless you work toward it in your own life."

The Virgin Mary's visitations at Guadalupe came against the backdrop of a particularly threatening context. The Spanish domination of the local Aztec population involved a fair amount of brutality and violence. Just before the Virgin Mary appeared to Juan Diego, the Aztecs had secretly planned to revolt against the Spaniards and to kill them all. This mass bloodshed may have been inevitable, considering the intense conflict between the two cultures, had not the Virgin Mary appeared to Juan Diego, offering him an important job to do to convey her ongoing love and presence among the locals. After her appearance, almost the entire Aztec population converted to Christianity, and the two cultures then found a way to coexist peacefully together.

Mary has also been likened to the bride in the Song of Solomon who said, "I am black, but I am comely" (or as some have translated the verse, "I am black *and* I am beautiful"). This image has been viewed as a precursor to the much-loved Black Madonna icons, as well as to Mary's prominent position among people of color. This image has been seen as a powerful antidote for the Western European art that often portrayed Mary as a pale, blue-eyed European, an image that had no real grounding in her actual historical, geographical, or cultural setting.

The Virgin Mary's role among the nations is one of peace, unity, and love. Not only is she shared by many nations, but within each context her visitations have conveyed her desire that the nations work toward peace and unity despite significant historical, political, and spiritual struggles between them.

According to author Sally Cunneen, Mary's ability to transcend culture has powerful implications: "As God-bearer, she reveals that God both comforts and challenges us to new creation at all times. Her very capacity to be translated into images of every culture shows that she is what [St.] Ephrem called her, 'The daughter of humanity.'"

This is perhaps Mary's ultimate role—as bridge between heaven and earth, between God and human beings. The old and the new, man and woman, Christianity and Islam, and between all of the diverse nations around the earth—in each role, Mary bridges the gaps between the cultures and peoples. The Virgin Mary offers the possibility of healing historical divides and rifts through her prayers, love, and example. In this significant work she becomes accessible and available to all.

Appendix A

Glossary

Akathist Hymn

An Eastern praise hymn devoted to the Virgin Mary and comprised of twenty-four stanzas. During Lent, the hymn often is spread over four Fridays, and then the entire hymn is sung on the fifth Friday.

Annunciation

In Catholicism, the revelation to Mary by the angel Gabriel that she would conceive and bear a holy child who would be the son of God.

Apparition

A ghostlike manifestation that appears unexpectedly. Apparitions of the Virgin Mary have been reported in almost every culture and era in the world.

Ascetic

Monastic disciplines such as fasting, abstinence, prayer, and giving to the poor.

Assumption

The Roman Catholic dogma (proclaimed in 1950) that teaches that the Virgin Mary was assumed into heaven. This feast is celebrated on August 15, which is the same day that the Eastern Orthodox Church celebrates the Dormition, or the "Falling Asleep" of the Mother of God.

Canonize

A rigorous process by which the Roman Catholic and Eastern Orthodox Churches pronounce that a deceased person is holy and worthy of veneration.

Church Fathers

Some of the earliest Christian teachers and writers who were viewed as extremely influential, although not always saintly, generally connected to the first five centuries of Christianity.

Coredemptrix

A Roman Catholic belief that the Virgin Mary continues to participate in the salvation of humanity in a unique way through an ongoing ministry of intercession and intervention.

Ecstasy

A trancelike state in which a person experiences a transcendent spiritual encounter. During ecstasy, visionaries are unaware of their surroundings, unresponsive to pain, and their bodies do not receive injuries. They tend to focus on a specific spot, and their faces may shine in reflection of what they are seeing. The word *ecstasy* is taken from the Greek term *exstatsis* which literally means "to stand outside of oneself."

Eucharist

The gifts of bread and wine that the Roman Catholic and Eastern Orthodox Churches believe are transformed into the body and blood of Christ. The word *Eucharist* is taken from the Greek word *Eukharistia*, which means "thanksgiving."

Hallucination

A strangely real perception of something that is not visible to others, usually seen by only one person, and most often a result of mental illness or drug use.

Immaculate Conception

A Roman Catholic dogma that the Virgin Mary was conceived without the stain of original sin, or the sin that has been passed down to all humanity since Adam and Eve. This dogma was officially proclaimed by Pope Pius IX in 1854.

Laity

A term used to denote a non-clergy person.

Mediatrix

The Roman Catholic belief that the Virgin Mary continues to mediate on behalf of humanity.

Novena

Novena is a Roman Catholic devotional practice related to saying a prayer for nine days straight in an attempt to win special favor. Novenas have often been devoted to the Virgin Mary.

Panagia

The Eastern Orthodox term for the Virgin Mary's complete and total purity and holiness.

Rosary

A string of beads used in prayer to the Virgin Mary, which is viewed as an opportunity to meditate on Scripture and to pray the Lord's Prayer and the Hail Mary Prayer. This is primarily a Roman Catholic devotional pratice.

Scapular

Two strips of cloth that cross at the chest, a remnant from ecclesiastic garb that is worn for protection.

Stigmata

A spiritual condition in which the hands of a holy person begin to bear the same marks that Jesus' did when he was crucified. This temporary gift may cause great pain, and the wounds sometimes bleed. Experienced by Saint Francis and others.

Theotokos

An Eastern term for the Virgin Mary that can literally be translated as "The One who gave birth to the one who was God."

Transubstantiation

A Roman Catholic doctrine that teaches that the bread and wine of communion is transformed into the body and blood of Christ during the consecration. Within the Eastern Orthodox Church, it is believed that the bread and wine become body and blood in a spiritual sense while remaining bread and wine in the physical sense.

Veneration

An expression of devotion and love toward a saint or a holy item.

Vision

A state in which a person sees a person who is not visible to all, in which they enter into an ecstatic state where they are not able to feel pain or receive injuries.

Visionary

A person who experiences visions. According to records from the accredited apparitions of the Virgin Mary, these visionaries are consistently shown to be of sound mental health, without tendencies toward suggestibility or altered perceptions of reality.

Appendix B

Timeline

C. 4 B.C.	The Annunciation and birth of Christ (commonly the year 0, that is, the beginning of the calendar, since A.D. means "*anno Domini*," "in the year of the Lord").
A.D. 30	The death and resurrection of Christ.
C. A.D. 40	The first reported apparition of the Virgin Mary, who was very likely still alive when she appeared to Saint James the Greater in Saragossa, Spain.
C. A.D. 81	St. John's vision at Patmos, Greece, which served as the basis for the Book of Revelation. (There are many parallels between the "Woman Clothed with the Sun," as described in Revelation 12, and the Virgin Mary.)
C. A.D. 238	The Virgin Mary is reported to have appeared to Saint Gregory the Wonderworker in Neocaesarea, Asia Minor (present-day Turkey).
C. A.D. 300	The date of the oldest known prayer to the Virgin Mary.
A.D. 352	The apparition of "Our Lady of the Snows" in Rome, Italy, connected to the creation of Saint Mary Major Church.
A.D. 431	Council of Ephesus in which the Virgin Mary was officially proclaimed as Theotokos, "the birth-giver of God."

A.D. 911	The Protection of the Virgin Mary apparition at Blachernae Palace Church in a suburb of Constantinople.
1054	The Pope of Rome and the Patriarch of Constantinople excommunicate each other.
1061	The apparition at Walsingham, creation of "House of Nazareth" replica.
1204	The Crusaders sack Constantinople (during the Fourth Crusade, 1202–1204).
1382	The apparition at Czestochowa, Italy, connected to the famed Black Madonna icon.
1517	Martin Luther posts his *95 Theses*.
1531	The apparition at Guadalupe, Mexico.
1560	The apparition of "Our Lady of Good Health" at Vailankanni, India.
1798	Apparition at Lavang, Vietnam.
1830	The apparition to Sister Catherine Laboure at Paris, France, that served as inspiration for the Miraculous Medal.

1854	The dogma of the Immaculate Conception proclaimed by Pope Pius IV.
1858	Apparitions at Lourdes, France, in which the Virgin Mary is reported to have said, "I am the Immaculate Conception."
1917	Apparitions at Fatima, Portugal.
1950	Pope Pius XII proclaims the Dogma of the Assumption.
1962–64	The Second Vatican Council.
1968	Apparitions at Zeitun, Egypt.
1973	Apparitions at Akita, Japan, associated with statue that wept 101 times and also shed blood and tears.
1981	Apparitions at Medjugorje, Yugoslavia, often viewed as the fulfillment of the apparitions at Fatima.
1982	Apparitions at Damascus, Syria, associated with a myrrh-weeping icon and concerns over divisions within Christianity.

Appendix C

Pilgrim's Guide

This appendix offers helpful resources should you wish to make a pilgrimage to a Marian shrine.

Tips:

- Pack comfortable shoes.
- Pack lightly—you may have to walk a good deal.
- Go with an open mind and a flexible attitude—pilgrimages are never quite what you expect them to be.
- Consider traveling with a local church group or with an organization responsible for organizing pilgrimages.
- You are likely to get the best price, and have a better experience when you travel with experts than if you strike out on your own.

General Pilgrimage Planning Web Sites

Here is a listing of some Web sites that might be useful as you plan your pilgrimage.

✍ *www.thecatholicpilgrim.com*
✍ *www.unitours.com*
✍ *www.gocatholictravel.com*

Popular Marian Pilgrimage Sites:

Lourdes
✎*www.lourdes-france.com*

Includes information about ideal times to go, lodging, and, the history of Lourdes.

Medjugorje
✎*www.medjugorje.org*

Includes information about planning to pilgrimage to this holy site.

Fatima
✎*www.fatima.org*

Offers a good deal of information about the apparitions at Fatima as well as how to make a pilgrimage there.

Appendix D

Additional Resources

Mary and the Church Fathers

Gambero, Luigi. *Mary and the Fathers of the Church* (San Francisco, CA: Ignatius Press, 1999). This book is a wonderful resource for understanding the thoughts of the Church Fathers in relation to the Virgin Mary. This is one of the few resources in which you can interact with their ideas in their own words.

_____. *Mary in the Middle Ages: The Blessed Virgin Mary in the Thought of Medieval Latin Theologians* (San Francisco, CA: Ignatius Press, 2005). This volume offers an opportunity to understand the thoughts of medieval Latin theologians in relation to the Virgin Mary.

Mary in Roman Catholic Teaching

Bunson, Margaret (compiler), *John Paul II's Book of Mary* (Huntington, IN: Our Sunday Visitor, 1996). This book offers numerous glimpses into Pope John Paul II's love for the Virgin Mary. This book would be useful for devotions.

Catechism of the Catholic Church, Second Edition (New York, NY: Doubleday, 2003). (Available from various publishers or online at *www.scborromeo.org/ccc.htm*). This book offers the most authoritative Roman Catholic perspective on the Virgin Mary and the teachings of the Church.

Varghese, Roy Abraham. *God-Sent: A History of the Accredited Apparitions of Mary* (New York, NY: Crossroad General Interest Co., 2000). This very detailed book offers an exhaustive Roman Catholic perspective on the apparitions.

Mary and the Eastern Orthodox Church

Maximovitch, St. John. *The Orthodox Veneration of Mary the Birthgiver of God* (Wildwood, CA: St. Xenia Skete Press, 1997). Provides a doctrinal overview of Eastern Orthodox teaching on Mary.

Schmemann, Fr. Alexander. "The Presence of Mary" (Mount Hermon, CA: Conciliar Press, 1988). These two brief pamphlets offer extremely helpful perspectives on devotion to Mary in the Eastern Orthodox context.

Ware, Kallistos. "Mary Theotokos in the Orthodox Tradition" (Wallington, UK: The Ecumenical Society of the Blessed Virgin Mary, 1997). Available from Ecumenical Society of the Blessed Virgin Mary (ESBVM), *www.esbvm.org.uk*.

Mary and Protestants

Braaten, Carl E., and Jenson, Robert W., eds. *Mary, Mother of God* (Grand Rapids, MI: Eerdmanns, 2004).

Longenecker, Dwight, and Gustafson, David. *Mary: A Catholic-Evangelical Debate* (Grand Rapids, MI: Brazos Press, 2003). This book offers a fascinating glimpse into a debate between a Roman Catholic and an Evangelical. The book-length debate, respectful and honest, offers different perspectives on titles of Mary, the rosary, apparitions, as well as the role of Mary's intercessions in the lives of the faithful.

Williams, Rowan. *Ponder These Things: Praying with Icons of the Virgin* (Franklin, WI: Sheed & Ward, 2002). Written by the Archbishop of Canterbury, this book offers an Anglican perspective on the Orthodox tradition of iconography.

General Works

Cunneen, Sally. *In Search of Mary: The Woman and the Symbol* (New York, NY: Ballantine Books, 1996). This highly readable book offers a fascinating glimpse into many of the historical debates and evolutions surrounding the Virgin Mary.

Ford-Grabowsky, Mary. *Spiritual Writings on Mary: Annotated & Explained* (Woodstock, VT: Skylight Paths Publishing, 2005). This book is wonderful for devotional use. It's full of short quotations from an incredible variety of sources from many religions, regions, and historical periods.

Pelikan, Jaroslav. *Mary Through the Centuries: Her Place in the History of Culture* (New Haven, CT: Yale University Press, 1996). This academic book offers a helpful overview of Mary's place in time, culture, and the arts.

Tavard, George H. *The Thousand Faces of the Virgin Mary* (Collegeville, MN: The Liturgical Press, 1996). This scholarly book is useful for providing an overview of the theological evolutions surrounding Mary.

Mary in Literature

Kidd, Sue Monk. *The Secret Life of Bees* (New York, NY: Penguin Books, 2003). This beautifully written book is a work of fiction that captures some of the mood of Marian devotion—the experience of a "mother ache" that is fulfilled as one draws close to Mary.

Index

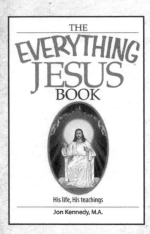